4/92

St. Louis Community College

Forest Park
Florissant Valley
Meramec

Instructional Resources
St. Louis, Missouri

SOFT SOAP, HARD SELL

SOFT SOAP, HARD SELL

American Hygiene in an Age of Advertisement

Vincent Vinikas

Iowa State University Press / Ames

In Fond Memory

Gary Ulozas

1948–1974

Vincent Vinikas is Associate Professor of History
at the University of Arkansas at Little Rock.

© 1992 Iowa State University Press, Ames, Iowa 50010

Manufactured in the United States of America
∞ Printed on acid-free paper

First edition, 1992

Library of Congress Cataloging-in-Publication Data

Vinikas, Vincent.
    Soft soap, hard sell : American hygiene in an age of advertisement/ Vincent Vinikas. — 1st ed.
      p. cm.
    Includes bibliographical references and index.
    ISBN 0-8138-1788-9 (acid-free paper)
      1. Advertising — Cosmetics — United States — History — 20th century. 2. Advertising — Toilet preparations — United States — History — 20th century. 3. Advertising — Soap trade — United States — History — 20th century. 4. Advertising — Women's health services — United States — History — 20th century. 5. Women's periodicals, American — History — 20th century.
    I. Title.
    HF6161.C77V56 1992
    659.1′966855 — dc20   90–48686

CONTENTS

PREFACE

SOCIAL INSTITUTIONS PROVIDE the framework of a people. Each defines a set of roles and social identities that tell individuals who they are and imposes an authority network of its own creation, telling folks not just who they are but how they fit in. The institution promulgates a cluster of social values and beliefs, and by promoting its own standard of normative behavior, a social institution also tells people where they should be headed and whether or not they are getting there. Social institutions are the media through which culture acts upon a people.

At some point in the early twentieth century, national advertising became a social institution in America. Advertising of some form or another has existed for centuries, and the moment at which this artifact of business transformed itself into a bulwark of community is impossible to measure. Social institutions are not invented; they evolve. Yet it is clear that advertising took on the functions of an agency of socialization as the century progressed.

Until quite recently, historians have generally eschewed the study of advertising and public relations. Despite several excellent analyses that have appeared in the past few years, our present understanding of advertising is akin to the proverbial grasp of an elephant by the blind men. Historians are currently in the midst of deciphering how advertising intrudes itself upon community; how it defines social roles and elicits standards of behavior; how it affects relationships, both among people and between people and the world of things around them; how it in turn is shaped and molded by the community it besieges. The work that follows suggests answers to some of these questions.

This study was first conceived in a paper written for a graduate seminar with David Rothman, some fourteen years ago. His genius was inspirational. Stuart Bruchey introduced me to economic and business history, and his guidance saved me from all sorts of wrong turns. Walter Metzger, Rosalind Rosenberg, Jim Shenton, and Viviana Zelizer helped me focus my thinking at critical points. Whatever merit the work possesses is due in no small part to these professors at Columbia University. I also want to thank Charlie Bolton for his intellectual generosity and for his amiable encouragement when I seemed to need it most.

Edna Emme and the National Hairdressers and Cosmetologists Association were gracious; Roscoe Edlund of the Cleanliness Institute was a pleasure to speak with; the Soap and Detergent Association provided a congenial atmosphere in which to examine the publications of the Cleanliness Institute. The reference staffs at Butler and Ottenheimer Libraries were indispensable.

Scholarly debts are not the only ones I've incurred. A number of people deserve my thanks for their insights and encouragement over the years. To my brother Matt Vinikas, John Perza, Mark Burnette, Ralph Hyman, Eunice Pollard, Leonard Walloch, Jon Hartman, Edna Savoy, my parents, Aldona and Matthias Vinikas, and Jack Nagel, thanks.

AN INTRODUCTION

to Advertising as a Social Institution

ADVERTISING, whether outlandish gimmick or "simple" pronounce-ment, has become the vade mecum—the always with us—of Ameri-can life in the twentieth century. One can no more escape it than air or taxes. Radio, periodicals and newspapers, billboards, junk mail, and television[1] are but the clarions of consumer culture. Almost every label, can, box, jar, and bottle carries a brand name or trademark announcing the existence of a producer hoping to sell. Estimates of Americans' every-single-day exposure to advertisements vary. By the 1970s, the average American's daily exposure was about 1500 mes-sages.[2]

Scanning one's immediate line of sight, perhaps attempting to calculate one's own environment, something more than the number of ads becomes readily apparent: the world is of things. One's life is a steady uninterrupted stream of interactions with innumerable objects. In America, those countless accoutrements are mostly bought and sold. Just as surely as most things have been on a truck at some point, they have also been purchased. In the great urban centers, even the blades of grass and the pebbles in the park have been paid for by someone and placed there. Advertising is intrinsic to the way those myriad goods are exchanged. Americans could no sooner wish ads away than abandon white bread, automobiles, or the very clothes they are wearing. In the dollar democracy, advertising will always be with us.

Of course the volume and tone of advertising changed dramati-cally in the early twentieth century. When he surveyed the state of the Union in 1928, Calvin Coolidge proclaimed that "the requirements of existence have passed beyond the standard of necessity into the region of luxury." That same year, Republicans won the presidency with visions, not of the full dinner pail they had promised in 1900, but with expectations of "A Chicken in Every Pot, a Car in Every Garage." American industry, by then, was organized to produce commodities and services far beyond the necessaries of subsistence. "A luxury or surplus economy cannot be built upon the physical needs of society. It is dependent primarily on the psychological needs and wants of consumers." As C. H. Sandage has concluded, "If capital, labor and natural resources are to be combined to produce non-necessities, the consuming public must be informed of their existence, educated to their want-satisfying qualities, and persuaded to buy them."[3]

Advertising assumed the challenge, and as it met these functions in the 1920s, the demands made upon the mechanism only increased. Although one cannot precisely measure the discrepancy between advances in productivity and the advances in purchasing power required to absorb that increased output, Ross Robertson has concluded that by the late twenties, "it must have been substantial. Between 1923 and 1929, productivity in the new manufacturing industries may have risen three times as fast as real wages . . . by the end of the twenties domestic markets were incapable of absorbing the nearly full employment output of industry." Business was preoccupied with this problem well before the decade's end. "Testimony abounds that the crucial difficulty in modern business lies in the 'selling end,'" recounted Wesley C. Mitchell in 1927. "The sincerity of this opinion is attested by the rapidly increasing volume of selling costs." Once the basic challenge of profitable enterprise shifted from manufacturing all the products that purchasers could buy to selling all the goods that factories could produce, advertising took on a stridency, a shrill persuasiveness, that would last until a new age arrived.[4]

Ours is a business civilization. Its evidence surrounds us, there for the most casual observer to see. But to what degree is it inside us? Historians have pondered that question for a long time, and will continue to assess the relationship between the dictates of the marketplace and those of changing human desires. This work seeks to evaluate one powerful influence in American society, the advertisement of goods, on a group of behaviors that have come to concern most of us every day.

Advertising is so commonplace that we take it largely for granted. Enveloped by a cacophony of pleadings for one product or another, inundated by offerings of this deal or that, we amble our way through everyday life assaulted on all sides by messages designed to make us buy. Most of these countless suggestions perforce must miss their mark, and leave us unmoved or unconvinced. One could not survive in American society without an ability to tune out the incessant clatter made by the promoters of goods.

This was not always so. As an artifact of American society, the advertisement is neither novel nor unusual, but developments since the turn of the century have transformed a relic of American industry into a cultural phenomenon. Advertising altered its purpose, scope, density, and content so radically that it became something entirely new. Americans commenced an acquaintance with advertising that was unique to their experience. Because it no longer confined itself to announcing the availability of merchandise, but instead attempted to define wants and to fashion needs, what had been a simple convention of business enterprise became an agency of socialization. Advertising belonged to the age.

Or did the age belong to advertising? Of what tangible effect were those uncountable millions of messages, suddenly loosed, systematically reinforced at every turn, increasingly strident in their efforts to persuade?

What follows is an attempt to assess the impact of national advertising on a cluster of practices that mutated in the twentieth century: changing habits of personal hygiene and grooming. At the beginning of the century, the bath was reserved for Saturday night; it was a ritual undertaken in anticipation of the Sabbath. Toothbrushes were curiosities; people used tooth powders as medicinal compounds, employing them to cure pyorrhea rather than to prevent tooth decay. Washing one's hair much more than once a month was considered unnecessary and unwise. Mouthwashes were unheard of. Underarm deodorants were only making their initial and inhibited appearance on the American marketplace in 1900. What transpired in the interim between then and now constitutes a revolution in these personal habits, as well as a reinterpretation in our perceptions of self.

We can identify the period when many of the new usages were introduced to and accepted by a preponderance of the American people. In the 1920s, it was becoming not merely fashionable but also normative for Americans to brush their teeth, wash their hands, bathe frequently, apply deodorants, gargle with mouthwash, and generally consume large quantities of toiletries.

Trying to isolate those factors that facilitated and occasioned this reformation in habits of personal hygiene is far more difficult than pinpointing the era in which it occurred. A variety of innovations came into play. New technologies like modern plumbing and indoor bathrooms certainly made some of the changes possible, just as the mass production of toothpaste and eyebrow pencils made them available at an affordable price. Altered conceptions of health and advances in dentistry contributed to a heightened amenability to new customs. Life in an increasingly urban environment redefined "social space," bringing people into a physical proximity that would have been foreign to their ancestors. The well-being of the nation in the 1920s meant that people had more money to spend on discretionary purchases that would enhance the quality of their lives. These factors contributed to the cause of modern American hygiene, but they do not explain the immediacy with which Americans embraced the new standards nor the breadth of the transformation. This exploration examines the mechanism that advised Americans of new products and usages, informed consumers of the advisability of undertaking new practices, and actually convinced them to do so.

Modern advertising found its identity in these personal hygiene campaigns of the 1920s. By the middle of the decade, persuasive advertising for toiletries was second in volume only to food in the national medium. Advertisers in all product lines were learning new techniques of persuasion; the marketers of soaps, toothpastes, gargles, and the like were in the forefront of a redefinition of marketing. This work addresses the interplay between national advertising and new patterns of grooming in modern America.

It has been several decades since David Potter, writing in *People of Plenty,* urged historians to examine advertising more closely. It was, said Potter, the institutional idiosyncrasy of an abundant society. In particular, he castigated the students of media who treated ads as though they were some sort of "side issue," when it was the commercial function of the various organs of mass communication that underwrote their existence. Potter further insisted that advertising was "really one of the very limited group of institutions which exercise social control." He challenged historians to address the plausibility of this claim.[5]

Historians did not respond quickly to Potter's invitation. The dearth of scholarly examinations dealing with advertising and the media it engendered continued until fairly recently. Now, however, a spate of studies has appeared. Daniel Pope has traced the institutional emergence of national advertising in the late nineteenth and early twentieth centuries; Stephen Fox has assayed the individuals and agencies that came to dominate the profession; Stuart Ewen and T. J. Jackson Lears have drawn connections between the ways in which goods were promoted and the larger culture of twentieth century America. Roland Marchand has presented a particularly intriguing look into advertising for an articulation of the modern American Dream.[6]

This study addresses Potter's insistence that advertising is, in fact, an agency of socialization. In that regard, it is both more and less ambitious than some of the works preceding it. To prove that advertising has altered normative behavior is no easy task. Just to determine the impact of a single advertising message on the sale of a particular commodity can be a hazy undertaking. Do promotional campaigns mimic consumer desires, or mold them? That has been an enduring mystery. Or does advertising achieve some murky combination of both "mirror and mind-bender"? Fox called it "the fundamental chicken-and-egg riddle in advertising history," and Marchand, in the introduction to his analysis, regretted that he could not resolve it.[7]

Of course every society teaches its members about commodities to one degree or another. But in the wake of the industrial revolution and the prospect of an ever increasing accumulation of goods in America, one witnesses the evolution of a formal mechanism for instruction in the meaning of goods. In that sense, modern advertising can be considered a social institution, and one could liken advertising as it emerged in early twentieth century America to other agencies of socialization like religion or formal education.

There are obvious similarities between each of these vehicles for the transmission and acquisition of cultural values. Each provides a characteristic setting, or environment; we have churches, schools, and magazines. That the magazine is a fluid place, a setting as mobile as its membership, makes it all the more engaging. In addition, each of these institutions also provides affective content; that is, within each environment, we find the instrumentalities of instruction that convey messages appropriate to the functions of the agency in question. The church has ministers and prayer books to indoctrinate adherents; the school employs teachers and textbooks; the magazine utilizes advertisers, stories and articles, and the advertisements themselves. In terms of supplying a context, content, and a cast of characters, the three institutions are comparable.

Each of these agencies of socialization also has a larger agenda, which can be achieved through specific instruction, to be measured in its effect on people's behavior. Advertising inculcates a materialistic sensibility that guides our relationship with the innumerable commodities with which we interact through every moment of our lives. It acts to encourage an ever increasing consumption of goods in much the same manner that schooling encourages an ever increasing acquisition of learning, or religion promotes an ever increasing attention to the soul. As Potter puts it, "advertising . . . trains the individual for a role — the role of consumer — and it profoundly modifies his system of values, for it articulates the rationale of material values in the same way in which the church articulates a rationale of spiritual values." Although these tendencies are implicit in the institutions themselves, measuring them would involve considerations far too cosmic for the rather humble monograph that follows.[8]

But the immediate effectiveness of each of these agencies can be tested. Pupils recite the alphabet, and eventually read and write; congregations murmur litanies; consumers conditioned by advertising brush their teeth, gargle and spray, wash and bathe, and learn to wash again. Advertising is process. It inundates us, and in its perpetual waking, it alters the store of accumulated shared experiences of a people. The magazine, the advertisement, and changing habits, in this view, are all part of a piece. To separate the component parts may have some limited analytical utility, but to understand advertising one must examine all three.

If advertising could be proven to have actually created a new need in the consumer consciousness, that would support Potter's contention that it is a genuine agency of social control. The opportunity to do that presents itself with an examination of Lambert Pharmacal and the Listerine phenomenon. This product had been on the market as an all-purpose antiseptic for hospital and home for decades before it became a household word. Listerine's lengthy existence as a commodity with severely limited appeal makes an analysis of its innovative advertising all the more revealing; it allows one to isolate the impact of new directions in promotional technique and witness the results. This is especially so because the product itself remained unchanged; its price, packaging, and contents went virtually unaltered. And yet, almost overnight, consumers began to gargle as never before; soon several imitators of the product joined in the craze to induce Americans to deodorize. Because Listerine's sales took such an abrupt leap so quickly, without any change in the commodity beyond the manner in which it was defined, we can also consider those extraneous variables of historical context that intervened to encourage consumers to adopt a new habit of everyday life. The marketing of Listerine in the 1920s exemplified and epitomized an advertiser's ability to shape novel wants, to conceive needs that only the manufacturer could sate.

Historians must be careful not to confuse this specific effect with an assessment of the influence of advertising in general. Because Lambert Pharmacal created demand does not imply that all promotional campaigns were nearly so successful, nor does it mean that such an outcome occurred with any degree of frequency. Students of the subject would then be misreading the potentials of advertising as surely as businesses of the 1920s did. They seized on Lambert's accomplishment as a key to the New Era of endless prosperity, manufacturing both needs and commodities in an ever accelerating spiral of profit. That the business community of the twenties made this mistake is of course quite significant. As Marchand points out, "the company's style and strategy gave rise to a whole school of advertising practice." Listerine's remarkable success "held the advertising trade enthralled." It contributed to a reinterpretation of the functions of American enterprise during the twenties, when the illusory promise of "demand creation" gripped the minds of merchandisers across the land. Yet this study makes no claim for demand creation save to insist that it did have a historical realization in the 1920s. However isolated the example, that point seems well worth making. It illustrates the acme of effective advertising and the ultimate power of persuasion.[9]

We all realize that the more common relationships between the media and Americans are less mechanistic. The mundane interaction between the consumer and the literature that advises purchasers how to fulfill their longings is as complicated as it is commonplace. But in these more ordinary instances, advertising does not perform a creative role of its own. To understand the boom in cosmetics in the 1920s, for instance, we must look beyond the ways such commodities were promoted. Advertising certainly stimulated demand for lipsticks, powders, rouge, eye makeup, and the rest. But the phenomenal surge in the sale of cosmetics cannot be credited to the new vehicles of mass persuasion that appeared in the early twentieth century. Instead, we must look to structural realignments in gender relations, as women assumed a more public identity than had been accorded them in the past. This reinterpretation in the meaning of female in America was signaled by the Suffrage, the birth control movement, new conceptions of motherhood, and the development of a new framework of opportunity for women beyond the confines of the home. It is only within the context of this fundamental change in the apperception of woman's place — the conditional acceptance of the "New Woman" — that the cult of feminine beauty becomes comprehensible.

The new look of the American female was the most striking alteration in personal grooming in the 1920s. To see women making obvious use of cosmetics in 1900, one would have had to frequent the theater or a vice district; rouge and lipstick were signs of the marked and fallen. By the 1930s, however, the typical American woman would have preferred not to go out without some form of makeup. The "painted woman" was no longer abnormal. The second case in this study explores the cosmetics boom of the twentieth century, relating changing concepts of woman's place to an unusual receptivity to commodities that emphasized distinctions of gender. This investigation considers the widespread utilization of lipsticks, powders, hair dyes, nail polish, perfumes, and eye makeup as an innovation in American perceptions of gender relations. It tries to trace the interplay of the marketplace and collective identity.

Advertising in this instance did not create need. Rather, the marketplace responded in a fairly traditional manner, providing goods to meet the changing desires of consumers. Cosmetic ads told American women that they could now purchase a group of commodities that suited a new category of wants. Once one appreciates these shifting needs of purchasers, independent of promotional campaigns, one does not discount the role of advertising entirely. The cosmetics revolution is perhaps a model of the Ewens' vision of the residual impact of the mass media on American life: it is "a world where it increasingly *makes sense* that if there are solutions to be had, they can be bought." In the case of cosmetics, we observe the New Woman searching for and then buying answers from businesses eager to supply them.[10]

Of course all advertising is ultimately designed to increase demand for a product or service. And yet, various campaigns had quite different objectives. Lambert Pharmacal hoped to create new needs; cosmetics promoters, by contrast, tried to meet new needs. The distinction between the two is noteworthy. Occasionally one may discover a combination of both goals, and an interaction of markets, entrepreneurs, and changing American values that coalesce to alter the landscape. Such is the case with the contemporaneous boom in beauty parlors in America.

The promotional activity on behalf of gender-specific barbershops, however, requires that we move beyond the pages of the magazines to explore advertising of another magnitude. It might be called public relations. The purpose and net effect of this campaign on behalf of the beauty parlor was not merely an increase in sales. An alliance of cosmetologists, hairdressers, beauticians, and manufacturers and distributors of beauty parlor equipment succeeded in a herculean effort that is almost astounding in its scope. They tried not merely to stimulate demand, or even to manage markets, but to guarantee the existence of demand for their goods and services for as long as law might last. They redefined demand and enforced this rereading of consumer need by making government a tool of the marketer.

In the early 1920s, women began to have their hair bobbed as never before. This invasion of the barbershop was an act of liberation, signaling the integration of what had been an exclusive male world apart from womankind. Barbers aspired to meet the new demand for women's haircutting by expanding their operations. At the same time, however, an alert magazine publisher saw an opportunity to ensure the continuing profitability of both his journal, *The American Hairdresser,* and the businesses of the readers he served. He organized a national association of hairdressers and cosmetologists determined to draw a line between man's hair and woman's. The distinction they sought to instill, moreover, was legal rather than social: they planned to segregate the barbershop on the basis of sex. They succeeded. Taking their crusade to the courts and state legislatures, the American Hairdressers Association recognized their objectives through careful and consistent promotion of the notion that barbering and bobbing, cutting men's hair and women's, were and should remain separate endeavors. As a result of their achievements in public relations, state after state enacted legislation that dictated the growth of the beauty parlor by forbidding female patronage of barbers. This was an advertising achievement of considerable consequence. It is of particular interest because the campaign on behalf of the beauty parlor was a step removed from the ultimate consumer, and, having succeeded, it made direct appeals to the purchaser redundant. These business interests cemented a national marketplace by using legislation to invent and enforce a national standard of behavior—in this case the subsidization of hairdressers. A woman seeking to buy a haircut would necessarily solicit a beauty shop, and a man would seek only a barber.

The marketplace of the 1920s was not entirely stable. The surge in demand for deodorants and cosmetics posed a direct challenge to soap consumption. But the soap industry also hoped to ride the crest of American prosperity. The fourth survey looks at the cooperative campaigns undertaken by the leading soap manufacturers in America, designed to ensure that consumers use soap lavishly. These remarkable endeavors won widespread acclaim for both creative marketing and community service. Joining together, soap manufacturers formed Cleanliness Institute to instruct the public in the importance of applying soap as often as possible. Using promotional devices that ranged from magazine advertising to what can be considered the precursors of the soap opera, Cleanliness Institute became a wellspring of expert advice and admonition, all of it aimed at more soap consumption in America.

Investigating these various practices is fairly difficult because the track of change and continuity in standards of personal hygiene has escaped historians' notice. One good reason is that sources concerning such rudimentary aspects of everyday life are lacking. People do not often write about brushing their teeth, or record their thoughts on deodorizing, or reveal how they feel when they have their hair cut or paint their lips. Precisely because they have come to invoke normative sanctions, these activities are performed rigorously but without question. The topic of personal hygiene itself makes some people uneasy and others giddy. Such reactions attest to the weight invested in the simplest routines, demonstrating that these procedures are neither so simple as they seem nor so trivial that they need be ignored. They constitute a framework through which we operate; they are part of the norms and mores that mediate our existence.

This is not a discourse on public health. Though closely connected, personal hygiene bears only a tangential relation to the general welfare. Rules regarding sanitation, inoculation, or expectoration, for instance, are civic concerns enforced by law. They guard the body politic. Personal hygiene is an intimation of self. It is once removed from law, the subject not of debate so much as of gossip. Individual identity as distinct from corporate interest is at issue. This does not mean that the two are not linked; the public health movement of the early twentieth century resonated with novel perceptions of appropriate behavior in the realm of hygiene. As Paul Starr observes in his study, a practice like hand washing could be and was promoted as a corollary of public health. But the two are as different as political coersion and social compulsion. Although those developments were concordant with and concurrent to changing habits, one must look elsewhere for an explication of advances in preventative medicine and public health.[11]

Nor is what follows meant to imply that Americans were somehow mere victims, molded like plastic furniture by the imperatives of industry. Whether Americans as a people were any more or any less manipulated and constrained by the growth of national advertising than they would otherwise be, any more or less "free" than before, is not argued here. The boundaries of existence were different, to be sure. But webs of expectation may be as intricate and extensive in the simplest societies as in the most complex. Conformity to changing patterns of behavior may be all the more rigorously enforced the closer a culture approaches the edge of desperation. Those sorts of questions are best left to the anthropologists or to philosophers. It is clear that a new agency was at work.

It is also apparent that the terms of existence were changing, and the alterations were so fundamental that the American character seemed to require a reorientation, which advertising was instrumental in effecting. If, as Potter noted, our character is inexorably intertwined with the world of goods, any marked alteration in the manner in which commodities were produced and distributed would also register in the "psychic economy" of the American people. Several scholars have tracked this realignment. David Riesman traced a shift from "inner-" to "other-direction" as Americans enured themselves to the age of consumption by making the approval of others the end-all of existence. More recently, Warren Susman advised that "one of the things that makes the modern world 'modern' is the development of consciousness of self." He proceeded to demark the emergence of an ethos that stressed that "true pleasure could be attained by making oneself pleasing to others," as a "culture of personality" evolved in the twentieth century. In his study of *The Culture of Narcissism,* Christopher Lasch portrayed a people desperate for the adulation of the world around them. Although the precise dimensions of change in the American character will be debated for some time to come, its broader outlines have been divined. These changing dynamics of self and its presentation resonated with conceptions of hygiene, which stressed the urgent importance of alluring and appeasing others. The new means of communicating these values, the national media underwritten by the promoters of goods, became a primary conduit for the dictates of the new order.[12]

The impact of mass communication may have seemed especially awesome by virtue of its novelty. Competing perhaps with attenuated networks of kith and kin, the ads claimed to and probably did tell people what their best friends would not. When parents, peers, or priests dictated behavior and demanded compliance, though, it seemed by contrast not nearly so menacing. Those ancient tyrannies were quite familiar. National advertising was new.

It was also comparatively impersonal, despite its pretense to intimacy — a sort of correspondence course in correct behavior, need adjustment, and the social graces. Its first textbook was the mass-circulation magazine, and the omnipresence of the periodical is a theme that runs through the analysis that follows. Because the magazine provided the first platform from which the promoter enticed the nation to embrace new usages, it is the logical point of departure for this investigation.

SOFT SOAP, HARD SELL

1

The Development of Promotional Magazines:

National Vehicles of the Early Twentieth Century

he distribution revolution called for a new relationship between the producers and consumers of goods. By the turn of the twentieth century a novel form of literature, the mass-circulation magazine, began to direct the communication between sellers and purchasers. Millions of these promotional vehicles appeared in homes across the country, carrying news of merchandise to a national marketplace. The advertising that subsidized these publications came to exert immeasurable influence on the ways in which Americans chose to buy. Proliferating across geographic and economic boundaries to entice Americans everywhere, the periodicals themselves contributed to the development of a national community of consumers.

Throughout much of the nineteenth century, America was still a loose amalgamation of many small groups, living in and around relatively self-contained towns and cities. Each community was largely its own society, a little world in which men and women acted out their lives in seclusion from the larger world beyond. The populace met their own needs as regional conditions and customs permitted, producing most of their material requirements within the confines of their town and its hinterland. The exchange of goods was familiar, personal, and independent of the vagaries of life a few hundred miles away. If one wanted shoes, the cobbler probably anticipated it. For those few who did not knead their own, the baker knew everyone who needed bread and how many loaves and cakes to make. The seamstress tailored garments to suit a buyer's individual specifications. Procuring a self-sustaining existence through their local markets, these clusters of people have been called island communities. [1]

In the latter decades of the nineteenth century, however, railways, roads, telephones, and telegraphs bridged the distance between island communities at an accelerated rate. By 1890, around the time the frontier finally disappeared, four transcontinental railroads integrated the country, linking Americans together in a vast national network. Physical proximity had ceased to be the chief determinant of who provided one with a material competence, or of what was available to consume. Markets merged, as heretofore disconnected towns distended each into another. Products made in Massachusetts might readily find their way to Wyoming. Manufacturers and distributors of everything from beans to burial vaults could now operate on a national scale. This change in the real and possible scope of making things and selling them altered the context of American life.

This broad transformation cannot be isolated in time because self-sufficiency is a relative condition. Until the 1870s, however, most businesses were small firms that "bought their raw materials and sold their finished goods locally." Pinpointing this new orientation to a national market can create other difficulties by obscuring historical continuities. Yet as Stuart Bruchey advises, it is clearly during those years between 1870 and 1900 "that we can first speak of the mass demand of a national urban market." Nor was it just an ability to move goods great distances that occasioned the change. It required a reinterpretation of American law in the late nineteenth century, hastened by the interests of large manufacturers, to strike down barriers to interstate trade. Indeed, if the marketplace is characterized as an area of free trade instead of an integrated network of transportation, then "the rise of big business was a prerequisite for the emergence of a national marketplace" instead of the other way around. It was ultimately up to the courts, under pressure from these corporate interests, to identify the boundaries of the marketplace with those of the nation.[2]

One of the casualties of the development of a national marketplace was the traditional relationship between makers and users of goods. In earlier years, producers were guided by an intimate knowledge of local needs. The emergence of national manufactories, however, necessitated major adaptations in the communication between buyer and seller. Relative to the neighborhood baker, for instance, the national producer who labeled his biscuits "Uneeda" was only guessing. He no longer knew to whom his goods were sold, let alone their specific wants and desires. The national producer had somehow to gauge demand for goods by purchasers who could not directly communicate their needs.[3]

The obvious risk involved in producing goods is that no one will buy them. This risk increased enormously when commodities were made at a distance, when a sewing machine maker in Philadelphia had to develop a market in Minneapolis. If hundreds of miles separated them, how could a prospective buyer know the product existed? Or if the purchaser knew it could be bought, then where to find it? And at what price? To manufacture or produce goods without a ready market close at hand entailed unusual elements of chance. To reduce the hazards of the distribution revolution, sellers had to build their own bridges between islands.[4]

Advertising could do that. In earlier years, merchants sometimes had reason to announce the availability of goods. When a ship came in, or a craftsman finished a piece, or the crop had been harvested and was on its way to market, the seller might run an ad in the local press, put a sign on his door, or disseminate broadsides to the crowd. The pronouncement followed a fairly predictable format, offering a brief description of the product's characteristics and the place where it could be procured. To tell consumers that they could now make their purchases, where and at what cost, shopkeepers had relied on advertising for several hundred years. As one of the early exponents of national campaigns explained it, "The efficacy and economy of advertising is as great as the difference between the use of the tongue and the use of type in the distribution of ideas."[5]

The first published solicitation in America appeared in 1704, according to Frank Presbrey. It sought advertisements. Incidentally defining the marketplace, it proclaimed that "all Persons who have any Houses, Lands, Tenements, Farmes, Ships, Vessels, Goods, Wares or Merchandizes, & c. to be Sold or Lett, or Servants Run away; or Goods Stoll or Lost, may have the same inserted at a Reasonable Rate." But this sort of effort to reach others had a slow start. It was limited by its function; in self-contained communities where everyone is famous, so are many of their goods.[6]

When advertising was employed, it was not meant to exceed the boundaries of local life itself. Retailers hoped to inform the audience close by. A need to reach beyond one's island to the larger world was rare; until the eve of the Civil War, national magazine advertising did not exist. Until the 1880s, businesses did not have much reason to use national advertising. Many thought that sort of publicity amounted to a confession of weakness. Magazine publishers thought ads degraded a journal. An ad campaign might consist of a two-inch column run once in three or four publications. It did not require much space to list new articles for sale, so quarter-page and half-page ads were scarce. To use a full-page advertisement, as peddlers of patent-medicines sometimes did, was sensational.[7]

But the nature of communicating the availability of goods altered with new conditions. Chief among them were "the increasing distance between the producer and consumer due to the concentration of manufacturing at large centres" and the consolidation of production and distribution in great firms catering to a mass market. The vertically integrated concerns that first appeared in the field of consumer goods initiated the trend. Horizontal combination of small companies into large organizations, often a function of the need to stem overproduction and ruinous competition in the rapidly expanding nexus of trade, gave manufacturers both a reason to pursue national campaigns and the wherewithal to do so. Businesses came to realize that mass production for a national marketplace requires national advertising; "that the hardest part of the distribution of merchandise is the distribution of the information which must precede the selling. That what the automatic machine is to making goods, the advertisement is to selling them." Thus would the distribution revolution alter not only the world of things, but of thoughts as well.[8]

Although newspapers had already existed in scattered cities and towns, providing an advertiser with local organs of communication, there was only one vehicle with a reach as wide as America had become. Unlike the newspaper whose audience was strictly regional, the magazine "could present simultaneously identical facts, uniformly treated, in every locality." Until the 1890s, however, magazines had a readership largely of the leisure class; they were edited "for gentlefolk of means." The largest one, *Century,* had a circulation of 186,257 in 1888. Although millions of Americans read Sunday newspapers, hardly 250,000 out of 80 million read magazines with any regularity. But in 1893 the requirements of the national marketplace converged with publishers' misfortunes to revolutionize the notions governing the periodical industry.[9]

When the Panic of 1893 hit, Frank Munsey found himself with two failing journals and debts amounting to $100,000. He had to stimulate demand for his product. With the October issue of his *Munsey's Magazine* he gambled, slashing its price from twenty-five cents to ten cents an issue. That month he sold 40,000 copies. By the following February, he was selling 200,000 copies a month. Advertisers clamored for space in this unequivocal success. *McClure's Magazine* and *Cosmopolitan* tried the same tactic with equally promising results. McClure, Munsey, and the *Cosmopolitan*'s Curtis had discovered the basic premise of the modern magazine and its role in the marketplace: it was possible to achieve an enormous circulation by selling periodicals for far less than they cost to produce, and then profit from the high volume of advertising that such circulation attracted.[10]

Of course this sort of enterprise involved considerable risk. Initial losses, incurred before advertising rates caught up with mounting circulation, could be substantial. Earlier attempts to implement this equation failed repeatedly; since most advertisers had been local firms, they had no use for out-of-town circulation and refused to pay for it. But "the consolidation and combination that took place toward the end of the century brought enough production under the control of one management to warrant large scale expenditures on advertising." Although the Panic was not conducive to publishing—thousands of magazines folded in 1893—this time the experiment worked. The need to stimulate demand in an economic downturn made manufacturers willing to try this means of reaching potential purchasers. "As advertising grew," concluded Theodore Peterson, "it made the magazine a part of the system of marketing in the United States." Technological improvements in printing—the halftone, Linotype, rotary press, and process engraving—made mass production of quality publications reasonable, at the same time that the increasing tempo of consolidation in industry enhanced the profitability of providing manufacturers with a national audience. In 1900, *Harper's* ran more ads than it had in the previous twenty-two years combined. Cyrus Curtis bought the *Saturday Evening Post* in 1897. Capitalizing on the same formula that he, Munsey, and McClure first employed in 1893, Curtis managed to raise the *Post*'s readership of 2200 to 2 million by 1920. Algernon Tassin estimated that between 1890 and 1910, "two hundred and fifty thousand regular monthly buyers of periodicals became two millions, and the reader of one magazine became the devoted devourer of half a dozen and more." In these twenty years, the modern magazine came to be. Periodicals like *Ladies' Home Journal, McClure's, Cosmopolitan, Comfort, Munsey's,* the *Delineator,* and *McCall's* became regular reading across the country.[11]

Effecting the "introduction of everybody to everybody," millions of magazines went into homes all over the nation. Precisely how many, and to whom? No one could be sure. What defined a magazine and, in particular, how did that differ from a national "newspaper"? It was neither price nor principle of operation, as both relied predominantly on advertising revenue to turn a profit. Was it the shape, or the quality of paper employed? Frequency of issue? The distribution of national newspapers came to parody that of magazines, or did that actually make them magazines? What were magazine sections of newspapers?[12]

Confining oneself to magazines that called themselves such and actually appeared in print, insurmountable difficulties still remained when tracking their distribution at the turn of the twentieth century. The profit in manufacturing a periodical hinged very much on its circulation. Its capacity to reach people was what advertisers bought; rates were based on the number of people who might read the periodical and on their ability to buy the goods it promoted. So the magazine maker had an interest in inflated circulation figures, and there was little but his word to go on. One publisher inadvertently identified the problem of relying on industry sources: "The facts about national magazines speak, convincingly, for themselves." Figures were quoted to suit the occasion.[13]

This imprecision was intolerable from a business's point-of-view. Coming to appreciate that a magazine's diffusion was its chief economic value, businesses discovered what Charles O. Bennett called "an almost complete absence of trustworthy figures on the amount of circulation the advertiser would get for his money." Ingenuity rather than efficiency dominated advertisers' efforts to ascertain the actual number of copies a publisher issued. One patent-medicine maker sent salesmen to stand outside print shops, counting the vibrations caused by revolutions of the press inside. Bribing the pressmen, however, seems to have been the preferred method of auditing the exaggerated claims of magazine publishers.[14]

Institutional efforts to rationalize the growth of this national medium succeeded in 1914. In that year, two regional enterprises, the Bureau of Verified Circulations of New York and the Advertising Audit Association of Chicago, merged to form the Audit Bureau of Circulations. The ABC represented advertisers, ad agencies, and the publishers of newspapers, magazines, farm journals, and business papers. These buyers and sellers of advertising space set out to provide standard definitions of paid circulation, to establish uniform auditing practices, and to report unbiased results — all on a voluntary basis. A board of directors was designed to represent all the various interests, but buyers rather than sellers of space had to constitute a majority of the board. Of space sellers, the bureau confined membership to publications with "paid circulation." It further refined that qualification by defining such a periodical as one with at least half of its distribution actually paid. To be paid, the final purchase price had to be at least half of the listed single-copy price. The bureau then required two systematic studies of each periodical. Publishers generally submitted statements on circulation semiannually. The bureau itself then undertook audit reports of company records to verify the statements on an annual basis. The investigation furnished the world with standard and certified accounts of how many magazines a publisher printed, how the particular periodical circulated, where it went, and the price people paid for it. By means of this yardstick of "audited paid circulation," the ABC provided the industry with both a sound basis for devising ad rates and an empirical framework from which to conduct consumer research. With these achievements in mind, the Audit Bureau of Circulations billed itself as "the greatest stabilizing force" in the advertising and publishing business.[15]

The bureau's standards were about as stringent as they could be. It confined its counting to magazines with paid circulation, because advertisers could use "paid circulation" as an index of reader interest. If people actually purchased the literature, they probably read it. The industry considered copies sold singly, over the counter, as the most effective national medium available. These periodicals were sure to be looked at, and by sizeable numbers of people: "Armies greater than the Expeditionary Forces sent to Europe in 1917 must go to the newsstands once a week, put down five cents and call for us by name."[16]

The agency's name—the Audit Bureau of Circulations—is not the only factor that might lead one to place it in the Progressive context of the early twentieth century. Although it differed from many traditional Progressive efforts to regulate in its principal aspect—it was private and voluntary—the ABC set out to enumerate reality with a Progressive enthusiasm. It standardized and defined terms, counted and recounted subscribers, measured and weighed circulations, and disseminated authoritative and auditable facts to interested parties. Celebrating its efficient search for "fact, without opinion," the bureau referred to itself as "the" outstanding example of successful self-government in industry, a designation that may have been deserved. The bureau became largely responsible for transforming advertising from a speculative venture into something of an investment.[17]

At the same time, the volume of magazine sales continued to mount. According to Peterson's estimate, the aggregate circulation of all magazines in 1900 was some 65 million. By 1923, that figure doubled, and by 1939, it had almost doubled again, reaching about

240 million readers. (Table 1.1.) If these figures are accurate, the industry published almost two magazines for every man, woman, and child in America by 1940.[18]

TABLE 1.1   Aggregate circulation of magazines, 1900–1939

Year	Circulation	Year	Circulation
1900	65,000,000	1931	183,527,000
1923	128,621,000	1933	174,759,000
1925	153,375,000	1935	178,621,000
1927	165,702,000	1937	224,275,000
1929	202,022,000	1939	239,693,000

SOURCE: Theodore Peterson, *Magazines in the Twentieth Century,* 2d ed. (Urbana: University of Illinois Press, 1964) 58–59.

NOTE: As Peterson states, estimating such circulation is "a highly speculative pastime."

By the 1920s, one could find at least one journal on almost any subject. Part of a magazine's function was to identify a particular group with recognizable needs, baiting its pages with matter that might attract a specific market. If readers with special interests could be isolated and solicited on the basis of their idiosyncracy, the advertiser had an easier time of it. Promoting picks and shovels in *Pictorial Review* would be frivolous, but the same products displayed in *Pit and Quarry* might command the attention of a ready buyer. The logic of the industry — to lose millions of dollars by selling magazines for far less than the production cost, only to make even more in ad revenue — lent itself to specialization according to categories of goods and purchasers. Mothers, fishermen, weightlifters, brides; Americans, adolescents; people who liked to knit, others attracted to exotic animals; campers and college students, each became the target of a magazine. The publisher who addressed a group of readers with homogeneous desires could count on the support of manufacturers whose products gave material reality to the group's interests and eccentricities.[19]

The magazines with the greatest distribution did have a truly national reach. A study undertaken in the mid-1930s demonstrated the embrace of the national market for mass-circulation magazines. (Table 1.2.) Using seventy-six cities and twenty-two periodicals, researchers discovered considerable variety in the reading habits of urban Americans, at least in terms of which magazines they received. In Omaha, for instance, *Good Housekeeping* sold 280 issues for every thousand families in town. In Fall River, only thirty-three families out of a thousand got that particular journal. But in both cities, despite

TABLE 1.2   Extremes of magazine concentration in urban America, 1933–1935

Issue date	Magazine	High city	Copies per 1000 families	Low city	Copies per 1000 families
2/17/1934	*Liberty*	San Diego	255.0	Buffalo	136.0
11/1934	*Popular Mechanics*	Grand Rapids	35.2	New Orleans	11.8
10/26/1935	*Literary Digest*	Salt Lake City	50.9	Fall River	16.5
3/2/1935	*Saturday Evening Post*	Seattle	251.5	Fall River	67.8
2/1934	*True Story*	Paterson	183.8	El Paso	52.0
3/1935	*McCall's*	Duluth	146.0	New Orleans	33.6
3/2/1935	*Collier's*	Grand Rapids	200.2	Jersey City	41.4
1/1933	*National Geographic*	Hartford	78.0	Memphis	16.1
2/1935	*American*	Flint	165.8	Jersey City	8.6
2/1935	*Woman's Home Companion*	Flint	197.6	Lynn	34.2
9/1935	*Esquire*	San Francisco	26.5	Fall River	4.3
12/1934	*Detective Group*	San Francisco	70.0	Jersey City	10.5
3/2/1935	*Time*	Minneapolis	57.7	Jersey City	8.6
6/1934	*Atlantic*	Providence	7.5	New Haven	1.0
3/1935	*Good Housekeeping*	Omaha	280.1	Fall River	33.1
4/1935	*House and Garden*	Dallas	12.4	Gary	1.5
3/1935	*Redbook*	Spokane	75.6	Lowell	8.7
4/1935	*Vogue*	Dallas	15.8	Gary	1.7
3/1935	*Cosmopolitan*	Omaha	239.0	Lowell	17.9
10/1935	*Better Homes and Gardens*	Duluth	146.9	New Orleans	10.9
4/1935	*Vanity Fair*	New Haven	13.5	Fall River	1.0

SOURCES: "How Cities Differ in Their Magazine Reading Habits," *Sales Management* (15 February 1936): 220. "How Magazines Differ—As Shown by City Preferences," *Sales Management* (1 March 1936): 296–97, 322.
NOTE: Magazines are arranged from least extreme in distribution to most.

regional conditions, historical development, and a distance of some 1500 miles between them, people regularly read the same pages, saw the same promotions, and if advertisers' expectations were reasonable, sought the same goods.[20]

A number of factors may have determined the reach of the medium. A related study of ninety cities discovered significant correlations between the size of a city and the extent of its readership. The more extreme a city's size, whether larger or smaller, the fewer magazines its inhabitants were apt to read. The highest density of circulation could be found in cities with populations ranging from 60,000 to 100,000. Perhaps the great cities offered more diverse amusements, as the study contended, for people in the largest cities were the least likely to read magazines. Then, too, the higher proportion of poor in the vast urban districts might have contributed to the lower readership. Those in the most populated cities also had access to a greater variety of newspapers than those living in less populous places. Besides, if the chief economic function of national magazines was to convey news of merchandise, one would expect to discover fewer readers in the largest cities. They already knew about the range of goods and had already been exposed to, were the core of, the mass market.[21]

Other factors also seemed to have affected magazine readership. The older a population, the more it tended to read. A rise in the number of movie theaters corresponded with rising readership of the magazines sampled. The occupational structure of the locality also influenced circulation; those cities with the most industrial workers were least likely to read magazines. This no doubt had something to do with income, which also showed a definite correlation with magazine readership. As one might expect, the higher a community's aggregate income, the higher its readership. The authors admitted to finding "a confusing jumble" when subjecting these correlations to more detailed analysis. They concluded that one central factor — income — might underlie all the correlations they computed. If so, then their findings exaggerated the importance of the other factors they isolated.[22]

If the hopes of the national marketers of goods had substance, income should have been the primary determinant of who saw their promotional vehicles. This was especially so for the popular literature designed for the broadest audiences. If a reader could not buy the soaps, applesauce, furniture, canned olives, convertibles, and other accoutrements of existence that the advertiser offered to sell, then the ads were largely useless in terms of stimulating immediate sales. (That advertising might have other significance, including potential and future market influence, one could take for granted. The magazines themselves could have a considerable pass-along readership.) Evidence indicated that a family's income had much to do with what they read.

By the 1920s, students of the medium tried to devise some precise measurement of those whom the various magazines solicited. Daniel Starch, one of the first professors of advertising and professor of business psychology at Harvard from 1919 to 1926, undertook this assignment with some care. Working with the American Association of Advertising Agencies, he discovered that all income-brackets were reading something, though the magazines' penetration was a function of household income. (Table 1.3.) The most popular periodical with the wealthiest families was *Saturday Evening Post,* and according to Starch's calculations, this organ reached a remarkable 46 percent of all families with an annual income in excess of $10,000. That made it powerful indeed. The most popular magazine among poorest American families was *True Story,* and it reached 4.7 percent of them, a

TABLE 1.3 Distribution of top ten magazines to families by income group as determined by subscribed circulation, 1930

Rank	$0–$999 to 4.29%	$1000–$1999 to 7.02%	$2000–$2999 to 7.17%	$3000–$4999 to 13.90%	$5000–$9999 to 31.63%	$10,000 + to 45.83%
1	Household	Household	McCall's	Saturday Evening Post	Saturday Evening Post	Saturday Evening Post
2	People's Popular Monthly 3.91	Woman's Home Companion 6.46	Pictorial Review 7.16	Ladies' Home Journal 11.22	Literary Digest 19.22	Literary Digest 35.96
3	Comfort 3.54	Pictorial Review 6.25	Woman's Home Companion 7.04	Collier's 10.98	Collier's 19.20	Ladies' Home Journal 31.15
4	Gentle-woman 2.77	McCall's 6.05	Ladies' Home Journal 6.22	Woman's Home Companion 10.82	Ladies' Home Journal 18.75	National Geographic 29.94
5	Woman's Home Companion 2.70	Ladies' Home Journal 5.30	Delineator 5.79	American Magazine 10.75	Woman's Home Companion 17.49	Delineator 24.34
6	Mothers' Home Life 2.64	Saturday Evening Post 5.17	Household 5.74	Delineator 10.33	American Magazine 17.10	Good Housekeeping 24.29
7	Pictorial Review 2.51	Delineator 5.07	American Magazine 5.64	McCall's 10.27	Good Housekeeping 15.93	Woman's Home Companion 23.54
8	Needlecraft Magazine 2.47	American Magazine 5.02	Collier's 5.57	Pictorial Review 9.02	Delineator 15.63	American Magazine 22.15
9	American Magazine 2.45	People's Popular Monthly 4.62	Saturday Evening Post 5.22	Good Housekeeping 8.46	National Geographic 14.97	Pictorial Review 20.26
10	Ladies' Home Journal 2.42	Comfort 4.38	Woman's World 3.93	Cosmopolitan 7.57	Pictorial Review 14.17	Collier's 19.73

SOURCE: Adapted from American Association of Advertising Agencies, *Magazine Circulations—Qualitative Analysis by Incomes of Readers* (New York: American Association of Advertising Agencies, 1930), 6–16.

NOTE: Income categorizations were derived from occupational income of family members combined with rental value of homes. These figures apply only to subscribed circulation. Because *Liberty* and *True Story* had little or no subscribed circulation, figures for their distribution were derived from investigation of newsstand buyers. The authors estimate that *Liberty* regularly reached 4.14% of $0–$999 families, making it their third most popular; 4.56% of $1000–$1999 families, making it eleventh; 6.67% of $2000–$2999 families, making it fourth; and 13.14% of $3000–$4999 families, making it second. For *True Story*: 4.70% of $0–$999 families, making it their most popular magazine; 9.72% of $1000–$1999 families, making it their fifth most popular; 6.27% of $2000–$2999 families, making it their most popular magazine. See p. 27.

figure that one could regard as a significant number of those with the least income to spend. The national consumer magazines circulated across the spectrum of the American social structure; a sizeable number of publications crossed not only geographic but economic boundaries to embrace consumers from all segments of the population.[23]

All of these magazines had a purpose. Cyrus Curtis, perhaps the most successful periodical publisher, once defined it. "Do you know why we publish the *Ladies' Home Journal?* The editor thinks it is for the benefit of the American women. That is an illusion, but a very proper one for him to have. But I will tell you." Curtis explained that "the real reason, the publisher's reason, is to give you people who manufacture things that American women want and buy a chance to tell them about your products."

The editor of the *Ladies' Home Journal,* at any rate, seemed to know what was going on. Edward Bok claimed to have invented "tailing" fiction articles into the back pages of the *Journal* in 1896, to increase the readership of promotional material. Until then, advertisements were largely segregated in the back pages of magazines. If readers objected to the intrusion, one would have difficulty proving it. In circulation, *Ladies' Home Journal* was among the first magazines to pass the million mark.[24]

The volume of periodical advertising skyrocketed even faster than magazine sales in the early years of the twentieth century. In 1909, promoters invested roughly $54 million to pay for periodical promotions. Within twenty years, that figure had increased almost six times over. By 1929, periodicals carried some $320 million worth of advertising copy. Not until 1916 did an advertiser spend a million dollars to promote his product in thirty leading magazines. But by 1930, twenty firms were spending a million dollars, and some of them considerably more than that. By then, advertisers saturated the pages of national magazines with their offers of goods for sale.[25]

Browsing through the leading periodicals of the twenties and thirties, one would readily discover that as much as 50 or even 60 percent of their content was explicitly commercial. (Table 1.4.) Scanning the various publications in April 1931, one would learn that advertising constituted well over half of the *Saturday Evening Post.* Reading *Woman's Home Companion* was little more than armchair window shopping, with 57 percent of its pages promoting some product or other. And yet it was one of the most popular magazines with every income bracket in America. *Harper's* magazine, which in 1869 turned down an offer from Singer Sewing Machines because ads "degraded" a journal, now devoted a third of its contents to the blandish-

TABLE 1.4   Preponderance of advertising in selected magazines, April 1931

Magazine	Issue date of weekly magazine	Total pages	Pages read-ing	Pages ads	Ads to total (%)
American Magazine	. . .	188	106	82	44
Atlantic	. . .	222	161	61	27
Collier's	4/11	76	39	37	48
Current History	. . .	196	182	14	7
Harper's	. . .	229	154	75	33
Liberty	4/11	76	55	21	28
Literary Digest	4/11	50	27	23	46
Nation	4/15	48	43	5	10
Saturday Evening Post	4/11	168	72	96	57
Time	4/13	84	29	55	65
Class Magazines					
American Golfer	. . .	98	50	48	49
Arts & Decoration	. . .	104	42	62	60
Better Homes and Gardens	. . .	144	76	68	47
Field and Stream	. . .	132	79	53	40
Theatre	. . .	114	92	22	19
Women's Magazines					
American Home	. . .	98	46	52	53
Delineator	. . .	130	61	69	53
Good Housekeeping	. . .	304	137	167	55
Ladies' Home Journal	. . .	210	87	123	59
Needlecraft	4/5	36	28	8	22
Pictorial Review	. . .	124	59	65	52
Woman's Home Companion	. . .	180	78	102	57

SOURCES: Volume of advertising in particular magazines can be found in "Summary of Magazine Advertising for April," *Printers' Ink* (9 April 1931): 139, 140, 142. For total pages per volume, see Hugh E. Agnew and Warren B. Dygert, *Advertising Media,* 133–34.

ments of the marketplace. If this was degradation, as people imagined it to be some sixty years before, it also led to an upward spiral in expenditures by promoters who wished to get people to purchase their goods.[26]

The advertising pages purveyed everything from canned beets to bath soaps. In 1935, not the best of times, the automotive industry invested almost $17 million on advertisements in the leading magazines. Advertisers spent a roughly equal amount to tell Americans which foods to buy. Taking expenditures for toilet goods and soaps and cleansers, and adding them together, one would realize that this industry spent some $20 million that year, letting people know which products would clean them, which ones would render their bodies sanitary or beautiful, which ones to apply to their clothes, their homes, themselves. (Table 1.5.) Electric fans, clothing, refrigerators,

TABLE 1.5 Aggregate expenditures on most-promoted goods in thirty-five leading magazines, 1935

Goods	Amount
Automotive	$16,775,729
Foods	16,581,173
Toilet goods	13,628,080
Passenger cars	7,570,412
Electrical	7,240,089
House furnishings	6,775,042
Soaps and cleansers	6,060,992
Canned goods	5,698,264
Smoking materials	5,219,047
Wearing apparel	5,001,082
Insurance	2,554,671
Transportation	2,324,156
Refrigeration	2,165,182
Dentifrices	2,105,698
Deodorants and antiseptics	1,982,135
Structural	1,961,309
Cereals	1,857,900
Furniture/flooring	1,852,053
Shoes and sundries	1,826,958
Face creams/lotions	1,799,984
Office equipment	1,765,089
Desserts/flavorings	1,747,881
Tires	1,669,876
Cleansers	1,618,435
Radio and musical instruments	1,557,336
Toilet soaps	1,553,000
Flour and bread	1,490,193
Household soaps	1,480,929
Textiles	1,323,462
Jewelry, silver, and timepieces	1,294,481
Wrappings	1,223,095
Powders, rouge, lipsticks	1,151,527
Soft drinks	1,145,072
Coffee and tea	1,021,321

SOURCE: Adapted from *Leading Advertisers, Showing Advertising Investments of Advertisers Spending $20,000 or More in Thirty-five Leading National Publications in the Calendar Year 1935* (Philadelphia: Curtis Publishing Co., 1936), 7, 18–19, 25.

watches, lipsticks, flooring, shoes and sundriés, a cornucopia of goods arrayed itself before consumers.[27]

Above all, advertising seemed to work. Advertising was to the distribution revolution as a tube was to toothpaste. Studies of the most recognized trademarks in America, 1923–1933, revealed that of the firms possessing these brands, the great majority relied heavily and sometimes exclusively on magazines to promote their wares. In 1931, investigators from Curtis Publishing surveyed 3,123 pantries for seventy-four commodities in homes across the country. They discovered a preponderance of nationally advertised brands on the nation's cupboard shelves, ranging from 48 percent of all goods surveyed in households from the lowest economic brackets to 67 percent for the well-to-do. A review of consumer spending by economist Richard Gettell, 1935–1950, suggested a close correspondence between change in spending and change in advertising revenues for national media. Fluctuations in consumers' and advertisers' expenditures "paralleled one another through depression and recession in the thirties, through mobilization and war in the early forties, through reconversion in the late forties." National advertising had come to be closely associated with the goods people purchased.[28]

Advertising stimulated the development of the national market, enlisting Americans in a continental community of consumers. By the 1920s the American marketplace was the wonder of the world. Although the United States lagged behind every country of northern Europe in the number of books published and sold per capita, it led the world in the circulation of periodicals and newspapers. Advertising facilitated the transformation from island communities to a nation. In fact, advertising itself was "so wholly American" that with a few minor exceptions, only in America were textbooks written on the subject, or courses on advertising psychology offered, or copywriters organized to define professional standards and goals. But one cannot precisely isolate the part played by advertising in promoting the material prosperity that came to be the hallmark of life in America. The two developments — the expansion of the national marketplace and of the promotional magazine industry — were coincidental aspects of the same thing.[29]

Other repercussions of the extension of media, their ultimate impact unforeseen and aside from the point of profit, must also be considered. Those who with historian Robert Wiebe search for a "new middle class" in the early twentieth century would do well to reflect on the influence of the magazine. The identity revolution that beset the professionals — the core of this new middle class — was promoted by the contemporaneous proliferation of business and trade journals, some 800 of which had appeared by 1897. These publications broke down the isolation of the island communities of the late nineteenth century, redirecting professionals to their peers throughout the nation. The advertisements announced the transcontinental accessibility of the tools, instruments, equipment, and paraphernalia that substantiated and shaped one's professional capacities. Their newly articulated occupational interests, if one wanted to share in them, might well be found in their magazines, sandwiched between the ads. But the middle class was more than its job skills, and its membership more than the professionals whom Wiebe isolated as its core. They were not the only ones to undergo this horizontal integration, nor was this integration confined to the occupational aspects of life.[30]

Whatever else happened to the structure and context of class in this era, it went national with the promotional magazines. If Starch's figures were roughly accurate, about one out of two families in the wealthiest group, wherever they happened to live in America, systematically and simultaneously received identical copies of the *Saturday Evening Post*. Fifty years before, such a reach was inconceivable. Magazines also integrated Americans vertically. Although different income strata preferred different magazines, some of their preferences were very much the same. *Ladies' Home Journal, Woman's Home Companion, Pictorial Review,* and *American Magazine* were among the favorite reading of all the groups across America. (See Figure 1.1.) As early as 1909, Frederick Dwight eulogized the old order. The national market was "the local genius of a people finding less and less expression in their clothing, their utensils, and their customs."[31]

The period most closely associated with rising magazine readership had another central characteristic. According to one scholarly observer of the teens and twenties, "The outstanding spiritual phenomenon of the times was the remarkable intensification of nationalism." Magazines had an influence. Karl W. Deutsch, a student of nationalism and its foundations, discovered that "all the usual descriptions of a people in terms of a community of languages, or character, or memories, or past history, are open to exception." According to Deutsch, "membership in a people essentially consists in wide complementarity of social communication. It consists in the ability to communicate more effectively, and over a wider range of subjects, with members of one large group than with outsiders." In this light, the promotional magazine should be viewed as a bulwark of the nation.[32]

As it proliferated, the new medium embraced and informed Americans up, down, and across the social structure. When Hornell Hart surveyed the "Changing Attitudes and Interests" of the American people for President Hoover's Research Committee on Social Trends, he thought it entirely appropriate to rely almost exclusively on magazines as the index of American values. For the student of such matters, said Hart, "the volumes of leading periodicals may well be regarded in much the same way in which a geologist looks at strata of the earth's crust." He then presented content-analyses of *Readers' Guides*. Years later, in his examination of the teens and twenties,

$10,000 and over	$5,000–9,999	$3,000–4,999	$2,000–2,999	$1,000–1,999	$0–999

--------------------*Literary Digest*-------------------

---------------*National Geographic*---------------

--------------------------*Good Housekeeping*--------------------------

---*Collier's*---

---*Saturday Evening Post*-------------------------------------

--*Delineator*-------------------------

--*Ladies' Home Journal*-----------------------

-------------------------------------*Woman's Home Companion*-------------------------

--*Pictorial Review*-------------------------

--*American Magazine*-------------------------

----*Cosmopolitan*----

----*Woman's World*----

--------------------------------*McCall's*--------------------------------

-----------------------------*Household*-----------------------------

-------*People's Popular Monthly*-------

--------------------*Comfort*--------------------

------*Gentlewoman*------

-*Mothers' Home Life*-

-------*Needlecraft*-------

1.1. Top Ten Magazine Preferences per Income Group as Determined by Subscribed Circulation, 1930
(American Association of Advertising Agencies, *Magazine Circulations—Qualitative Analysis by Incomes of Readers* (New York: American Association of Advertising Agencies, 1930), 6–16)

William Leuchtenburg recorded "a change in manners and morals that shook American society to its depths" as traditional behaviors disintegrated. To understand this "'revolution in morals,'" said Leuchtenburg, one's "best source is contemporary periodicals." That the new medium spoke for and articulated a national culture could almost be taken for granted. In his look at *America's Heroes,* Theodore Greene chose the mass circulation magazines to study because they are "the best periodical measures of the concerns, the tastes, and the standards of an era." The sheer increase in the number of journals, from 600 titles in 1857 to some 6000 by 1947, from reaching thousands to reaching thousands of thousands of Americans, going everywhere, enmeshing the national marketplace, actually may have effected the "introduction of everybody to everybody" else. The islands had been bridged.[33]

2

Socialization and Demand Creation:

Disinfectant as Deodorant

s magazines inundated America in the early twentieth century, the advertising that subsidized these promotional vehicles took on an added function. Besides announcing the availability of merchandise, advertising sought to fashion wants and create new desires to sell more and more of the goods that otherwise threatened to accumulate. By the late 1920s, when Americans produced more than they could buy, advertising had acquired this larger social dimension. Advertisers, enamored of their new profession and its potential, talked confidently about "demand creation."[1]

Others accorded persuasion a much less powerful role. To be sure, housewives and husbands who never conceived of a vacuum tube or internal combustion engines relied on ads to tell them of the wonderments of technology. A need to sweep the floor, however, or to travel from place to place, was nothing new in the constellation of American values. New products owed their very invention to prior wants of a similar sort. In this view, ads did not engender demand but met the demand for information required by a continental community of consumers.

In the 1920s, however, demand creation did occur in the deodorant market. In 1920, if a mouthwash habit existed, its material manifestation in the distribution of goods is hard to find. People perhaps chewed parsley after fish. Within a decade, however, a number of firms began promoting the consumption of mouthwash and producing various concoctions for a national market. Ads for the solutions appeared everywhere. But these solutions were clearly answers to problems of the advertisers' own making.

Lambert Pharmacal, the manufacturer of Listerine, initiated and exemplified this phenomenon, demonstrating that in addition to a commodity, a company could also produce demand. Listerine had been a disinfectant for home and hospital since the 1870s. When ads for the product appeared in earlier decades, their message was orthodox. Providing a vague list of uses, perhaps including a picture of the container, ads alerted Americans to the existence of the merchandise. In the 1920s, though, Listerine ads changed radically and specifically to effect new markets. Introducing the consumer to "halitosis," advertising copy moved from disinfectant to deodorant, from medical to romantic, from hygiene to hedonics. These promotions virtually dispensed with the original intention of acquainting demand with supply—a buyer with a bottle of disinfectant—and instead began generating a general demand for deodorization as a remedy for the social disaffections and personal inadequacies of the nation's consumers. Brand identification became secondary to promoting a consciousness the company itself first conceived, then articulated, and subsequently reinforced.

The ads did indeed fabricate a novel disease and an unverifiable social symptomology in order to secure customers. They also constructed a particular association of values clustered around the consumption of Listerine, none of them bearing an obvious or previous connection with a bottle of disinfectant. Love, friendship, fame and fortune, status, our secret selves afraid of rejection and loneliness: these needs and avoidances became the primary topics of Listerine promotions. By structuring old wants and anxieties in a novel manner, reinforcing this fear, playing upon that ambition, and undermining old self-confidence in unprecedented ways, these advertisements did more than stimulate demand for a product that had been on the market for decades. They created a demand that did not exist before.

Advertising of this sort must be viewed as an agency of socialization. It promoted more than just a product; it transmitted cultural values of an advertiser's own design. By selling its peculiar version of human interaction and social adaptation, it would also sell goods. To the degree that it succeeded, this type of solicitation taught consumers something about who they were and how they related to the world at large, to that world the advertisers themselves construed.

To understand this alteration in advertising, one must appreciate the changing dynamics of the American marketplace. In the decade after World War I, a number of observers felt that the world had witnessed two economic revolutions of major import. The one in Russia, self-conscious and deliberate, rejected capitalistic organization and the primacy of material possessiveness. The revolution they perceived in America, on the other hand, came disguised as a flush of goods. The change in the United States was not structural; it was not so much a transformation in the kind of business enterprise, as it was a matter of degree. "But it is this degree of economic activity," counseled the Committee on Recent Economic Changes, "this almost insatiable appetite for goods and services, this abounding production of all things which any man can want, which is so striking." There seemed to be more things than ever to be bought and sold; in particular, there seemed to be a profusion of goods that were little used or wholly unknown a generation beforehand: radios, refrigerators, and rayon; a maze of devices for the home; gas stoves and oil furnaces; wrist watches, phonographs, and cigarette lighters; mechanical pencils; airplanes, autos, and antifreeze; trucks and tractors; conveyor belts, spray painters, and excavating machines. Although its origin was hazy, the effect of this so-called friendly revolution was clear. America provided "the greatest physical well-being that any nation has ever been able to accord its people."[2]

This abundance was no optimist's illusion, and that became obvious as the figures emerged. Total national wealth, measured in constant prices, rose 68 percent between 1912 and 1929. Gross National Product (GNP) per capita, in constant dollars, rose from $710 to $857 between 1919 and 1929. The combined production of all sources of power in the United States, in terms of thermal units—the "power wealth" of the nation—constituted almost half the world's total. This put American "not at the head of the class but in a class by itself." In addition to wealth, income also showed an actual and marked advance over previous levels. Annual income per capita, adjusted for inflation, rose from $336 in 1914 to $396 in 1929; the real increase in income per person gainfully employed averaged 28.7 percent in those same years. The evidence of abundance seemed incontrovertible and everywhere in sight.[3]

Moreover, prosperity reached down to include a large segment of the population whose previous purchases had been confined to basic needs. Yesteryear's luxuries seemed essential to everyday life in the 1920s. Electricity was only one of them; once introduced, it prompted a new order of wants and desires. Electrification occurred almost at once in historical time: in 1912 only 16 percent of the population had electricity in their homes; by 1927, 63 percent of their homes were wired. Hence, another network, and yet another web of expectations, entangled the overwhelming majority of Americans in the first decades of the twentieth century.[4]

This material well-being made for more than ready access to electricity, modern plumbing, and automobiles, although all three represented visible and striking departures from the everyday experiences of the average American at the turn of the century. The National Industrial Conference Board tried to measure "Changes in Minimum Standards of Living, 1869–1938." Not to its surprise, for this was a rigorous study of enterprise and social progress, the Conference Board reported fairly steady increases in workers' discretionary income from Reconstruction right through the Great Depression. Measuring change is fraught with difficulties, but these pale in relation to defining a minimum standard of living. The term itself is political.[5]

The figures in Table 2.1, for instance, do not control for changing conceptualizations of a material minimum over the course of the study. In the 1870s, soap, underwear and overcoats, eyeglasses, a telephone, and proper medical care were optional accoutrements of existence. By the 1930s, however, the American wage earner would have preferred not to live without them. Discretionary income, in that sense, cannot be confused with excess income, or money that one could spend on whatever one pleased. New "necessities" of life — from curtains on the window to toilet tissue to white collars for the new class of wage earners — accompanied a rise in pay that measurements of discretionary income can only intimate.[6]

These figures on standards of living nonetheless bear scrutiny. They are based on scores of family studies undertaken since 1869, all of course with problems of their own. Proportions spent for food,

TABLE 2.1   Change in relative costs by wage earners' families, 1869–1935

	Percent of Average Total Expenditures				
Period	Food	Housing	Clothing	Fuel and light	All other expenditures
1869–1879	51.3	16.8	14.9	5.9	11.1
1880–1889	44.0	15.7	18.7	5.8	15.8
1890–1899	42.3	14.3	15.9	6.2	21.3
1900–1909	43.1	18.1	13.0	5.6	20.2
1910–1919	39.9	13.7	15.6	5.2	25.6
1920–1929	37.3	14.6	14.9	5.0	28.2
1930–1935	32.8	16.0	10.9	5.5	34.8

SOURCE: *Conference Board Studies in Enterprise and Social Progress* (New York: National Industrial Conference Board, 1939), 153.

clothing, housing, and fuel and light, when isolated from all other expenditures, might give a crude notion of the money left over for "cultural" acquisitions, for goods in addition to the subsistence requirements of American wage-earning families. The data may suggest the degree to which those families could meet their wants in addition to their needs.

The most striking advance came oddly enough from 1930 to 1935,[7] when over a third of a family's income could be used for all other expenditures. To the working families of the 1870s, their departure from basic need — as indicated by their possible range of incidental purchases — must have been almost imperceptible. Their 300-plus percentage increase in discretionary income over the next sixty years meant the gradual but inevitably increasing appearance of pocket combs, toothpaste, perhaps an extra pair of shoes, a pack of cigarettes, toasters, fans, nail polish, consumer goods of all descriptions, which distinguished American wage earners from their forebears both here and abroad. No other country in the world could approach the American standard of living in the 1920s.[8]

The evidence seems to indicate, from another perspective, that wage-earning families of the twenties and thirties could go without a third of their wages and still manage to subsist. So long as one's unemployment — and loss of ability to buy — was not carved out in one or three or five year lapses of perpetual idleness, Americans could buy more goods and more types of goods than ever. As Lynd and Hanson noted, "The great bulk of the things consumed by American families is no longer made in the home and the efforts of family members are focused instead on *buying* a living."[9]

The productive capacity of the nation guaranteed that there was more than enough to purchase. Although the population increased only 65 percent between 1900 and 1930, the quantity of manufactures was up 151 percent. Between 1919 and 1925, output per worker advanced 15 percent in transportation, 18 percent in agriculture, 33 percent in mining, and 40 percent in manufacturing all sorts of goods.[10]

Recognizing this "revolution in our midst," this "almost unprecedented progress," commentators sought explanations for this meteoric leap in the production of goods. Rexford Tugwell recorded over thirty contributors to America's remarkable rise in productivity. Notions of scientific management earned first place in Tugwell's list of specific causes: the standardization of facilities, the introduction of a "standard task" with measured movements for each worker, the "functional foremanship" of supervisory personnel, and the incentive of differential wages. But the cause of revolution is multiple.[11]

Tugwell's explorations were exhaustive, from an "enlarged reliance on paperwork," to an American eagerness to eschew obsolescence, to eight-year cycles in the astrological conjunctions of Venus. Others cited their favorite explanation for the unparalleled onslaught of making, selling, and buying goods. Some felt that the roots of American prosperity could be unearthed in America's abundance of natural resources; others cited the continental expanse of an area of free trade. Only in the United States could someone travel 3000 miles in one direction, and then go 2000 miles another, and still find people speaking a language almost indistinguishable from first stop to last. Such an immense region with a common language permitted the development of "national consumption habits" and thus the large-scale production required to meet the needs of a national marketplace. Mechanization itself seemed principal to others. The World War had to be credited in several ways—the wartime records of industry became goals to which business aspired when peace returned; European need for goods after the conflagration provided a ready market. The influence of the Federal Reserve System, the growth of economic services that traced curves of business and prognosticated, and Republican administrations in Washington also seemed to contribute. There were almost as many reasons for America's spectacular advance as there were commentators to discover them.[12]

Advertising underwent a transformation of its own. It took on an increasingly complicated social role as the feverish acceleration in the number of goods to sell required a corresponding demand. To merely let a buyer know a business had something to sell had been sufficient when business believed that general overproduction was impossible. But the world had changed considerably. In his study of advertising, Ralph Hower observed that, "as never before in history, the consumer was faced with more goods than he knew what to do with. . . . Early in the 'twenties there were signs that the flow of goods was being checked—not at its source as had so often occurred in centuries past but at the outlet—through the consumer's failure to absorb all the commodities which were thrust upon him."[13]

In the island communities of a century before, this situation was hardly conceivable. "They not only produced what they consumed, but they consumed what they produced." To at least one economist as late as the 1890s, the very existence of a supply of goods evidenced consumer desire and ultimate consumer demand. "Want is always the prior fact in economic development," as George Gunton explained it. "It needs no special study to see that things are not demanded because

they are made, but that they are made because they are demanded."
But if some nineteenth century Nostradamus had foreseen the actual
output of American industry in 1928, he would have been regarded as
foolish.[14]

In the 1920s, it became increasingly clear that a glut of goods
threatened to undo the "friendly revolution" of prosperity in
America. By the 1930s it was obvious that "there was not only
enough, but too much gasoline, too much cotton and copper, too
much of practically everything." The machine was making more
goods than people could possibly buy. Advertisers, scrambling to sell
their wares, hoped not only to meet demand, but also to create it.[15]

The lure of demand creation—the manufacturing of material
want in addition to the supply that would sate it—began to entrance
advertisers in the 1890s. During the last years of the nineteenth century, as the potentials of mass production became apparent, advertisers realized that the masses were big buyers of goods. Promoters
came to appreciate that the middle and lower classes were a far larger
market than their previous gallery of the well-to-do. The promotional
magazines began to reflect this new interest, and in the years that
followed, perspectives governing advertisers altered fundamentally.

Around 1900, advertisers learned to speak to the consumer as
one person rather than a vague anonymous aggregation. "You" became their audience. During the Progressive years, as advertising took
on the ideological apparatus of a profession, the perceived objective
of promoters moved from alerting customers to one's commodities to
attracting and influencing possible purchasers. As Daniel Andrew
Pope reports, "it shifted from a means of information and announce-
ment to a tool of persuasion and demand creation." The ideology of
demand creation was expressed only "in embryo," however, before
World War I. When the war was over, advertisers "proclaimed their
social purpose in bold terms."[16]

The war itself altered the ways in which people regarded promotional possibilities. Income and excess profits taxes, legalized in 1913,
mounted along with the war effort. Realizing that a large portion of
their profits would otherwise go to the government, many businesses
became willing to spend sums that might pave the way for even
greater profits after the war, when the government turned to peaceful
and less costly pursuits. So advertising made good sense. At the same
time, the government itself seemed to demonstrate that advertising
had an almost illimitable potential. In its crusade to sell both the war
and liberty bonds, asserted *Printers' Ink,* the government proved it
could "sway the minds of whole populations, change their habits of

life, create a belief in a given policy or idea by the use of the right methods of advertising." In the 1920s, promoters would attempt to effect the same results.[17]

Influencing how Americans would dispose of their incomes became a very big business. As one accountant of American prosperity put it, "Educate the world and his wife to want, and the productive capacity of the country will actually groan under the burden of enormous demand." Magazine advertising revenues took off in a spiral of heady anticipations. Vehicles of mass communication proliferated to announce not only the availability but also the desirability of goods. There seemed to be few limits to the possibilities of profitable production of commodities and desires.[18]

Could an advertiser actually create demand for goods? Make people want a product—and want it enough to go out and buy it? Lambert Pharmacal did so, with a product that had known only an indifferent market for the previous fifty years. Jordan Wheat Lambert had studied chemistry and, in the 1870s, developed an antiseptic dressing safe for human tissue. He went to England to seek out Joseph Lister, whose work on antisepsis had spurred Lambert's own curiosity. Lister agreed to loan the use of his name to this "professional preparation to be used in surgery." The firm used some advertising to convey its existence to Americans; indeed, it had acquired a powerful trade name in days before branding a difficult product became a common practice. (Fig. 2.1.) Listerine provided Lambert a comfortable income until his death.[19]

Young Gerard, his son, had known few wants. As he remarked, "I was quite used to having any material thing I wanted." As a student, he rode in a chauffeured limousine to get from building to building at Princeton. The economic downturn in 1921, however, left him strapped for funds and heavily in debt. As he considered the alternatives, Gerard Lambert decided to make the family business pay as it never had before.[20]

A senior member of the firm discovered the term "halitosis" in a clipping from a British periodical; the company decided that Listerine could cure it. The terminology lent the authority of medicine to the disorder, giving a semantic legitimacy to the condition. Lambert himself claimed to have written the first ad. Reciting the case of a pretty girl and a tale of woe, he alerted Americans to the secret crippler of their dreams. The debility, halitosis, required an asterisk that referred to its explanation, but its meaning was clear from the copy. Although the company invented the story, the results were a ready demonstration of the effectiveness of this approach to the marketplace.[21]

2.1. A SAFE ANTISEPTIC
(*Saturday Evening Post*, 29 January 1916)

When the agency passed the ad around its offices, most of the staff predicted that the campaign would fail because it defied the well-established practice of avoiding disagreeable topics. "While he probably was not the first to use this type of appeal," said one business journalist, "Milton J. Feasley, who promoted the halitosis campaign, originated the idea of applying it to an actual commodity." To test this new technique, this expression of larger social values instead of listing product uses, coupons were used on both the old and new type of ad. (Fig. 2.2.) "Halitosis" outpulled its predecessor by four-to-one. Sales climbed 33 percent the month after the firm first alerted Americans to the cause of their failures and defeats.[22]

Lambert decided to take promotion into his own hands, convinced that most ad men "don't know a damn thing about it themselves, and couldn't earn a dollar on their own at the game." He increased advertising expenditures by $5000 a month until in 1928 they exceeded $5 million. "We never failed to take in a profit in any one month that was greater than the increased advertising cost for that month." In time, halitosis seemed to afflict an enormous number of people; "our advertising created a demand from the consumer so great that the dealer *had* to carry it, even if he did not like the terms of the sale."[23]

By then, halitosis and a cluster of social values associated with avoiding it had become common fare in popular periodicals. "A few years ago," asserted an ad for mints in 1925, "bad breath was condoned as an unavoidable misfortune. Today it is judged one of the gravest social offenses." The figures used to convince consumers of their offensiveness made the blight seem endemic. Of 1000 dentists supposedly asked how often they used Listerine "in self-defense" on a patient with this malady, 83 percent said frequently; 15 percent did so occasionally; only 2 percent said never. "Don't fool yourself by thinking you never had it," warned the advertisements. The "*face to face evidence*" of 120 hotel clerks proved it. (Fig. 2.3.) "Nine people out of ten" suffered either chronic or acute sieges of this "unforgivable social offense." Ads told Americans the worst thing about their breath: "it builds a barrier not only between acquaintances and friends, but between loved ones as well."

Fighting and overcoming bad breath was a simple matter of "using Listerine every morning and night. And between times before social and business engagements." The ritual was an investment in popularity, "your assurance that you will be welcome by others." Why be "a nuisance" and offend? Listerine no longer advertised itself as such; its ads began to look more like messages of public service underwritten by antiseptics manufacturers.[24]

The results were twofold. In 1921, Lambert Pharmacal did not rank among the 100 largest advertisers in leading national magazines. In 1922, it moved just ahead of International Harvester, ranking

If your friends were entirely frank with you

THERE are some subjects that your most intimate friends habitually dodge in conversation. Even wives and husbands often back away from them.

Halitosis is one of these.

What is it? Why, halitosis is the medical term meaning offensive breath. And nine people out of ten suffer from this trouble either chronically or from time to time.

One of the most trying things about halitosis is this: the victim of it is usually not aware himself of the fact that his breath is not agreeable to those about him.

Halitosis may come from a disordered stomach, from bad teeth, catarrh, too much smoking, eating or drinking. It may be temporary: it may be lasting. When it is chronic it's a case for your physician to look after. Let him get at the seat of the trouble.

For temporary relief, however, and for that comfortable assurance that your breath *is* sweet and clean, there is one simple, ready precaution you may yourself observe.

Listerine—used as a mouth wash.

Thousands of people now know this delightful toilet aid for its wonderfully effective properties as a breath deodorant. They use it systematically as a mouth wash and gargle because it relieves them of that uncomfortable suspicion that their breath may not be just right.

By doing so, of course, they are at the same time observing a sensible method of preserving mouth hygiene, guarding against sore throat and the more serious germ diseases that find entrance to the system through the mouth—all of which the antiseptic properties of Listerine combat.

If you are at all sensitive about your breath, you will welcome Listerine. It is the most agreeable and effective way to counteract halitosis.

To those who are not familiar with this use of Listerine we shall be glad to forward a generous sample if you will fill out and mail to us the coupon below.

Once you have tried Listerine and enjoyed the fresh, clean feeling it leaves about your mouth, throat and teeth, you will never be without it—at home or in your traveling bag.

LAMBERT PHARMACAL COMPANY, SAINT LOUIS, U. S. A.

LAMBERT PHARMACAL CO., 2118 LOCUST ST., ST. LOUIS, MO.
Please send me a sample of Listerine as you suggest in this advertisement.

Name _____ Address _____

City _____ State _____

2.2. THAT UNCOMFORTABLE SUSPICION
(*Cosmopolitan,* November 1921)

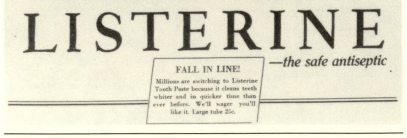

don't fool yourself

It ruins romance

Did you ever come face to face with a real case of halitosis (unpleasant breath)? Can you imagine yourself married to a person offending this way?

Halitosis is the unforgivable social offense, and don't fool yourself by thinking you never have it. The insidious thing about it is that you yourself never can tell.

The way to avoid such offense is to rinse the mouth with Listerine, the safe antiseptic.

Immediately it removes every unpleasant odor—even a powerful one like that of the onion.

Keep a bottle handy in home and office—so that you may always put yourself on the safe and polite side. Lambert Pharmacal Co., St. Louis, Missouri, U. S. A.

> $\frac{1}{3}$
>
> **Had Halitosis**
>
> **120** hotel clerks, 40 of them in the better class hotels, say that nearly every third person inquiring for a room has halitosis. Who should know better than they?
>
> *Face to face evidence*

LISTERINE

—the safe antiseptic

> **FALL IN LINE!**
>
> Millions are switching to Listerine Tooth Paste because it cleans teeth whiter and in quicker time than ever before. We'll wager you'll like it. Large tube 25c.

2.3. FALL IN LINE
(*Better Homes and Gardens,* September 1927)

seventy-ninth. By 1924, it ranked sixteenth. It fluctuated between fourth and sixth place for the rest of the decade. Meanwhile, a new consciousness awoke in America, illustrated on page after page, reiterated month after month, year after year, and on its way to making deodorization part of everyday life. Lambert Pharmacal's advertising in newspapers and magazines was reaching a combined circulation of 110 million a month.[25]

After a point, the firm realized that new appeals for the same product, run when the commodity neared a saturation point with one group of users, "would be like plowing virgin territory." It employed sore throat, dandruff, and after-shave appeals, and sales kept rising. The business introduced a "saw-tooth" method of campaigning. A three-month cycle began with almost no ads and gradually intensified until the end of the third month, when expenditures reached $600,000. Then they would drop again to nothing. The profits, said Lambert, rose another $1 million that year.[26]

As Lambert Pharmacal's ranking in the list of leading magazine advertisers rose from seventy-ninth place to number four, profits also registered impressive gains. Annual earnings jumped from $115,000 to over $8 million in those same seven years. Not all of this success could be attributed to the halitosis campaigns. When Lambert decided to take charge of the firm, he introduced efficiencies of production that reduced costs by one-third. As it increased its advertising, the firm reduced the sales force from twenty-two people to five. The tax on the alcoholic content of the concoction was reduced since Listerine was not for drinking, and the firm saved another million dollars. The line of goods was expanded to include heavily advertised toothpaste; Lambert noted that the profitability of the toothpaste campaigns far exceeded mouthwash, although they were much less spectacular. Nonetheless, effective advertising was the key contributor to the company's success.[27]

Lambert was sure of it, asserting that earnings would have remained at $115,000 a year if not for the firm's reliance on advertising. Others in the company agreed: "There is no question as to the cause of the recent phenomenal success of our Company. The product has been unchanged for many years. . . . There is but our advertising—it is right in appeal, it is right in presentation, and right in the medium that carries it to the public." Lambert relinquished Listerine in 1928, although he continued to feel a personal responsibility for the term "halitosis" once it began to appear in the dictionary in addition to the vocabulary of the common culture. When he sold his shares of stock, he settled for a certified check in excess of $25 million, "all of which I had made in six years."[28]

By that time, promotions for all sorts of consumer goods had become especially intense. Conditions affected production and distribution differently, and began to lend a quality of marked unpredictability to the marketplace. In the early 1920s, before advances in income registered in the American shopping spree that followed, business faced considerable sales resistance. The situation called for increasing sales volume along with quantity production. The development of large-scale industry depended upon a "social habit of consumption" attuned to the use of goods that could be mass-produced, thereby lowering the unit costs of production. Advertisers had realized at the turn of the century, in the heyday of the trusts, that advertising expenditures were more related to the amount of output of a product than to the number of firms competing to sell it. Total volume of advertising actually doubled between 1918 and 1920, from $1.5 billion to $2.9 billion.[29]

By the midtwenties, times had improved substantially. Excited by visions of unparalleled productive capacity, observers discovered a new logic to the mass market. Removing the limits on production had resulted in increased purchasing power, which in turn spurred production, which in its turn would increase purchasing power, and so on. It seemed that America could expect an endless cycle of buying, selling, and buying more. This optimistic understanding of market mechanisms suited the inflated expectations of an era of unparalleled prosperity. Around 1926, expanding distribution "became an obsession. . . . An overwhelming desire for volume at all costs affected numerous organizations like a feverish disease, producing frenzied efforts to sell, sell, sell, anywhere and everywhere." Manufacturers in many fields of business began to eye a potential market for their wares that both reflected the optimism of the age and belied sound judgment.[30]

Indeed, consumer need was not necessarily the initiating force in industry. Now goods were often made, said Tugwell, "almost altogether in anticipation of demand," before knowing with any real certainty that anyone was willing to pay for all the innumerable commodities that would otherwise accumulate as dust on the shelves. Personal credit, secured only by a faith in the ability to pay tomorrow for property transferred today, was introduced on a grand scale. Indebtedness in America mounted as never before. Installment buying—converting future earning power into present purchasing power—hastened the rush to overproduction and precipitated a day of reckoning.[31]

But overproducing seemed relatively inconsequential—even perhaps impossible—when wants were inexhaustible, and it seemed that way in the 1920s. If a shadow clouded the horizon, it was underconsumption—a need for more purchasing, not a need for less production—a difficulty for the individual producer that suasion might cure. As late as 1929, even so scholarly an analysis as *Recent Economic Changes* asserted that its "survey has proved conclusively . . . that wants are almost insatiable; that one want satisfied makes way for another." The editors summed up a decade of friendly revolution, what many called a New Era: "We seem only to have touched the fringe of our potentialities." Their acclamations had some basis in fact. A few years later Frederick Mills discovered that between 1922 and 1929, rates of change in production and population were such that "the doubling of the individual's portion would have required only 29 years." That sort of phenomenon, however, would have also required appropriate adjustments in the system of distribution, an alteration in the means of getting all those goods into the hands of purchasers.[32]

Signs of trouble ahead, and a larger role for persuasion, were there to divine. During 1929, machines were so underemployed that manufacturers were only making 80 percent of what their factories could turn out, and this increased the advisability of exerting influence upon popular habits of consumption. Lynd and Hanson explained that, "in a rough sense, plant expansion follows consumer demand; actually, however, guided by guesses and plans for capturing the volume market, expansion tends to leap ahead of actual demand; and it often outlasts demand. Once built, on the basis of whatever expectations, correct or inaccurate, expanded plant facilities increase overhead and become a compelling stimulus to sales pressure on the consumer." Advertising appeals often became dissociated from the products themselves, as promoters sought to accord their particular commodity the widest cultural meaning to wrest the largest demand from a marketplace glutted with goods. "Not goods, but social value and 'service' were sold in the advertisers' copy; not clothes, but the advantages of neat appearance; not foods, but health; not labor-saving devices in the home, but visions of leisured women engaged in sports; not dancing or saxophone lessons as such, but social popularity." The glut gave rise to a "ceaseless quest for what advertising men call 'million dollar merchandising ideas,'" that is, "'halitosis' as applied to Listerine."[33]

Of course we now know that the Listerine phenomenon was idiosyncratic. Advertisers do not generally create new needs, despite their best efforts to do so. But the fluke was by no means inconsequential in its historical context. Lambert Pharmacal's success epitomized the entrepreneurial optimism of the New Era. Its campaigns introduced a new social function for advertising, and this manipulation of consumer desire seemed to work. It actually generated demand. Contemporaries did not overlook the formula. It encapsulated a new "understanding" of the marketplace that other businesses were quick to embrace and mimic.

Traditional economic thought hinged on the understanding that industry was guided by the producer's incentive to fulfill consumers' needs. This older conceptualization, however, assumed that customers' needs were independent of the enterpriser. Once possessed of the ability to manipulate demand, the entrepreneur no longer had to abide entirely by the consumer's choice. Success might come to someone who could fashion wants and cash in on changes in demand that advertising effected.

The focus of productive energies shifted, undermining the notion that production was geared to prior need. To the degree that returns to be made depended upon persuasion, "they are not derived from catering to wants, but from cultivating tastes for commodities, the supply of which the individual producer controls." It was, an economist commented, about as easy to augment one's slice of the pie by manipulating taste, as by meeting it. And indeed prior understandings of the marketplace did need revision. The fall devastated a society made breathless by its ascent.[34]

Foster and Catchings had explained in 1925 that collapse inevitably followed the climb. They spoke of the day when distribution would be so out of kilter that industry would benefit by actually giving goods away, dumping them overseas, "or even by burning them up." That hardly seemed reasonable in the dollar democracy of the American marketplace. Every day was a new election; the candidates — merchandise of all descriptions — stood to win or lose depending upon the ballots cast, the dollars spent, by purchasers across the land. Foster and Catchings insisted that the wise producer both recorded today's results, and expected tomorrow's. By the late 1920s, however, it seemed just as important to be out campaigning. Total advertising volume peaked at $3.4 billion in 1929.[35]

But demand is not mere desire. An individual without purchasing power is disfranchised in the marketplace. When the stock of goods produced in excess of effective demand accumulated past a certain point, there was no hope of profit in keeping people employed making still more things that they were unwilling or unable to purchase. Abetted especially by the stock market crash, the lopsided distribution of income in America, the overextension of credit, and the fiscal short-sightedness of the Federal Reserve, what might have been a "garden-variety" downturn resulted in economic collapse. Employment dropped precipitously. The spiral of making, selling, buying, and making more switched course; "in the midst of plentiful supplies of most necessities and many luxuries of living, a large share of the total consumer population was reduced to the level of bare subsistence." Creative advertising could not stem the tide. The fabled day of "enough and to spare for all" had arrived, but the dream was a nightmare in the dollar democracy.[36]

Although Gerard Lambert left Listerine in 1928, the company did not alter its formula for success substantially. The Lambert Company was the third largest advertiser in leading American magazines in the midst of the worst economic retrenchment this nation has known. Ads became more adamant and less related to the product itself. As measured by the noticeability of a brand name in their copy, in fact, the actual item the firm had to sell was increasingly indiscernible in its advertising. (Fig. 2.4.) It seemed that as long as people worried about halitosis, they would think of Listerine. The company tried to ensure that no one would forget what the significant others whom it had invented could not forgive.[37]

Compelling factors—quite independent of Listerine's creative promotion—undoubtedly influenced the public's amenability to the company's campaigns. Perhaps Americans actually began to need deodorants as never before. Industrialization had reshaped both the workplace and the marketplace. Urbanization sharply redefined social space. The terms of subsistence had been transformed. Complementary messages from the promoters of other goods reinforced the claims of Lambert Pharmacal. The very degree of change in the order may have made Americans willing to accept new habits of everyday life.

Diet underwent substantial modification. Foods were processed by unprecedented means and preserved in unprecedented fashion. The output of canned fruits and vegetables was up 524 percent from 1899 to 1925. After the war, between 1919 and 1926, official estimates recorded a rise of almost 58 percent in total consumption of fresh milk. Milk products also showed large increases: per capita consumption of butter was up 23 percent; cheese up 27 percent; ice cream up 45 percent. Sugar consumption soared from a war-time low of 75–77 pounds per capita to 114.67 pounds by 1925/1926. Fresh fruits and

"If you want the truth—

—go to a child." And the old saying is certainly true, isn't it?

Here was the case of a young woman who, in spite of her personal charm and beauty, never seemed to hold men friends.

For a long, long time she searched her mind for the reason. It was a tragic puzzle in her life.

Then one day her little niece told her.

* * *

You, yourself, rarely know when you have halitosis (unpleasant breath). That's the insidious thing about it. And even your closest friends won't tell you.

Sometimes, of course, halitosis comes from some deep-seated organic disorder that requires professional advice. But usually—and fortunately—halitosis is only a local condition that yields to the regular use of Listerine as a mouth wash and gargle. It is an interesting thing that this well-known antiseptic that has been in use for years for surgical dressings, possesses these unusual properties as a breath deodorant. It puts you on the safe and polite side.

Listerine halts food fermentation in the mouth and leaves the breath sweet, fresh and clean. The entire mouth feels invigorated.

Get in the habit of using Listerine every morning and night. And between times before social and business engagements. It's the fastidious thing to do. *Lambert Pharmacal Company, St. Louis, Missouri.*

For HALITOSIS use LISTERINE

2.4.   A TRAGIC PUZZLE
(*Ladies' Home Journal,* June 1936)

vegetables now could be eaten all year, and were. Consumption of poultry rose millions of pounds. To the degree that one's breath related to what one ate, as deodorant ads intimated, a changing diet may have altered exhalations. More importantly, the variety of a diet freed from the dictates of seasonal and regional availability ensured that the relatively homogeneous menu of the island community was gone for good.[38]

Prohibition created its own market for unliquored breath. The ban on imbibing took effect in January 1920. In the six years before that in Massachusetts, which apparently kept unusually complete records, arrests for drunkenness had declined. But by 1924, the law logged double the number of arrests made in 1920. Prohibition, furthermore, induced "a curious and almost comical inversion of class relations," the drinkers no longer being the poorer sorts, but the college crowd and the upwardly mobile. The same social stratum was probably the eye of Listerine's target market.[39]

Cigarettes became a very popular addiction. The war made smokers of many men, and women started too. Between 1911 and 1915, sales were less than 15 billion cigarettes per annum; from 1921 to 1925, more than 65 billion were sold each year. By 1925, the increase in output of cigarettes over 1899 was an astonishing 2038 percent. In 1928, sales reached 100 billion a year. How this may have affected washing one's mouth is immeasurable. Ads for Listerine cigarettes appeared in a handful of magazines in 1931. "What? You haven't tried a Listerine cigarette?" Impregnated with the essence of antiseptic, these cigarettes were just the thing for "super-sensitive throats."[40]

Contemporaneous efforts to sell toothpastes and brushes also echoed Listerine's breath campaigns. When Borden sought to measure advertising's economic effects, he chose to study dentifrice because in spite of the many brands on the market, 90 percent of demand went to a dozen heavily advertised brands. The major development in the dentifrice market occurred between 1914 and 1931, courtesy of persuasive advertising for toothpastes, white teeth, film, pretty smiles, and pyhorrea, which increased thirty-fold. This outpouring was especially great in the 1920s and "quite clearly must have been an important factor in bringing about the marked growth in primary demand for dentifrices."[41]

The specific effects of toothpaste promotion on brand sales did not contradict its positive impact on demand for dentifrice in general. Borden's compilations insist upon an extremely close correspondence between consumption of particular types of toothpaste and their producers' advertising outlays. The sources he used require that qualifications be made when interpreting his results. Borden relied primarily upon a Scripps-Howard inventory of 53,000 homes in sixteen cities served by that particular network, which may or may not be comparable to cities entwined in another part of the web. The home inventory forms were distributed to parent-teacher associations and church groups, who for a consideration canvassed an apparently sound sampling. The respondents, however, completed the inventories themselves. But they had to select a trade name if they claimed to have a tube of toothpaste. So even if the results of the survey are nothing more than an index of the housewives' material dreams (this was 1938), that fact would not alter a conclusion that the amount of advertising and brand identification corresponded closely.[42]

Dentifrice advertisers ran campaigns to coincide with the vogue of women smoking, with copy like "Can a Girl Smoke and Still be Lovely?" A daily brushing would help. Advertising for Listerine toothpaste in its own small way probably contributed to the accelerated adoption of brush and paste in the 1920s. Although in the teens Listerine itself offered to clean where a brush could not reach and was an oral antiseptic, Lambert Pharmacal formulated its own brand of dentifrice in 1921. (Fig. 2.5.) These ads undoubtedly added to the compulsion to brush that other advertisers incited and magnified the firm's own efforts to sell gargle and a concomitant concern for fastidious attention to one's mouth.[43]

Lambert's employment of the negative appeal may have been a special key to the company's success; the business was largely responsible for its revival after years of increasing disuse. Attempts "to stimulate the reader to the avoidance of a repulsive situation" were in general disfavor in advertising circles, and never more so than in 1920, perhaps because of a general belief in the efficacy of positive thinking. Later, experimenters would find no major benefit to positive advertising. Evidence even suggested a slight preference for negativity among women (who probably purchased most Listerine consumed in the home), and some enhancement in effectiveness of the negative appeal as the subjects advanced in age.[44]

A particular twist to the negativity of Lambert Pharmacal's copy was its contention that the effects of bad breath, though supposedly experienced often, were never articulated. Not even your best friends would tell you. It was, ads importuned, a matter polite people did not discuss—not even husbands and wives. Halitosis was "an invisible Judas, unsensed as well as unseen, yet always with her; it betrayed her to others as a careless and sometimes objectionable person," but she

Once an active social leader ~ now a helpless invalid

HOW ABOUT YOURSELF? Have you seen your dentist lately? Are you aware of the fact that many, many grave diseases trace their origin directly to neglected, abscessed teeth? Your doctor and dentist will tell you so.

One eminent authority in this field estimates that 78 out of every 100 adults today suffer from tooth abscesses—many totally unaware of the dangers lurking in such infections.

Among the troubles traced to these hidden wells of poison in your mouth are rheumatism and joint diseases; heart and kidney trouble; stomach and intestinal derangements; to say nothing of more minor ailments ranging from simple headaches to insomnia and nervous affections.

The age to which you are going to live may depend very largely upon the kind of attention you give your teeth.

Don't neglect seeing your dentist

In spite of these grave dangers that lurk in tooth abscesses, relatively few people today ever think of visiting a dentist until pain drives them there. Whereas, only a good dentist can really place you on the safe side.

The right dentifrice and faithful tooth brushing can, of course, do much to keep the teeth clean and the gums exercised and healthy. But when abscesses have developed, only a dentist and the X-ray can cope with the trouble.

Choose carefully

However, it becomes very important to choose the right dentifrice because clean teeth will not decay and cause trouble. For this reason more and more dentists are today recommending Listerine Tooth Paste.

Listerine Tooth Paste, and this tooth paste only, contains all of the antiseptic essential oils of Listerine, the safe antiseptic. These healing, antiseptic ingredients help keep the gums firm and healthy and discourage the breeding of disease bacteria in the mouth.

Quick results—and safe!

This is an age when people want quick results. Listerine Tooth Paste is so formulated that it cleans your teeth with a *minimum* of brushing, calling for much less effort than is ordinarily required.

Also, this paste cleans with absolute safety. The specially prepared cleanser it contains is just hard enough to discourage tartar formation, yet *not* hard enough to scratch or injure tooth enamel. And, of course, you know how precious tooth enamel is!

Finally, Listerine Tooth Paste is sold at a price that is fair—large tube 25 cents—the right price to pay for a good tooth paste. Try it. Enjoy really clean teeth. But don't forget the importance of seeing your dentist regularly.—*Lambert Pharmacal Company, Saint Louis, U. S. A.*

If your dentist has not already handed you our booklet on tooth abscesses and a sample of our dentifrice, you may have both of these by addressing a postal to the Lambert Pharmacal Co., Saint Louis.

WILL <u>YOU</u> BE ALIVE FIVE YEARS FROM NOW?

2.5. A PUBLIC BENEFIT
(*Saturday Evening Post*, 14 March 1925)

herself was utterly unaware of it. At least until the advertising made her wonder.[45]

Urban Americans of the 1920s must have been fairly coarsened, caught in the act of inuring themselves to the constant jostles and freak encounters of city life, pressured into learning how to consume conspicuously to assure both their status in a fluid society and that the machines would keep turning out goods. One of the perils of prosperity, said Leuchtenburg, was that "it undermined facets of the American character which had developed under an economy of scarcity; in particular, it encouraged an anxious concern for social approbation." Urbanization entailed a propinquity of people—and strangers at that—so tight as to be imaginable only at the most congested camp meeting of the nineteenth century.[46]

Several scholars have noted a reorientation of American character in the early twentieth century that would have made Listerine's pitches especially appealing. David Reisman, in *The Lonely Crowd,* tracked the emergence of what he called "other direction," as modern Americans began to rely on the external approval of others rather than internal determinants of self-worth. Christopher Lasch, in his study of *The Culture of Narcissism,* drew similar conclusions. Americans began to invest in the acceptance and attention of others as the basis for their own self-esteem to the degree that it became a cultural preoccupation. Warren Susman also examined this fundamental shift in the psychic economy of the nation in the early twentieth century. "The social role demanded of all in the new culture of personality was that of a performer," said Susman. This development of an acute self-consciousness implied that "true pleasure could be attained by making oneself pleasing to others." The externalization of an individual's sense of self-worth gave special urgency to commercial pleas that promised popularity on the one hand while threatening ostracism on the other.[47]

Romance also seemed to be on the rise in the 1920s; necking and petting were more in evidence. The good-night kiss apparently became a commonplace. Social scientists coined the term "companionate marriage" to refer to the American model, which by then had been stripped of many of its nonaffectional functions. If romance was on the rise, however, so was divorce. The ratio of divorce to marriage had climbed from 1:10 to 1:6 between 1914 and 1928. Perhaps impossible expectations, to which advertisers surely contributed, made marriage more incompatible with the everyday drudgeries of life. At least as early as 1931, for instance, ads announced that halitosis had been cited as grounds for divorce—extreme cruelty.[48]

Shortly after Lambert Pharmacal introduced its stark note, Lever Brothers initiated their BO campaign for Lifebuoy. But Americans had been exposed to perspiration in ads since the turn-of-the-century, in tiny ads for Mum and later Odorono discretely tucked in the back pages of the ladies' magazines. In the teens, a doctor's or nurse's advice often lent legitimacy to underarm deodorization. Profuse perspiration was not healthy, one ad would say; another might warn that it was the result of local physiological weakness. In the twenties, ads got bigger and bolder; one could come across a whole page of "The Most Humiliating Moment in My Life." The ad supposedly quoted a Chicago girl: "Many times I have heard women criticize you for publicly discussing such a delicate personal subject. . . . I know that many of these women who criticize you would benefit by taking your message to themselves." Delicacy became harder to find as time went by. It became a fact of life, according to ads; "underarm perspiration odor is harder to excuse because it is so easy to avoid."

By the thirties, even moisture alone seemed to taint. Only thirty-five cents would have saved the dress she liked and the man who liked her. Looking at stained and faded clothes, however, was nothing compared to seeing others' looks, trying not to seem offended by the odor. And excessiveness no longer had much to do with it. Mum announced that "you can offend with *underarm odor* even if you don't perspire." A daily bath was no protection. And BO, said the ads, only began at the armpit.[49]

The burgeoning trade in perfumes also hastened the manipulation of attitudes about personal odor. In 1915, the traffic did not amount to much. The use of fragrance was limited to the wealthy and aristocratic, people of the stage, and "the deviant fringe of society." But ten years later, its scents were ubiquitous. By the midtwenties, some 71 percent of American women over eighteen used perfume. As one perfumer postulated, "Never before in history has such tremendous buying power been concentrated as it is in America, and never has a buying power been educated so quickly to the need for luxuries." This general acceptance of artificially altering one's aromas with perfume probably made mouthwashing seem unexceptionable too.[50]

All of these factors may have favored American adaptation to mouthwashing. The very abundance of an urban society that could suddenly provide widespread access to record players, manicures and mechanical pencils, built-in bathrooms and electric power made the American consumer eager to accept the new usages. Franz Boas suggested that "the stability of a general trend of mind is likely to be the greater, the greater the uniformity of culture. In a complex culture, in which diverse attitudes are found, the probability of change must be much greater." Thus innovation facilitated innovation. A receptivity to novelty was no doubt conditioned by the nationalization of American culture in the early twentieth century, accelerated by the accretion of magazines, movies, radio, roads and roadsters, national brands, the wages of war, and any number of other integrative instrumentalities. "The creed of change became the catechism of the religion of progress." This made Americans unusually predisposed to new conceptualizations of the fabric of day-to-day life. Gargling, after all, was just another habit.[51]

This specific habit, though, was directed in its development and rigorously so, from its inception. The folkways, said Sumner, evolved through a sort of offhand empiricism. The members of a community established a usage by selection and approved it by experience, employing the simplest judgments. "It is not possible that the love of luxury, excitement, social intercourse and amusement is any greater now than it always has been, but popular literature has spread the hunger for it to classes of people who never felt it formerly. The hunger enters into the mores and becomes a characteristic of the age." The hunger for adulterated breath, however, was carefully cultivated. Of course a number of conditions might have made Americans amenable to it — whether diet, prohibition, smoking, toothbrushing, attention to underarms, urbanization and its attendant stress on social space, the emergence of "other direction," a rise in romance, a general proclivity to conspicuous consumption, the negative appeal, or an unprecedented range of goods. Virtually all behaviors compliment some larger social context. In this case, however, an orchestrated campaign no less intimate for its relentlessness usurped the place of shared experience.[52]

To the degree that advertisements invented and insisted upon one response to an altered milieu over other responses, and also convinced consumers of the appropriateness of their particular solution, they did not merely stimulate demand — they created it. As one publishing firm acclaimed, advertising began working on babies and kept up to the grave. In time, effective promotion made "a product part of our national life: part of our national eyes, palate, fingertip feel, sensory habit, rooted in the popular flesh and nervous system as well as in the popular mind."[53]

3

Cosmetics and the Crisis of Gender Identity

in the Early Twentieth Century:

Escape from Androgyny

Vaguely she wondered why she did not cry out that it was all a mistake.
—"BERNICE BOBS HER HAIR," 1920

The tendency of contemporary merchandising is to elevate more and more commodities to the class of personality buffers. At each exposed point the alert merchandiser is ready with a panacea.
—LYND AND HANSON, 1933

y the 1920s America possessed a national market-place serving consumers with ready cash or credit and an optimistic industriousness committed to the view that wants were endless. This optimism belied structural dislocations in American society that were often painful, mystifying, and not soon to be resolved. Magazine advertisers sought to redress them, however, as the national medium did its best to identify readers and markets, to articulate their wants, and to promote the goods that would sate them. An advertiser could actually create demand for a product by defining old elusive needs in novel fashion, as in the case of Listerine. Cosmetics advertising, however, came to stimulate demand in more traditional manner; it acquainted possible purchasers with the availability of merchandise rather than trying to fashion new desires of an advertiser's own invention. Although in that sense, the function of this toiletry advertisement was orthodox, the sheer volume of advertising messages could act as an agent of social change. This unprecedented outpouring of commercial pleadings assaulted potential purchasers. By associating products with their conventional uses in the unconventional milieu of a culture in flux, the results of such campaigning could have an enduring impact on American habits of every-

day grooming. Tapping a flood of social change and guiding its course, advertisers could direct consumer needs to profitable ends; when effective, advertising could establish and freeze patterns of consumption throughout the nation though the storm of structural instability within American society raged on. Such was the case with the cosmetics boom.

Amidst all the change they saw around them, Americans also changed themselves. Perhaps nowhere was this more evident than in the appearance of the "New Woman." The certainty of her existence was matched only by the elusiveness of her role. Scholars studied her while commentators derided or championed her, but no one could define her with precision. They knew she was different: first she bared her ankles and then almost bared her knees; she danced, drank, and smoked with an apparent abandon; she cut her hair; she employed contraceptives to avoid a large family; she could work outside the home and admit to being married; and she used the ballot, although she voted unpredictably.[1]

Women of the early twentieth century made marked advances toward full participation in American society, freeing themselves from the restrictive and circumscribed statuses that had confined them to the private domain of the home. Compared with traditional conceptions of gender, the distinctions between appropriate male and female behaviors became obscure. As this process of emancipation continued, Americans sought assurance that woman would retain her femininity. They found it, in part, in the widespread acceptance of cosmetics. Ten or twenty years before, only prostitutes, or "painted women," made obvious use of cosmetics; during the 1920s women of all persuasions were doing so. Urged on by advertisers who made the volume of beauty promotions second only to food in the national magazines, women used this easy means of expressing sex difference to alleviate a crisis in gender identity.

Developments provided a functional fit that was occasioned by the conjunction of the national magazines, toiletry manufacturers, and structural changes in the roles of homemaker, mother, housekeeper, wife. These changes were crystallized in the 1920s by the Suffrage, birth control, behaviorism and its impact on child rearing, cigarettes and casual sex, electrification and labor-saving devices, and the intrusion of the magazine itself. With rouge, lipsticks, powder, and nail polish, women could demonstrate that although they were not the women of twenty or fifty or a hundred years before, they were women just the same. Only different.

Women won the right to vote in 1920 as the result of a fleeting consensus on the nature of their special contributions to the polity. In the years that followed, this general agreement on women's appropriate concerns failed to withstand the changes that underlay its formulation. Although the Suffrage campaigns had extolled motherhood and the home, developments in modes of production and changing material circumstance reduced the traditional significance of women as childbearers and homemakers. In an urban, industrialized order, offspring were an economic drain and home production was not a chief means of livelihood. Private and public spheres melded. As women entered the world outside the home, they had to expand and in some ways reject previous notions of their proper place. The consensus symbolized by the Nineteenth Amendment dissipated quickly.

Almost immediately, writers tried to explain the "revolution" — though not in the polling booth — of a "new generation" of women. The home has become largely a place for eating and sleeping. Bearing children mattered less than raising them well. Marriage was no longer the inevitable means of obtaining a living. Maintaining the home itself involved an ability to mediate between the family and society — at the supermarket, the department store, and beyond. The mixing of private and public aspects of life — unavoidable in a national marketplace and a machine age — blurred past ideals of women's concerns, and made notions of a separate female world of interests apart from men increasingly outdated. Women's collective identity and shared experiences diminished as the terms of their participation in society changed and moved beyond the confines of the home. Traditional conceptions of gender distinction, predicated upon a view of inherently delimited arenas for male and female activity, seemed anachronistic.

Perhaps her failure to fulfill the rhetoric of the Suffrage campaigns was the most obvious intimation that the meaning of female in America was undergoing a transformation. The extension of the franchise typified the crisis. As Aileen Kraditor discovered, apparent differences between the sexes had "led both men and women to expect women, if and when they obtained the ballot, to vote differently from men." What the Progressive nation seemed to need most was, in a sense, some serious devotion to national housekeeping. In large part, she succeeded in securing the ballot because of her special skills as nurturer, reformer and uplifter, housekeeper and homemaker, and her distinctive interests as the mother of the race. To a society preoccupied with rationalizing itself through the application of expertise, it seemed only natural for women to express themselves when pure food was an issue; when propagation and procreation became targets of legislative concern; when teaching immigrants the American way and raising their children to that standard seemed compelling; when the need for protective legislation in the workplace seemed pressing; when Americans wanted to forget war, celebrate peace, and preserve their sense of national purity. With their ready willingness to invoke the authority of the state in the marketplace, workplace, and home, Progressives thought it appropriate that American women take direct political action. Once government was itself viewed as a chief instrument of current conceptions of progress, perhaps it was not so much their right as it was their duty for middle-class American women to seek and use the ballot.[2]

The aftermath of victory had to be a letdown to those who viewed it as a means to other ends. The passage of the Nineteenth Amendment did not revolutionize American politics. Because women's concerns were not so much different from men's, then they had to be different from the idealized "woman" whom the gender ideology of Suffrage had articulated. It was not that women did not care about political issues, but that as with men they too were influenced by factors more forceful than gender—class, occupation, race, religion, nativity, and so on. In the sense that Progressives had assigned women particular political responsibilities, many of the issues which might have elicited a consensus had already been passed upon—like pure food and drugs, eugenics, peace, antiprostitution, and prohibition legislation. At the ballot box, Americans discovered that females were not only similar to but were essentially indistinguishable from males. This was but the most obvious indication, however, of what one commentator called "the interpenetration of man's world and woman's."[3]

That a New Woman was on the scene seemed a surety. "Few doubted that a new day had dawned for women." J. Stanley Lemons reports that "the periodical literature abounded with comments on woman's 'New Work,' 'New World,' 'New Society,' 'New Politics,' 'New Social Vision,' and even the 'New Man,' who must appear as the complement to the 'New Woman.'" A contemporary account of the change, written in 1927, took a less dispassionate view:

> There are many who would have us believe that she does not differ from her mother or her grandmother. It is significant that she is on the defensive, for she does not claim to be better. We may try to deceive ourselves and close our eyes to the prevailing flapper conduct. We may call boldness greater self-reliance, brazenness greater

self-assertion, license greater freedom, and try to pardon immodesty in dress by calling it style and fashion, but . . . When women can gaze upon and indulge in the voluptuous dance of the hour; when young girls can sit beside their youthful escorts and listen to the suggestive drama of the day and blush not; when they spend their idle hours absorbed in sex-saturated fiction; when women, both married and single, find their recreation in drinking and petting parties; when mothers clothe their daughters in a manner that exposes their physical charms to the voluptuous gaze of every passing libertine; when they can enter the contract of marriage with the avowed purpose of having no children; then surely the "New Woman" is different, and it is a libel on the generation that has gone to hold the contrary.

Whether this emancipation of American women struck observers as an appalling disgrace or the ultimate achievement of freedom or neither or something in between differed with their individual perspectives. Perhaps the best evidence of the confused condition of women in the era can be found in the work of those who have sought to describe it; Estelle Freedman has concluded that writers claim "all things and nothing for women in the 1920's." Most Americans could agree, however, that women were not the same.[4]

Some felt that the differences were probably ephemeral and ultimately inconsequential. Declared Charlotte Perkins Gilman in 1923, "Motherhood will keep." She was not implying that women should eschew maternity, but was instead attempting to dismiss the significance of recent changes in manners and morals that were superfluous to the reproduction of the species. If the new status of women was actually to "militate against motherhood," then one might be alarmed, but in the meantime, "the laws of nature are apt to have their way." As carriers and bearers of the race, women's discrete interests apart from men would prevail. Others concurred, reassuring alarmists that one could not generalize about women from "the anti-Christian neo-pagan" behavior of the few; "the waves from the passing storm are not to be confused with the deep tides of the ocean."[5]

And yet, as these plaintive certitudes attest, maternity had never been so unimportant to middle-class American women. The controversies surrounding birth control in the 1920s only exacerbated the confusion concerning woman's place, and particularly because the issue was so intimately related to concerns of class. Family size shrank as people came to appreciate that in a cash economy the more they multiplied, the further they had to divide their income; all else being equal, adding to its size reduced the family's standard of living.

Children had become an economic liability. "As increasingly optional expenditures," said Lynd and Hanson, "children have come into direct competition with other consumption goods." Those least needful of planned parenthood, the upper and middle classes, were most likely to employ birth control, however. Those most tenacious of older values, the lower classes, were the least able to afford them. They not only produced more children, but in so doing, produced more poverty as well. As Gilman admonished, if it was a "free ticket" for "misbehavior" on the part of more affluent American women, contraception was a positive benefit to "the crowded poor." The same practice was viewed by commentators as a necessity for one woman but license in another, depending on one's place in the class structure — and often altogether in contradistinction to what any woman specifically might believe to be right for her. The debates over birth control only undermined the notion that an individual woman and women, race mothers, had distinct and transcendent values in common.[6]

As the family acquired its contemporary characteristics, so did the home. The census of 1920 revealed that, for the first time, most Americans lived in urban communities. Once the city was the locus of life, and industry outside the home the chief means of livelihood, the home ceased to be the foundation of existence. With the advent of electricity and modern plumbing, some commentaries depicted the housewife as an engineer working in laboratories with advanced technologies; others recorded the relative meaninglessness of it all as the home itself lost import as a unit of production, an educational center, an agency of social welfare. The decline in the centrality of the home was of course decades in the making; the trend seemed certain by the 1920s. Yet at the same time that the home and family lost their nonaffectional functions, the homemaker was acquiring professional status.[7]

Exaggerating the ambiguities attending "woman's sphere" were changing notions of "motherhood" itself. As fecundity became less and less important, mothering came to focus on raising rather than bearing children. Emphasis shifted from quantity to quality of progeny as the sociological aspects of motherhood gained at the expense of the biological. "If care for children in the home was less extensive than formerly," said Preston William Slosson, "it was also more intensive." Women were forced to question ideas of child care that they had long taken for granted; this process was accelerated in the 1920s when an objective, almost clinical, approach gained ascendancy. It was difficult — child rearing was "the most difficult of all professions" — but psychologist John B. Watson vowed that he could take any baby and turn it into whatever and whomever he pleased. Once mothers studied the principles of behaviorism, which many did once Watson's *Psychological Care of Infant and Child* appeared, they too could hope to raise bankers, artists, and merchant chiefs. "Children are made not born," the author insisted.

The conditioning required for success, however, explicitly rejected older conceptions of motherhood. As the family was shedding its nonaffectional attributes, it was a mother's affections that made most of them fail. In this new paradigm, coddling, kissing, comforting babies had the most pernicious consequences; the origin of that behavior in women, furthermore, was almost perverse. Mother doted on her offspring because "it is at bottom a sex-seeking device in her, else she would never kiss the child on the lips." Invalidism was the certain result. The new mother, according to the tract that Lois Banner has identified as "the standard reference on childrearing for a decade or more," saw her task as an objective experimental procedure. Indeed, claimed its exponents, as motherhood became a profession, it became something for which most mothers were probably unfit.[8]

Woman was individuating. As Leta Hollingsworth put it in 1927, "the essential fact about the New Women is that . . . they are women, not woman." This process of individualization was perhaps inevitable. The achievements of liberation were to be found not so much as woman, but as voter, purchaser, student, patron; scientist, gymnast, nurse; depositor, juror, customer, and client; speaker, revivalist, writer. Yet to the degree that they entered the public sphere, women were unrelated individuals in an impersonal world. Freeing themselves from (or feeling free to choose) the fixed statuses and ascriptive roles within the confines of the home, women lost identity by acquiring more roles to play. Alienated from old stereotypes, they were catapulted by the demands of a national marketplace and a machine age to undertake new tasks and visions. They had voiced a gender rhetoric as participants in political battles for Suffrage that, once its immediate goals were won, made the army seem anachronistic. New technologies in subsistence and social and sexual functionings altered their roles as mothers, homemakers, and wives. Woman confronted a collective identity crisis of major proportions.[9]

Though political expression had been a goal of feminists before Suffrage, in the 1920s the New Woman began a concerted search for self-definition. Assertions that women were still "woman" seemed somehow unconvincing, if only because they required their repeated articulation. Martha Bensley Bruere averred that "Nature passes her creatures on from stage to stage and keeps only to a few rigid fundamentals. Among them is sex. . . . As for the suffering which results from the loss of home work, female pride no longer centres in the patchwork quilt nor woman's ecstasy in the perfect pie crust, and yet our sphere is the sphere of the human female still." She moved in circles and the circles moved. Another more adamant advisor, Joseph Jastrow, insisted that there were "no human beings—only men and women." Nonetheless, many women felt caught in transition. One's feelings and thoughts and aspirations were a battleground, said Elsa Denison Voorhees; "hence one frequently seems totally inconsistent to oneself."[10]

In her study of *The Grounding of Modern Feminism,* Nancy Cott explains the paradoxes that confronted the New Woman. "As much as feminism asserts the female individual—by challenging delimitation by sex and by opposing the self-abnegation on behalf of others historically expected of women—pure individualism negates feminism because it removes the basis for women's collective self-understanding or action." The very success of the movement threatened it with self-destruction. As Cott puts it, "the singular conceptualization of *woman* in the woman movement came into crisis: the more women gained the rights and access it had pressed for, the less operable its premise of unity." By the teens and twenties, says Cott, the movement was "at the historic turning point."[11]

A chief concern expressed by many contemporaries was the marked loss of femininity that seemed to result from too much mixing with the world outside the home. Many had feared just that in the years before Suffrage. As early as 1893, Edward Bok warned of the influence of business on women to readers of the *Ladies' Home Journal.* "The number of women in business who lose their gentleness and womanliness is far greater than those who retain what, after all, are woman's best and chief qualities." By the mid-1920s, the crisis seemed at hand. Among the repercussions of woman's "encroachment" in the world of men was an accentuated masculinity, critics insisted. Interaction with the world at large brought out the combative, predatory qualities and repressed the dependent, passive, sequacious aspects of character. Said one commentator, "thus the paradox is reached that for women Feminism really spells Masculinism." At least one historian, James McGovern, has been forced to agree. Undergoing this process, women "joined men as comrades, and the differences in behavior of the sexes was narrowed. She became in fact some degree desexualized."[12]

Physiological complications, at least according to one alarmist, led to "premature ossification of the pelvic structure and to morbid rigidity in the pelvic and upper femoral regions." In her study of *Disorderly Conduct,* Carol Smith-Rosenberg has noted that this, too, was an old worry. She traces the evolution of beliefs that "gender inversion" would manifest itself in female physiology. In the minds of many Americans of the early twentieth century, these concerns were not to be ignored. The freedom women were gaining might cost them the race, not to mention society as they knew it.[13]

Not all women objected to that prospect. Writing in 1930, Beatrice Forbes-Robertson Hale projected "a marked decrease in their secondary sexual characteristics in proportion as their energy is deflected into the fields of intellect, affairs, and sport." On the other hand, within the first tenet of Dorothy Dunbar Bromley's credo for "Feminist — New Style" was an explicit assurance that it did not "necessarily follow, scientists tell us, that a woman with a flair for the creative or the scientific, or with a genius for abstract thought will have a masculine physique." The best that another commentator could do was to recognize "the fire-like rapidity with which she has adopted modes and mannerisms which identify her with the man," and assume that, just as quickly, woman would return to her feminine form.[14]

Many Americans were not so sure. The twenties witnessed a number of attempts, some vain and others vacuous, to rediscover ideal American womanhood, "The American Woman." After its rekindling in 1915 and revivification in 1920, the Ku Klux Klan elevated "pure womanhood" to a cardinal place of honor in its crusade against "modernism," enlisting millions of men and women in the struggle. Even they may have suspected that "pure womanhood" was much like the hoopla and ballyhoo about "pure soap" in the newspapers and magazines: the modifier "pure" had no real meaning. If and once one argued that femininity was a relative quality — that one woman could be more womanly than another — then the topic was not biological. But many Americans feared that New Woman was somehow manlike; the KKK was not alone in seizing upon the relativity of gender distinction in the 1920s.[15]

A more enduring effort in search of real woman resulted in the perennial quest for Miss America, instituted in 1921. The contest is mired in ambiguities, "maligned by one segment of America, adored by another, misunderstood by about all of it." In his capable though unscholarly investigation, Frank Deford warns that when trying to study the meaning of this American invention, one faces an obdurate ambivalence engrained in its very origins. *"Miss America* is confusing — and it is either purposely confusing or congenitally so. Surely, no U.S. institution could be riddled with so many inconsistencies by accident." The pageant is, for instance, a beauty contest "embarrassed to death about sex, bathing suits, and possibly even girls." Even its name is confusing; not a Queen or a Lady is "crowned," but a "Miss" who can only intimate monarchy to the republic. Although promoters keep adding distractions — talent, gowns, interviews, certified judges, and scholarships — the contest still glories in girl watching. "Personality" — said to be the most important factor in winning — is never judged officially at all. Indeed, the process of evaluation is "so incredibly arbitrary, imperfect, and inconsistent that it fairly revels in its own whimsy." Despite the shadowy nature of the endeavor and its ultimately arbitrary meaning, year after year, a new personification of some supposed expression of American woman is crowned the "queen of femininity."[16]

But the beauty pageant was by no means the major expression of the crisis of gender identity of the early twentieth century. "What the human nature of males and females really consists of," explains Erving Goffman, "is a capacity to learn to provide and to read depictions of masculinity and femininity and a willingness to adhere to a schedule for presenting these pictures, and this capacity they have by virtue of being persons" quite independent of their physiology. According to this view, as another student of the subject defines it, "Becoming a socialized person means acquiring thespian skills — knowing what the part of male or adolescent or doctor calls for, making the performance so believable that the role will seem authentic to the audience, guarding against discrepant gestures that would give the play away." Perhaps nothing changed so visibly in the late teens and twenties as the schedule for portrayal of female in America.[17]

To envision the New Woman, one must turn not only to short skirts, bobbed hair, and pocketbooks, but to the phenomenal boom in cosmetology, the business of beauty culture, and the production of goods whose purpose was to exaggerate obvious gender distinctions. If a consensus on the meaning of womanhood was lacking, women could acknowledge their new status yet guarantee that they were not men. The 1920s witnessed a rapid rise in the consumption of lipsticks, nail polish, perfumes, mascaras, rouges and powders, eye paints, lotions, face masks and hair dyes, permanent waves, creams, balms and bath goods, all designed to undermine or erase the sartorial similarity of the sexes.

The increase in output of products that women could use to aggravate superficial differentiation of gender was staggering. Per capita output of perfume, cosmetics, and toilet preparations trebled between 1919 and 1929.[18] (Fig. 3.1.) The value added by firms producing such goods leaped fourteen times over in fifteen years. (Table 3.1.) The effort promoters expended to ensure that women consume all these goods was compelling. Expenditures for drug and toilet advertising in leading magazines rose from $2.5 million to $25 million between 1915 and 1929. Throughout the midtwenties, toiletries were the second most advertised class of goods in the national medium. As the most effective rhetoric regarding women in the teens had been political in its origin and humanitarian in aim, by far the most persuasive utterances of the 1920s were generally commercial and specifically cosmetic.[19]

Although both idealizations stressed woman's distinctiveness, the switch in emphasis had conspicuous consequences. Paula Fass observed that "the cosmetics most popular with young women emphasized artificiality and tended to draw attention to their use. Face powder was indispensable. It smoothed out an uneven surface and covered a shiny nose, giving the face a smooth, whitened finish. Rouge and lipstick then added the necessary color. The result was a heightened contrast between pale skin and rouged lips and cheeks." Fass notes that "there was nothing natural about the effect. Rather it contrasted surface contour and color sensuality. The plucked brow further accented this effect, as the uneven line of the natural brow was replaced by a precise arch. Lips, too, were sometimes artfully bow-shaped. Each feature stood out against a smooth white surface. It was an artificial scheme that produced a doll-like painted look when cosmetics were used to excess." Insofar as excess is a relative judgment, any discernible application of cosmetics would have seemed excessive a mere decade or score years before. "They were associated with prostitutes."[20]

Of course the history of cosmetics had dimensions of continuity. In her study of *American Beauty,* Lois Banner has traced the use of makeup of one form or another back to the sixteenth century. Indeed, in her study of *Confidence Men and Painted Women,* Karen Halttunen indicates that this sort of body ritual is a sensitive barometer of subtle social changes. During the 1700s, middle-class women made regular use of paints and lip colorings, beauty patches, and eye brow pencils. By the 1830s and 1840s, though, arbiters of fashion and propriety utterly rejected such disguises of the flesh, extolling instead the

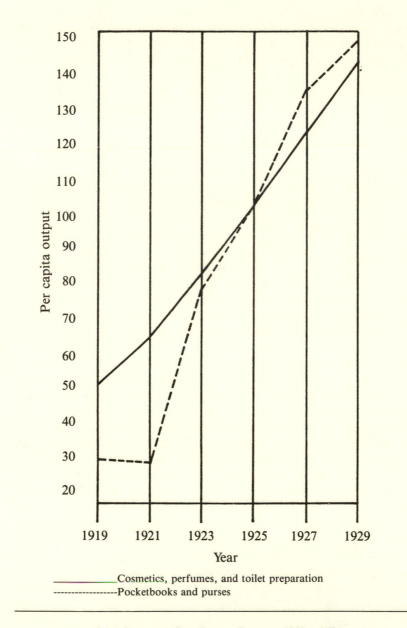

3.1. INDEX OF PER CAPITA OUTPUT, 1925 = 100

(Robert S. Lynd, with the assistance of Alice C. Hanson (Jones), "The People as Consumers,"
Recent Social Trends in the United States (New York: McGraw-Hill), 1933, 898, 900)

TABLE 3.1 Toilet preparations

Year	Value added by manufacturing (millions of dollars)
1909	8.6
1914	9.4
1919	33.3
1921	44.5
1923	62.6
1925	82.6
1927	108.5
1929	135.1

SOURCE: Solomon Fabricant, with the assistance of Julius Shiskin, *The Output of Manufacturing Industries, 1899–1937.* (New York: National Bureau of Economic Research, 1940), 619. Also see p. 232; looking at toilet preparations as a percentage of the total value added by the entire group of chemical industries, the major shift occurred after 1919 rather than before.

"moral cosmetics" of clean living and clear skin. During the 1850s, cosmetics staged a slight comeback, as advice books and fashion guides suggested an easing of earlier proscriptions by endorsing moderate use of these commodities. But "sometime in the 1870s fashionable women abandoned cosmetics and, after a lapse of a decade or so, once again came to identify paint with promiscuity." By the turn of the twentieth century, as Banner and Fass have demonstrated, the visible application of cosmetics was deemed highly inappropriate by middle-class Americans.[21]

The widespread reintroduction and acceptance of cosmetics in the first decades of the twentieth century was a noticeable revision in the schedule for the depiction of female. This innovation can be interpreted as a ritual of feminization, and the timing of its appearance reveals its meaning. The use of cosmetics served to modify the recent changes in women's status in America; in applying them, women could both acknowledge recent alterations in gender identity and mute the more threatening ambiguities that accompanied the emergence of the New Woman.

Categorizations by sex carried the weight of centuries. American society customarily relied on those divisions of labor, status, and power. Discrimination of "male" from "female" was not only functional in years gone by; it was convenient biological fact. Unlike other human attributes like intelligence, strength, skill, or maturity, the difference between the sexes seemed truly dichotomous and absolute—a matter of either/or rather than more-or-less. In the early twentieth century, however, the line between appropriate male and female behaviors in the United States became quite blurred. An indeterminant era in the history of gender relations was at hand.

America verged on the transcendence of what had become invidious biological distinction. Though in roundabout fashion, Americans formally acknowledged this development in such measures as the Nineteenth Amendment and the Cable Act. Informally, through such means as new technologies in the home, newly accepted measures of controlling birth and nurturing offspring, and a shifting sense of the structure of appropriate educational and occupational pursuits for women, Americans faced a host of options and opportunities that undermined or offered to erase old boundaries between the sphere of female and the sphere of male. The New Woman challenged the order of the ages.

The resultant confusion sought resolution. Uncertainties and anomalies of such magnitude drive a people to render the universe more predictable and to make ambiguities amenable to understanding. Revision in the rituals of everyday life has a key function in this quest for clarification. When change threatens to topple old verities, innovations in ritual can redefine and sort through the confusion. Mary Douglas, studying concepts of pollution and taboo in simple societies, advises that "any given system of classification must give rise to anomalies, and any given culture must confront events which seem to defy its assumptions. It cannot ignore the anomalies which it produces, except at risk of forfeiting confidence." Adaptation in daily rituals can redirect and clarify change, making it somehow less awesome. "By ritual and speech what has passed is restated so that what ought to have been prevails over what was, permanent good intention prevails over temporary aberration. . . . Ritual creates harmonious worlds with ranked and ordered populations playing their appointed parts . . . it is primitive magic which gives meaning to existence." Cosmetics may have met this sort of need for Americans in the 1920s. This may account for the enthusiasm with which the new usages were greeted.[22]

This complex of body rituals was not merely negative, however, demonstrating that woman was not and would not become masculine as she left former barriers behind. The innovation was also affirmative of a new identity. These procedures for distinguishing gender anticipated new departures in the participation of women in American society. As Ross and Rapp observe in their analysis of "Sex and Society," even "the seemingly most intimate details of private existence are actually structured by larger social relations." In this instance, lipstick, rouge, and the rest served a "framing function"; they offered contextual clues to everyday experience, excluding unwanted ambiguities of gender identity while acknowledging and incorporating others. The use of cosmetics announced a uniquely qualified set of aspirations, at once contained and yet confirmatory of new roles and expectations. Makeup was a prop that allowed the New Woman to interpret her part correctly; the widespread introduction of these goods altered and modified change by expressing it. Unlike her American antecedents of earlier generations, the new user of cosmetics was no longer a "marked woman"; instead she was simply marked: woman.[23]

The avidity with which these products were purchased in the 1920s guaranteed their continued production. Noting that women were spending $5 million a day on beautification by 1926, an industry source estimated that of American women over age eighteen, 90 percent used face powder, 83 percent used talcum, 73 percent used toilet water, 71 percent used perfume, and 55 percent used rouge.[24]

By 1927, there were 7000 kinds of cosmetics on the market. According to one beauty budget that appeared in 1930, every woman should plan to spend $307 per year "to keep fit." By then, women were buying "enough lipsticks to reach from Chicago to Los Angeles by way of San Francisco," 52,500 tons of cleansing cream, 26,250 tons of skin lotion, 19,109 tons of complexion soap, 17,500 tons of nourishing cream, 8,750 tons of foundation cream, 6,562 tons of bath powder, and 2,375 tons of rouge.[25] Beauty parlors sprang up across the country; although none existed in Middletown in the 1890s, seven had appeared by 1925. Ten years later there were forty-seven. The cosmetics market, in fact, was depression resistant, eclipsing more mundane realities of want in the 1930s. When they returned to Middletown in 1935, the Lynds discovered third-grade girls attending school with cheeks of rouge, brightly lacquered nails, and Shirley Temple curls.[26] The "painted lady" had ceased to be deviant. Determined sex-typing had become an everyday routine for millions of American women. The growth of the business of beauty culture and its eager acceptance engendered a new cult of feminine beauty.

4

Temples of the Cult of Beauty:

Magazine, Market, and Law

he influence of the magazine was not confined to its advertising, nor to persuading consumers to support the market that underwrote its existence. Trade magazines and occupational journals integrated whole professions. These periodicals were subsidized by promoters of the specialized categories of commodities that distinguished one occupation from another and allowed professionals to perform their services. Besides informing readers of products, these magazines also told subscribers of changing conceptualizations of standard practice, innovations in technique and trade, and arcane news of national import.

By binding continental armies of experts together, enterprising publishers could have an impact on American life that far exceeded the immediate needs of their constituencies. They defined and directed occupational goals through the editorial content of their journals. By providing a voice for the national perspective that was intrinsic to the development of a national marketplace, they could in the meantime ensure a healthy circulation for their periodicals. As well-springs of professional action, as well as providers of a showplace for goods, they could exert a powerful influence on activities that would perpetuate their magazines' readership.

At times, as in the case of the *American Hairdresser,* the publisher was a catalyst for change that otherwise might have gone undeveloped. Bringing cosmetologists across the country together in 1921, Charles Meeker Kozlay founded a national organization of hairdressers, wholesalers, and manufacturers called the National Hairdressers Association. He provided it with an official forum—his

American Hairdresser magazine. The association's effort to manage its market was quite unlike the campaigns of Lambert Pharmacal, or even those of the cosmetics industry. It did not have to create demand for women's haircuts, nor did it try to stimulate consumer interest. Instead, the National Hairdressers Association hoped to enforce demand by rigorously regulating and restricting supply. If the organization's campaigns were successful, when women sought tonsorial services, they would fulfill their needs only within the confines of a beauty parlor. The association became a clearinghouse for activities that would, within a decade, give its founder's vision of normative behavior the weight of law.

By 1927, according to Dorothy Dunbar Bromley, "feminist" was a term of opprobrium. Old models of emancipation were inappropriate in the New Era. Women were no longer conscious of themselves as a sex, she said, so much as they were simply self-conscious. In her "modern woman's credo," Bromley set out to reassure her readers that once outside the home, woman need not abandon her sexuality. Sharing man's experience, woman did not have to imitate his appearance. The New Woman of the 1920s "is so far removed from the early feminists that she is altogether baffled by the psychology which led some of them to abjure men in the same voice with which they aped them." Comparing contemporaries to their counterparts of just a few years before, Bromley testified on behalf of the new cult of feminine beauty that was transforming the appearance of American women during the decade. "Certainly their vanity must have been anaesthetized, she tells herself, as she pictures them with their short hair, so different from her own shingle, and dressed in their unflattering manly clothes—quite the antithesis of her own boyish effects which are subtly designed to set off feminine charms." To the New Woman, a masculine appearance was just "bad taste."[1]

Undoubtedly at first, bobbing their hair could be viewed as both a symbolic and actual act of emancipation, a breakdown of previous barriers to women's full participation in every sphere of American life. Barbershops were sure institutional vestiges of an exclusive male world apart from womankind. By the late teens and early twenties, women across the nation were invading the barbershops. "Not long ago the men reclined in their barber chairs, gazing over lathered cheeks at maidens hurrying past the plate-glass windows with downcast eyes. But times have changed." The *New York Times* of 1924 noted that "the up-to-date barber shops now have special chairs for women, and the women, true to the ways of today, take their places beside the men." New styles of appearance "served at once a symbolic and a functional role in the new variety of relationships between the sexes," according to Paula Fass's study of college youth in the 1920s. "Bobbed hair, for example, which was the prevailing style for women on all campuses, was enthusiastically defended on the grounds that it was carefree and less troublesome than the long ponderous mane, which was de rigueur in the prewar period."[2]

But just as females began having their hair cut in record numbers, American hairdressers waged a strenuous and successful campaign to reinforce a world of women apart from the world of men, to protect their vested interests and to profit from the boom. By 1924, according to a speaker at the National Hairdressers' Convention, roughly half of the women in America knew what a beauty parlor was; of the other 50 percent, it fell to the hairdressers "to educate them that the hair dressing business is a means of beautifying themselves." During the 1920s, the number of hairdressers in the nation rose from 216,000 to 374,000 — an increase in excess of 70 percent. The profession became a field of special opportunity for women; official counts registered a "spectacular increase from 33,000 in 1920 to 113,000 in 1930 in the number of women in this type of work." By then, the National Hairdressers Association had largely succeeded in enacting the sex-specific barbershop, and its feminine form, the beauty parlor, was here to stay.[3]

The institutionalization of beauty culture had an intimate relationship with women's emergence from their place apart from men. The association, however, was largely negative: the beauty business encouraged an extravagant elaboration of gender distinction. The achievement of the Nineteenth Amendment — why it took seventy-two years in a society willing to extend the franchise to every man before any woman — was perhaps because, as Carl Degler observes, "the suffrage was a direct attack upon the doctrine of the separate spheres." Yet even so, the meaning of the vote was disguised by a gender rhetoric that stressed sexual differences. The assault on traditional values that the vote represented, once the victory was in hand, was diverted by the assiduous advertisement and acceptance of claims that women and men were obviously different. These views found concrete reality in the trafficking of gender-specific goods like cosmetics, which gave substance to such assertions. The cult of feminine beauty redefined and narrowed the meaning of recent moves toward women's emancipation. Charles Meeker Kozlay, the founder and first president of the National Hairdressers Association, was blunt about it: "In this coun-

try we want to venerate our women; we don't want to have this bringing down, as suffrage has done in some directions. Women have the
right to vote, but let them be women and vote." The *American Hairdresser,* the journal he published, and the organization he founded
can be said to have ensured the existence of the American beauty
shop.[4]

The hairdressing profession had existed for many years before
the beauty parlor became a cultural commonplace. In an earlier era,
however, the central function of the hairdresser was to coif hair rather
than cut it. American women traditionally wore long hair, and the
care and arrangement of "fashionable" women's coiffures required
some degree of expertise; the hairdresser could achieve the elaborate
designs that were in vogue in the nineteenth century. By the 1870s,
according to Lois Banner, "the woman of fashion had to have masses
of hair arranged in intricate displays." Many styles required the extensive use of artificial hair. These elite interpretations of beauty were "a
boon to the hairdresser, who played no small part in popularizing the
new styles." The *American Hairdresser* was founded in 1878, and the
first American school for the training of hairdressers opened in 1890.
The dressing of hair became a growing trade in response to the desire
for sophisticated and complicated coiffures.[5]

It was during those years that the hairdressing salon evolved.
This precursor of the modern beauty shop served as an establishment
where the labor-intensive task of creating stylish modes could be undertaken. Women of fashion were fitted with false braids and curls,
manicured, and advised of the latest trends in beauty. These early
enterprises served a limited clientele. As late as 1920, the editor of the
American Hairdresser defended the elite orientation of the business:
"we claim that our profession cannot be classified as a luxury, but as a
necessity to civilization. . . . It is therefore, these so-called luxuries,
still a little beyond the reach of many, that act as an incentive" to
inspire them to a higher standard of living. The beauty business did
not boom until women demanded a new look to accompany their new
status in America. When women sought to have their hair sheared,
seeking out the services of barbers, salon owners were quick to respond to this threat to their trade. It was when women wanted haircuts instead of elaborate coiffures that the modern beauty parlor was
born.[6]

When women began to have their hair cut, local associations
formed in a number of cities to accommodate and take advantage of
the unprecedented demand for women's barbers. (Fig. 4.1.) As the

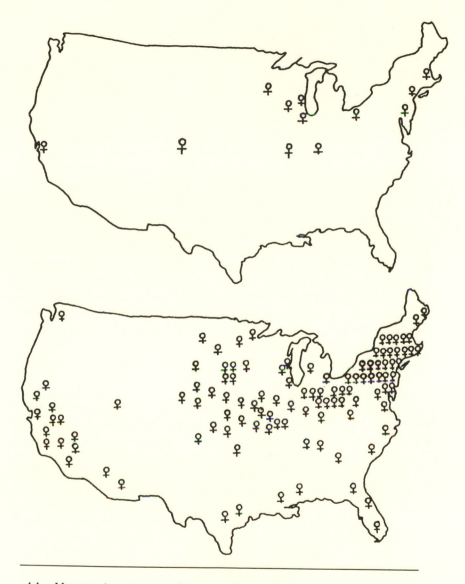

4.1. MEMBER ASSOCIATIONS, NATIONAL HAIRDRESSERS AND COSMETOLOGISTS
ASSOCIATION, 1921 (ABOVE) AND 1929 (BELOW).
LATTER MAP OMITS HAWAIIAN ASSOCIATION.
ALL LOCATIONS ARE APPROXIMATIONS.
(National Association of Hairdressers, Minutes of First Convention, 1921;
N.H.C.A. Bulletin, September 1929, 18–19)

common link between beauty shop owners around the nation, the publisher of their trade magazine appreciated the problems that might attend either an unchecked boom in this market or the development of competing regional efforts to direct its course. In correspondence with these local groups of parlor owners, Kozlay urged national cooperation and unification for the expressed purpose of "effecting uniform legislation throughout the United States." He appreciated that professional recognition was in large part a function of legislative dispensation and that, in a national marketplace, such regulation had to transcend the boundaries of city and state. Properly applied, the law could be a best friend of business. As T. Paul Titus, the man who later became the national association's legal counsel, put it, "there is in my mind none of the alarming thoughts that a laymen [*sic*] might have when he is confronted by any encroachment by the authorities upon his work or his person." Instead, government had to be viewed as an instrument for the management of demand. "It is my idea that the very fact that the authorities are encroaching and that they are trying to surround you with certain laws, rules, and regulations, is an asset to you." He explicated his faith in the benefits of an interventionist state.[7]

Perhaps more cynically, the second president of the National Hairdressers Association noted that politics teemed with crooks. Nonetheless, "we are responsible for them. . . . There are only two things in life that we don't get through politics and that is life itself and air. Everything else comes through politics. Now if politicians are crooked[,] we are responsible and we have only the politician to seek to remedy our evils of our profession today and we must necessarily work through politicians." He pleaded for the necessity of an active lobby on behalf of the beauty parlor. Enacting appropriate legislation while halting adverse acts became a primary goal of the new association.[8]

The beauty shop had much to gain by taking timely action. The demand for women's haircuts surged in the late teens and early twenties. John B. Watson, the psychologist turned advertising executive, observed that the new look was not mere fashion, but was indeed in the process of becoming normative behavior by 1921. The opportunities seemed endless. When demand overwhelms the capacity to meet it, the task of business is not so much to make production and distribution profitable, as to render it predictable—that is, amenable to continuing profitability. Unlike other fields of enterprise that faced underconsumption later in the New Era, in the early twenties the deliverers of beauty services and parlor goods feared the reckless profiteering that accompanied a lack of supply.[9]

Itinerants traveled house-to-house, head-to-head, in direct competition with those who purchased shops and maintained chairs, sinks, permanent-wave machines, and all the other capital accoutrements of the profession. The operator who owned merely a pair of scissors and perhaps a bag of beauty aids could charge less yet make more than those parlor owners who paid electric bills and rent and employees' wages. That the new practice might become a cottage industry was a serious menace. The "great curse of our business today," charged one critic, was not the transient but the bedroom beautician working from her home. Whether residential worker or traveling bobber, she "in each case out of ten clears more actual money than the woman who is running a shop." This immediate threat from unregulated entrance into the field could make the beauty parlor unprofitable despite the swell of demand, and make efforts to elevate the trade, to "raise the standard," fruitless.[10]

Unlicensed access to the craft also undermined the long-range professional interests of the calling. Until the law proscribed it, anyone might claim to be a cosmetologist. Shoddy workmanship could have a devastating impact on an occupation just attaining respectability. The vocation was only now emerging "out of the strata of business which it started in, one where a woman was ashamed to let it be known that she was a patron of a beauty parlor," and was becoming "a legalized, legitimatized, proud profession, where the woman or the girl who goes to it is proud of the fact." The hairdressing industry did not want to reverse that trend.[11]

"In such things therefore," mused C. W. Godefroy, "there arises the thought in our mind, is legislation desirable, or is it not? System is always desirable to chaos. Legislation is a form of system, because without it in this unregulated profession we have no system." He hoped that some day, when the beauty culturist came up in conversation, a certain respect would follow, "just like right now when a trained nurse is mentioned, women's noblest profession comes to mind." System would impart substance. Sharing the enthusiasm, another speaker exuded confidence: "Once the business in our trade has gotten legislation, it will only be a few years until manicure girls will marry among the rich men."[12]

A host of immediate problems intervened, though. Some of the more profitable procedures, like dyeing hair and permanent waving, required a fair amount of expertise. But rainbow-colored hair was a commonplace in those days, when would-be beauticians attempted to dye without the requisite training. The topic of corrective coloring, in fact, was worthy of special sessions at the national convention. Subjecting a woman's head to chemical wave treatments, particularly when the results were more-or-less "permanent," could be a tricky enterprise. The field was "being prejudiced daily by someone that has made a fizzle of a permanent wave. That travels faster than ten good heads." Perhaps more damaging to long-term goals were the fraudulent "schools" that sprang up to skim the demand for training by those who wanted to enter the rapidly expanding trade and thereby perpetuated inferior craftsmanship. Petty frauds abounded in the industry. When advertisers for wigs promised "convent cut hair," for instance, the phrase properly referred to hair cut from the head of a live nun in a convent. But wig makers often sold "second quality hair, and often times Chinese hair" instead. Regulations could stem all these abuses; "the enactment of beauty culture laws necessarily provides a licensing so as to separate the fit from the unfit."[13]

The fundamental threat to the beauty profession, however, was the barber. Once women sought bobs in record numbers, barbers also hoped to seize the new market. It was a field for which they were eminently qualified. They, after all, were the haircutters. They had ancient interests to maintain. A barber accompanied John Smith in 1607. Their union had been active since 1887. And their aim, too, was to profit. The struggle with the barbers was an immediate precipitant of many of the National Hairdressers Association's early efforts. To stem the widespread abuses in the business, perhaps the most rational thing for regulations to do, was to subsume the new trade within the barbers'.[14]

The barbers themselves were encouraged to cultivate the new field. The *Barbers' Journal* advised in 1922 that "This line is developing very rapidly; so wake up and make your harvest while the harvesting is good." If one wanted to segregate his clients, one might open a beauty parlor above his barbershop, or better still—since the appliances were essentially the same—the enterprising haircutter could simply install "a portable curtain which encloses your last two chairs." As for an ostensible distinction between male and female hair, the *Barbers' Journal* suggested that "there is a big difference between barber work and ladies' hairdressing work. To illustrate more clearly, we find hairdressers and beauty culturists getting as high as $2.50 and in some cases $3.00 for a massage. We find those same barbers that have learned how to do permanent waving earning as high as $35 to $40 for an hour and a half and two hours work." Barbers began to reap the profits to be made with enthusiasm, harvesting women's hair.[15]

The cosmetologists rallied against this attempt to "cop the business" by stressing the separation of the spheres. Beauty was "a form of christianity in a practical degree," said W. C. Snyder, the only actual hairdresser to head the association in the 1920s.[16] "It stood next to the ministry in his mind. [He] urged us to keep the ladies beautiful and in that way create more homes, harmonious homes, and keep the men loving the ladies." But the difficulties of enforcing sex-specific barbering were enormous. As one delegate asked in 1922, "If a barber is not connected with a ladies hairdresser, who is? You might as well give it up." That sort of logic had to be obliterated. Harry M. Spiro, a wholesaler of parlor goods and at the time a member of the association's bylaws committee, countered: "Because a barber happens to be used to cutting a man's hair and children's hair all these years, that is no reason why he should say he is the only one who can cut a lady's hair." Indeed, that was the major threat to the beauty shop. "The barber is no ally of ours, he works on men and we work on women; it is two entirely different branches of beauty work, and we should decide upon that today at this convention. . . . It is time to wake up to the fact and have it distinctly understood." Somehow, the association had to draw the distinction and drive it into the American mind.

Women's work done in barbershops did not merely undercut the beauty business. "Morally . . . it is wrong; it is going to encourage things which are not to be encouraged, and if anything, discouraged." Another delegate recalled meeting with the Barber's Board of Saint Louis. "We asked these men if they would allow their daughters to even go into a barber shop and have their hair bobbed and they said no." She did not reveal whether these men objected to a daughter's presence in the barbershop, or to the woman's bob itself (nor did she note that Saint Louis led in the world's production of beauty parlor and barbershop furniture).[17]

Laws in a number of other localities, however, were being passed, interpreted, or enforced in an antagonistic manner. Just a week before the association's second convention in 1922, a Minneapolis hairdresser was fined $100 because of a barber's law preventing her from bobbing hair. Another delegate asked, "Are we going to allow the hairdressing business to be carried on in barber shops? I think the best answer to that would be Mr. Spiro's idea of a moral standpoint." The delegate explained that some interpositions into the world of men were simply inappropriate for women. "In every city in the United States we have poolrooms. We have ladies in this assemblage, no doubt, who play a good game of pool, but those ladies would find it impossible to go into a poolroom and play pool where men are playing pool. A man's poolroom would be barred to those ladies, from the moral standpoint only." The delegate was not, however, advocating women's poolrooms. Another hairdresser suggested that, "to help this moral uplift along, it would be a very good idea to discourage wholesalers" from pushing beauty equipment on barbers. In Pittsburgh, where the price of a permanent wave "has never been less than seventy-five cents," the first thing a barber did after acquiring a machine was to advertise for fifty cents. The second convention resolved to condemn the extension of barbers' work to women as "traditionally inexpedient, as opposed to a proper devlopment [*sic*] of the work of our profession, as as [*sic*] [in] conflict with sound principles of propriety." The association spent much of the next year killing legislation that lumped barbers and beauticians together, or having hairdressers excluded from legislation appertaining to men.[18]

The association used this negative approach to the law until it could devise a "model bill" that could be applied with uniformity throughout the cities and states of the nation. "It has been well to try to avoid legislation of any kind on the part of any of the legislatures," advised counselor A. M. Davis in 1922. The profession did not want to act too hastily; while the association was in its infancy and unsure of its needs, the best procedure was to thwart unfavorable actions. The folkways were in flux, and their future uncertain. As an exchange as late as 1926 revealed, the hairdressers themselves questioned the course of their trade:

> *Madame Louise:* I remember years ago, when we had the long hair, and father or brother would not allow the young lady to lose one inch of the family's length of hair, no matter what a time they had of it. Now, some men go to the other extreme, and want it all cut off. . . .
>
> *Bernard Boch:* The bob is the outgrowth of utilitarian necessities of the war. The war workers found it a decided advantage. I don't want to speak against the trade, a great many might be making a fortune with the increasing mannish style, but I contend that women will never give up their love for the beautiful. . . .

Another hairdresser commented that the bob was but a fad and that long hair would be back. "It is only necessary to have the style changed, and they will leave it just as quickly as they adopted it." But Madame Louise suggested otherwise, that women did not want their hair long because it was simply uncomfortable.

Delegate: In the matter of the hair remaining short permanently. I do not think women are wearing their hair short to look good, but they are doing so to show their independence. It is the new woman of the day.

Madame Louise: You are right in a way, though some women do not care to cast aside the feminine and go to the masculine.

Delegate: Some women do, though.

Madame Louise: Oh, yes they do. You see father, mother and son from the back and they all look alike.

Delegate: They greatest problem is to educate the woman in the difference between a barber shop and a hair dressing cut shop.

Contrary to the delegate's perception, though, the greatest problem was formulating a legal rather than social distinction between barbed and bobbed hair. Barber bills had to be opposed because they generally restricted hair cutting to barber shops. "Now we all know," commented Kozlay in 1923, "that if you did not use the scissors in your establishments you could not do your work." Until the association itself could discover a definitive legal difference between the barber and the beauty shop, it did not endorse legislation so much as challenge it, resolved to "assert the right of engaging in all work pertaining to artificial hair, and all other work ordinarily done in the hairdressing and beauty parlor on women and children, free from the domination of barbers' laws."[19]

The association was aided tremendously by the courts and a determined hairdresser from Kansas who balked at having to become a barber to practice her trade. "Let us think of her as a mother—one of those rugged mothers of the pioneer days who would brave anything for her child." The child was the hairdressing profession of Kansas, about to be smashed by "the iron fist" of the State Barber Board. As Mary E. Keith explained it, she and one of her operators were arrested for violating the Barber Act, cutting hair without a license. "Threats of wholesale arrests of the members of the profession who failed to contribute to the treasure chest of the barbers, and who refused to submit to the indignities of physical examinations" provided by the Act, led her to countersue in 1923. The Supreme Court of Kansas recognized that Keith had, indeed, "been doing all of these different kinds of work which barbers in general do: cutting hair, massaging the face, clipping hair with barber clippers, singeing the hair, giving tonics, shampooing, manicuring." Yet Keith called her business a "Ladies' Hairdressing and Beauty Parlor," not a barbershop. As the court conceded, "There may be difficulty in stating the precise difference between the two, but we do not think the use of the term barbershop fairly indicates or suggests the kind of place kept by the plaintiff." If the legislature had meant to include beauty parlors when the law was enacted, "the strong probability is that specific reference would have been made to them." Ruling for Keith, the court found that "if persons who do work similar to that of barbers, but do not undertake to shave customers, are to be brought within the discipline of a regulating board[,] it should be by virtue of new legislation rather than by an extension of the scope of the existing law by interpretation." The Keith decision was a boon to the beauty business. Scores of barber bills were either "amended or hurled into the dust" immediately after the victory. "Only through the decision of Mary E. Keith was this possible—ladies' haircutting is *not* barbering!"[20]

The association made her an honorary member, and set to the task of providing model legislation to fill the void created by the Kansas court. The model bill formulated a national beauty profession. It defined the hairdresser's place of business, a place used only for business. It defined the participants—hairdresser, beauty culturist, manager, owner, operator, and apprentice—and distinguished them by their expertise. The bill elucidated everything from minimum age requirements "commensurate with the present well recognized, increased intelligence of the female sex," to minimum schooling, written and oral examinations, State Boards, and inspectors to uphold the various procedures. The bill provided exclusions for practitioners who engaged in the business prior to the Act, and revocation provisions for felons, frauds, drunks, and drug addicts. It also included a clause allowing one state to accept the credentials of another with a similar statute. Each member of the association was pledged to use the bill as the structure for regulation within his or her own state, so that when all the forty-eight states had laws, they would be so similar as to ensure a "perfect reciprocity" among them, guaranteeing that the association and its marketplace would indeed extend from sea-to-sea.[21]

The association made steady progress enacting its notions of the beauty trade. Within a year after composing the Model Bill, it was introduced in seventeen states; in nine, it became law. In other states, the barber threat was still severe. During the same year, between September of 1924 and 1925, twenty barber bills were introduced; eighteen died and one was amended to conform with the association's bill. Many government agencies still suffered "a general lack of understanding" as to the distinction between man and woman. The barbers' main argument was "that haircutting whether male or female is the same," so the hairdressers' task was to stress the difference. "To require us to take a barber's license" was akin to requiring "a surgeon to have a choropodist's [*sic*] license to operate on a toe." Their interests could best be served by "intensive campaign propaganda, and solicitation of political parties." Since government was bound to support the public welfare, it could "well be argued, without reflecting on the barber shop[,] that the patronizing by females of barber shops is as equally detrimental to public morals as the patronage by men of beauty parlors." The association in the meantime insisted on exemption clauses for women every time a barber bill applied to any person. The one word "any" was the key.[22]

In 1925, the association also engaged the Proprietary Association in the struggle against adverse legislation. The Proprietary Association employed a staff in Washington, D.C., and all the states' capitals. For $500 a year, it monitored legislation and alerted its members to bills that concerned all business and those that infringed on a member's particular business. The preeminence of the national marketplace was a chief preoccupation. "Detrimental legislation in any part of the country affects all other parts—so, should be opposed . . . no matter how innocent legislation may appear, if it affects their membership and is not self evidently beneficial, they oppose it on the general principle that it would merely be the nibbling into their rights, resulting harmfully as time goes on." The association endorsed this viewpoint; bills appeared everywhere that impinged on the beauty business.[23]

At times, the association even had to oppose its own local representatives who pressed legislation that deviated from the Model Bill. A number of local activists, overly aware of their individual situations, seemed bent on perverting the point of standard legislation throughout the nation, burdening their particular bills with "the penalty of excessive provision." Clouding legislation with immediate personal difficulties could wreak havoc with the future. By 1926, this problem was easing, though; "women, especially today, know more about legislation than they did two years ago." Other locals, in their enthusiasm, went the opposite direction, looking for easy victories by supporting bills that had been stripped of essential provisions and, specifically, the constitutional safeguards clause, the repeal of prior and inconsistent acts clause, the stipulation of fees clause, and the enforcement clause. As the president put it, "Better no law than a bad one." The national marketplace required conformity; a central task of the association's legal department was "to prevent a mania to enact bills, according to the fancies of individual grievances and conceptions." Law had to be prospective rather than retrospective. It did not have to "tie a knot around your neck to give satisfaction."[24]

Although the association often had to discipline overly exuberant supporters, the larger menace to the beauty parlor came from interests outside it. "Barber bills, anti-cosmetic bills and tax bills have flooded the country," noted the counselor in 1927. The profession also had to guard against "friendly enemies" with narrow self-interests. The American Medical Association, in particular, seemed determined to interfere in the business. "While due credit must be given them for sincerity of motive, your president [himself a producer of hair dyes] feels that the hairdressers are better judges as to the effects of the continuous use of cosmetics, and, in general, would recommend that such bills be opposed." The issue was complex, as the counsel noted in an address asking, "Where does Beauty Culture end and Medical Practice begin?" Although an operator had to diagnose each client, she could not "pose" as a diagnostician. "You all know that there are as many different types of acne as there are Nationalities in this country. Some of which can be treated by Beauty Culture methods, others cannot." Overstepping the boundaries of "beauty" could and would entail "unlooked for legislative actions." Indeed, attempts to classify cosmetics as dangerous drugs pressed heavily on the profession. In 1926, a prominent doctor noted that thirty-six cases of cosmetic poisoning occurred in the previous year. From the association's perspective, he failed to recognize that about $400 million worth of cosmetics were used by 50 million women during that same time. People die and people die. Godefroy noted that patients expired all the time at the hands of physicians. That did not mean society should do away with doctors.[25]

The boom in cosmetics complemented the parlor trade throughout the twenties and, although tangential to hairdressing, may have had much to do with the bobbers' ultimate success over the barbers. As a speaker at a sublegislative committee meeting in 1924 explained it, "You ladies and gentlemen must appreciate that the beauty business indirectly or through the advertising in magazines and through the great sale of cosmetics in this country is being forced on us. . . . It is being forced on us by the enormous sale of cosmetics in the United States." The craze fed the parlor trade. "There are manufacturers who never enter a beauty shop with goods but they run double pages, run full pages on Sunday. These manufacturers are creating business because they are making women accustomed to the use of cosmetics and the next step with the woman is that she is going to have them professionally applied." As she acquainted herself with the new usages, she availed herself of the temples of the new cult of feminine beauty that were becoming a commonplace across the nation. "She is not satisfied with her own use of them and she goes to a beauty shop and naturally that increases the beauty shop business and is going to bring about 30,000 beauty shops in five years. That is the reason, I think, we are all going to get our houses in order." For that reason, he concluded, "We are just on the threshold of a wonderful business in America and don't let's spoil it. Let us have it a standardized business."[26]

In time, the National Hairdressers Association succeeded in enacting its notions of the sex-specific barber shop. By 1933, the hairdressers had been so successful that, when the National Industrial Recovery Act, the NIRA, called for codes of fair practice in hairdressing, it was only reasonable to turn to the obvious experts in this particular search for order. The association's secretary, Edna Emme, became chairman of the Hairdressers' Code Authority, administering regulations that she and her colleagues had largely devised. "This was a signal victory for the National," and although the NIRA was eventually declared unconstitutional, it guaranteed the organization's position as "the 'Voice of Cosmetology in the Nation.' " By 1935, when the census of business tabulated the extent of this form of enterprise, it reported the widespread existence of beauty shops in every state in the union. (Table 4.1.) With over 61,000 parlors grossing some $172 million in receipts, the beauty business had become an institutionalized expression of femininity in the continental community of consumers.[27]

If he hoped to ensure a market for his magazine when he founded the organization, Charles Meeker Kozlay succeeded. The *American Hairdresser* was the official organ of the American Hairdressers Association during its formative years, despite heavy competition from a number of other trade journals. Its preeminence in the field endured as long as it served as the journal of record for the National Hairdressers Association. It still exists today, as the *American Hairdresser/Salon Owner,* bringing together the owners of shops and the manufacturers of parlor goods. In 1927, the association changed its name, too, perhaps to reflect the input of the manufacturers and wholesalers who had been among its most active supporters from the beginning. It came to be called the National Hairdressers and Cosmetologists Association. And it too exists today, occupying the previous headquarters of the House of Godefroy in Saint Louis.

TABLE 4.1   A census of beauty shops, 1935

State	Number of shops	Receipts (in thousands of dollars)	Active proprietors	Employees (average/year)	Payroll (in thousands of dollars)
Alabama	471	1,076	464	761	401
Arizona	160	422	166	152	118
Arkansas	516	938	529	531	294
California	5,089	16,768	5,246	6,557	5,762
Colorado	603	1,507	613	680	488
Connecticut	566	3,248	574	1,437	1,299
Delaware	139	306	137	127	92
D.C.	442	2,426	429	1,246	1,052
Florida	652	2,117	652	1,224	832
Georgia	684	1,791	680	1,234	717
Idaho	232	469	228	209	126
Illinois	4,432	12,874	4,493	5,868	4,470
Indiana	2,019	3,287	2,059	1,495	923
Iowa	1,436	2,875	1,483	1,120	715
Kansas	884	1,452	898	675	356
Kentucky	694	1,483	692	713	464
Louisiana	556	1,228	568	791	440
Maine	482	1,060	482	343	263
Maryland	1,010	2,202	998	1,002	698
Massachusetts	2,622	7,606	2,579	3,129	2,503
Michigan	2,534	6,140	2,484	2,631	1,974
Minnesota	1,168	3,516	1,235	1,621	1,130
Mississippi	361	527	364	321	153
Missouri	2,222	5,350	2,252	2,754	1,811
Montana	257	509	268	155	108
Nebraska	996	1,575	1,014	576	382
Nevada	62	147	66	43	39
New Hampshire	306	624	317	168	115
New Jersey	2,224	6,836	2,188	3,003	2,243
New Mexico	148	300	150	140	85
New York	7,685	32,952	7,519	14,231	12,816
North Carolina	651	1,813	648	1,055	642
North Dakota	282	514	293	220	136
Ohio	3,970	10,200	3,957	4,579	3,274
Oklahoma	1,239	1,891	1,248	1,121	589
Oregon	598	1,601	605	666	531
Pennsylvania	4,621	11,670	4,580	4,806	3,484
Rhode Island	300	864	281	351	279
South Carolina	304	673	297	430	226
South Dakota	304	549	321	233	135
Tennessee	812	2,082	821	1,304	743
Texas	2,753	5,554	2,854	3,290	1,851
Utah	281	503	298	204	132
Vermont	216	337	223	90	57
Virginia	626	1,750	591	1,024	670
Washington	937	2,524	953	1,041	807
West Virginia	536	1,119	553	491	292
Wisconsin	1,111	4,423	1,017	2,125	1,547
Wyoming	162	265	169	95	59
Total	61,355	171,943	61,504	78,062	58,323

SOURCE: U.S. Bureau of the Census, *Census of Business: 1935, Service Establishments,* Vol. 2: *Statistics for States, Counties, and Cities* (Washington, D.C.: GPO, 1935), 4–52.

With a few dozen dedicated people, a few hundred others who actively supported the effort, and the willing endorsement of America in the dollar democracy of the marketplace, Kozlay and his organization styled new standards of everyday appearance. One participant, himself a hairdresser, explicated the achievement best in 1925: "There is a little difference between a man and a woman. Where that difference starts you know, for the barbers do the work for the men, and we do the work for the women."[28]

5

The Cleanliness Crusade

All the soiled and spotted children, back yards, restaurants and streets of the country are to be sought out, imbued with the desire for soap and scrubbing brushes, and turned loose with appearance and self-respect improved several degrees.
— *NEW YORK TIMES*, 1927

The business of cleanliness is big business.
— ROSCOE C. EDLUND, 1930

hen new needs are added to the marketplace, they upset the stability of old ones. In the 1920s, the cosmetic enthusiasms of an abundant society threatened to undermine the demand for soap. Following what was becoming a common practice in many fields of industry, soap producers formed a trade association to protect their market and promote the consumption of their commodity. The Association of American Soap and Glycerine Producers, in turn, established the Cleanliness Institute to teach the public the importance of keeping clean. Combining popular concerns for health with its own concern for profit, the institute embarked on a remarkable campaign designed to ensure that Americans use soap liberally. Magazine advertising and radio broadcasts were only the most obvious efforts on behalf of the cause. Infiltrating the classroom with materials it sold at cost, dispensing "news releases" and expert advice on hygiene, this arm of the association gained acclaim, not just for innovative marketing, but for public service. For a historical moment, the Cleanliness Institute became a center of learning: of learning the need for more soap consumption in America.

The soap makers already faced difficulties promoting their particular line of goods; they had to surmount the obstacles inherent in marketing a branded staple, each specific trademark competing against essentially identical goods on the basis of marginal differentiations. The buyers' market of the late 1920s did not ameliorate the situation. When there were more products than people could afford to buy, competition for the consumer's dollar became more widespread than brand against brand, Lux against Lifebuoy, or even one cleansing agent over another, soap versus cold cream. Instead, lipsticks waged war with paper clips, and the makers of shoes and cigarettes and porcelain plates all competed with one another to gain the attention of purchasers.

In the 1920s, moreover, the manufacturer of soap faced the rise of a cosmetics industry that marketed goods which would truly "beautify." Soap promoters relied heavily on an elusive promise of loveliness. Since producers had to distinguish their particular brand of a staple commodity, they were compelled to offer a product that might somehow do more than other soaps, provide an extra charm or restore a schoolgirl complexion. Now another industry altogether threatened to deliver on those beauty promises, with products having nothing whatsoever to do with washing. The soap maker confronted a climacteric. "For over fifteen hundred years soap and water had stood as the accepted agent of cleanliness, yet now the time had come when it had to be constantly so maintained in the public mind. To so maintain it, cooperative effort was needed."[1]

The industry probably exaggerated its plight. Soap may have existed for fifteen hundred years—the word's first recorded English usage dates back to around 1000 A.D.—but one cannot assume that the ancients used it as one might today. Soap was not the same substance then; it was instead a lixivium leached through ashes. Modern soap made its appearance with the development of vegetable oils in the mid-nineteenth century. When employed in combination with animal fats, these oils eliminated the problem of perishability. Molding the improved product into cakes to facilitate transport, the manufacturer began to explore the possibilities of regional marketing, to develop a brand distinguishable from others, and to seek the support of consumers at the cash register. The growth of the trade presaged the national marketplace.[2]

The enterprising artificer quickly discovered that soap had an unusually large margin of profit, and the lure of even greater returns encouraged experimentation with advertising. Armed with unusual sales vision and the wherewithal to pursue it, soap makers became one of the first manufacturers (outside of patent medicines) to utilize promotions on a large scale; they were among the first legitimate industries to incorporate ads as a regular part of doing business. The soap-making trade can be credited with leading the way to modern advertising.[3]

The path seemed paved with profit. Enoch Morgan's Sons began running ads for its soap in 1869. Within a year, the firm found 500,000 regular users. It soon ceased producing anything else to meet the demand for Sapolio. Artemas Ward took charge of promotions in 1885; he made the product one of the most widely used articles in America through innovative advertising. By 1891, "Sapolio proverbs were second only to Solomon's in wide publicity."[4]

Sapolio was not the only soap to find an eager market. By the 1890s, abetted by effective advertising, Ivory and Pear's were also "known almost everywhere that merchandise was sold." Procter & Gamble discovered the importance of an alluring trademark when, in 1879, they changed the name of their White Soap to Ivory. Using simple slogans like "It floats" and "99$^{44}/_{100}$ percent pure" and underwriting a wide distribution for the messages, Procter & Gamble made their ads as famous as their product. They also sold soap. By 1890, 30 million cakes of Ivory were being bought annually. Pear's started taking full-page ads in the 1880s, when doing so was still considered a questionable venture by most businesses. Pear's introduced arresting pictures and attention-grabbing inquiries: "Good morning, have you used Pear's soap?" A few years later, the firm incited a vogue for testimonials by employing the endorsements of famous people. While the magazine industry grew, embracing the nation with news of goods for sale, soap makers stayed at the forefront of the ranks of· leading advertisers.[5]

By the late 1890s, Wool, Dr. Woodbury's, Cuticura, and Fairy stepped up on the soapbox of successful selling through ads. The initiative of the industry continued to dominate the national medium, adding innovation after innovation in the quest for increased revenues. Woodbury created the "Facial Purity League" in the late nineteenth century, augmenting campaigns with buttons for all of its "members." The modern premium owed its commencement to B. T. Babbitt and Babbitt's Best Soap. He conceived of ascribing a value to wrappers; anyone submitting twenty-five received a panel picture. Editions of some illustrations ran into the hundreds of thousands. Wool Soap inaugurated rebates in 1898, when the Women's Christian Temperance Union received a penny apiece for its Chicago temple every time someone remitted a wrapper to the firm. The jingles of "Spotless Town," made so hygienic by Sapolio, became a commonplace at the turn of the century, making rhymes a popular promotional technique. In the first decade of the twentieth century, an even more important contribution appeared in soap ads. Ivory's campaigns pointing out its wide range of uses gave advertisers ready proof of the effectiveness of that approach to the marketplace. By 1910, soap makers led the trend toward selling what a product did, instead of what it was. Their ads "began to talk cleanliness." When the industry anticipated a slump in sales in the 1920s, it was an old hand at eliciting consumer demand.[6]

The decline in demand it hoped to avert was probably attributable to a net drop in dirtiness in America. Based on a study he undertook in 1926, Walter B. Pitkin asserted that the automobile and the paving of streets were especially responsible. The old dirt road was dusty in dry weather, muddy when wet, messing up homes, draperies, furniture, clothing, and all sorts of things that had to be washed. People formerly rode horses or walked; those modes of transportation were inherently less hygienic than hopping into a flivver. The increasing popularity of the closed car accentuated the impact. As the filth and mire of road dirt and horseback dwindled, so did demand for cleansers.[7]

Changes in home technologies also threatened the soap market in the 1920s. "The tremendous increase in the domestic use of electricity vies with the automobile in its disastrous effects upon soap consumption." Replacing the kerosene lamp and coal stove with light bulb and range sharply reduced the soot and muck of everyday life. A primary reason Americans ripped up the carpet to lay linoleum or tile in the twenties was to cut down on cleaning. Paper napkins and tablecloths were discarded rather than washed. The abrupt shrinkage in the number of household servants employed after the war also may have influenced soap sales. They seemed "notoriously wasteful with soap." The housewife who did her own scrubbing perhaps used much less. Wash day was a thing of the past in many homes, and sending clothes to the laundry undermined the soap industry, too. Said Pitkin, "Mass production of cleanliness works like mass production anywhere else: it reduces the unit costs tremendously." Commercial laundries, furthermore, often used chemicals other than soap to clean clothes. The substitution of silks for cotton, and finer cotton for wools, and the dry cleaning those garments often required, detracted from soap sales. Changed fashions in clothing meant less soap consumed at wash day, even if the work was done at home, because the noticeable reduction in what women wore in the 1920s meant less extensive use of detergent when laundering. Improved home heating with central systems and better insulation (and an urban apartmentalized life) reduced both the likelihood of wearing heavy winter clothing throughout the cold seasons, and the need for frequently washing those weighty underwear, stockings, coats, and cloaks. All of these factors acted to the detriment of demand for cleansers in the 1920s.[8]

As women's work in the home changed with new technologies, so did men's work outside it. Another by-product of the machine age was the cleaner condition of the worker coming off his shift. Inventions that saved labor incidentally served hygiene. Tons of goods carried by back and brawn a few years before now moved by conveyor. Cellars and sewers were dug not by hand anymore, but by machine. "Thousands of jobs which, only a few years ago, were rough and grimy are today almost white-collar jobs." The less soiled the laborer, the less soap required to clean him up. For all these reasons, "the soap maker weeps."[9]

The dilemma that made the soap makers' condition untenable was posed by the boom in cosmetics. To stimulate demand for the product, the soap manufacturers had advertised for forty or fifty years. But their pitches had to be secondary to general soap-and-water hygiene, if they hoped to sell their individual brands of the staple. They were was forced by the logic of the marketplace to employ "special pleadings" extolling an ostensible difference between trademarks. They cared not about primary demand for all soap, so much as they sought to enhance the specific demand for Palmolive, or Resinol, or Camay. So the basic premise of cleanliness was lost to particular appeals, among them being loveliness. When the business of beauty culture emerged, though, lipsticks, powders, and face creams co-opted the message. Indeed, claimed the soap industry, cosmetics came into direct competition with hygiene itself.[10]

As an industry spokesperson explained it, other "products which would substitute for soap and water were so advertised against the weight of medical and health opinion; and still other processes and products were being promoted to tear down the use of soaps for household purposes." The industry's trade association decided that if producers hoped to continue making a profit as well as soap, they had "to stabilize the appeal of soap and water as the primary agencies of cleanliness, thus providing a basic and constant background for brand exploitation." Manufacturers had to let Americans know, not just that they were still soiled, but that they could never be sanitary enough. As the country became cleaner than ever before, manufacturers had to dig up dirt.[11]

The industry had some experience at cooperation to guide its assault on the marketplace. During World War I, the government encouraged cooperation in industry. Washington's interest in soap sprang from the Allies' need for glycerine, which was "exclusively a by-product of the soap industry" and essential to dynamite production. The Food Administration urged soap makers to get together; they in turn formed the Soap and Candle Industries War Service Committee, chaired by Sidney Colgate. The committee came to oversee soap production in America. This experience at wartime cooperation, though brief, was profitable. The industry made some practical discoveries, both major and minor, which it no doubt used later to good effect. Various efficiencies of production and packaging could increase output significantly with the same amount of labor. It learned about the use of fillers to substitute for more costly materials. It experimented with price-fixing. According to J. Donald Edwards's survey for the Bureau of Labor Statistics, the business learned how to hide "price increases for soap through changing the terms of sale," and how to use government to good advantage. It found that two small cakes of soap, equal in weight to a larger bar, did not last as long; virtually all manufacturers reduced the weight of their cakes during the war. "The Food Administration did not wish to conserve soap," Edwards noted, but on the contrary, it hoped to encourage production at home and export abroad. As measured by exports, the experiment was an astounding success. Soap exports "in 1916 amounted to about 70 million pounds with a declared value of about 5.2 cents per pound. By 1918, the volume of exports had increased almost one hundred percent and the average unit value had risen to 9.3 cents." Restricting imports of luxury toilet soaps after 1 April 1918, in the meantime, caused a drop of 70 percent over imports in 1916. When the soap makers formed a trade association a few years after the war, they could continue to capitalize on their previous experience at cooperative profit-taking.[12]

In the 1920s, that sort of enterprise became a standard procedure in all sorts of industries. It was called "the New Competition." "In an earlier day the consumer had been left pretty much to himself to make the selection of which of his wants and desires he would attempt to fulfill. . . . Essentially the new competition involved a shift from product competition within an industry to want competition between industries." The trend began with the trusts, which at the turn of the twentieth century realized that desires compete on a broader scale than brand against brand; one want fulfilled could crowd out another. In the teens, cooperative advertising by firms producing the same commodity became "a veritable epidemic" in fields as diverse as apples, floor coverings, and bicycles. Most of those efforts did not endure. Inexperience, poor organization, a lack of whole-hearted interest, a dearth of systematic financial support, anticipations of too much too soon, and a lack of coordination between advertising and selling led to their demise.[13]

After the war, however, manufacturers seized on this means of enlarging their markets. They learned that competitors in the same business were in a fundamental way allied — they all hoped to stimulate demand for similar sorts of goods. Voluntary coordination of industry through the trade association was one determinant of the prosperity Americans celebrated in the 1920s. Referring to this innovation in business organization as a predominant contributor to the cause of abundance, Wesley C. Mitchell recounted "a marked increase of readiness to join co-operative programs of research and publicity, to interchange trade information, to standardize products where standardization is good business, to consult about methods and practices — in short, to treat the industry for many purposes as a unit in whose prosperity all members have a common interest, and to inspire good will in the public by open dealings." One could debate how open those dealings were, but that trade associations were everywhere in the New Era was a matter of fact. Lynd and Hanson estimated the existence of 1000 to 1800 such organizations. Of those, they singled out the Association of American Soap and Glycerine Producers. The workings of its Cleanliness Institute, they concluded, "exemplify new types of trade association consumer stimulation."[14]

The *New York Times* heralded this "new public welfare organization of national scope" immediately after its founding in 1927. Through the Cleanliness Institute, all the "slovenly folk, who have been going on the theory that they can take a bath or leave it, are to be brought to their senses." Trumpeting the venture, the *Times* went on; "The American standard of cleanliness has not been attained or even thought desirable by thousands of our citizens. To discover the sections of the population that are unaware of the blessings of sanitary conveniences, to make them discontented with their unwashed condition, and then to supply them with running water, open plumbing and soap, is the purpose of the present investigation. Such work is a real public service." What could be more progressive? To effect research, education, and "betterment work," soap producers "have joined hands."[15]

They must have been wearing gloves. If soap makers read the literature distributed on their behalf, saw the ads, or heard the speeches, they surely knew that hands were filthy organs. Microbes were everywhere, omnipresent, ever-ready to spread disease, debility, death. Ill-considered commingling was a certain route to an untimely end. "As a social procedure, handshaking may be acceptable, but from the standpoint of health it is a pernicious custom." As an institute spokesperson put it, "we Americans might well learn something from the Chinese, who, in greeting each other, shake their own hands, and if it is present, their own dirt." There was no greater sin in the cleanliness catechism than infesting a fellow traveler with those microscopic multitudes of germs that most Americans inevitably carried. "I call this a biological discourtesy, and I wonder how many of us are biologically discourteous every day."[16]

The institute's first concern was for the children. Habit-formation was the heart of its hopes, and school kids were a captive audience. No approach could better meet the industry's ends than inculcating every youth in America to a tale of soap-and-water. Once habituated to regular and frequent consumption, the children could guarantee a market for years to come. As the institute advised, "the objective of all cleanliness teaching is the establishment of lifelong cleanliness habits." To convince the children, Cleanliness Institute committed its primary effort.[17]

Every school day in America, 50 million hands attended class. Once there, these hands handled books, pencils, paper, chalk and erasers, maps, toys, innumerable and unmentionable other things; they played at recess; they carried food to 25 million mouths. Yet how many of those hands touched soap? And how many held soap "as often as health and decency demand?" To discover the extent of soap-and-water hygiene in American educational facilities, the institute investigated a sample of 145 schools enrolling 124,088 students in fifteen states. Although about 44 percent of the schools had hot and cold water, 57 percent had soap, and 70 percent had drying equipment for general use, less than one-in-three schools (31 percent) supplied all three together. In most of those cases, moreover, the supply was inadequate from the institute's perspective: one sink for everyone, or not enough towels to go around. Even more startling was the fact that only one school in the entire sampling observed the cardinal rule of the soap makers' vision of health: in only that one school alone "do *all* the children wash their hands regularly after toilet and before lunch." According to the institute, the implications were staggering. "In 92 percent of the deaths caused by communicable diseases the organism enters or leaves the body through the mouth or nose; and it is the human *hand,* in many instances, that carries it." To get every student in the nation to wash his hands at least twice during the school day — before lunch and after toilet — was an enormous undertaking. But even that goal was not enough. "The object should be not merely to make children clean, but to make them love to be clean." The institute took to the task with determination.[18]

The regimen was unrelenting. The institute promulgated schedules of habit formation for each grade level, providing a cleanliness curriculum that could be integrated with other subjects, a system of carrots-and-sticks to enforce behaviors, and hundreds of thousands of texts and storybooks—which it sold at cost—to convey the message. Posters, fliers, pamphlets, and teachers' guides complemented the crusade. This prodigious outpouring of cleanliness guidance was "the major effort of Cleanliness Institute." It delineated motor, attitudinal, and cognitive objectives for every stage of a child's education. At the end of third grade, ideal students washed their hands before eating and after toilet, kept their faces clean with daily ablutions, and assisted in taking an all-over bath at least twice a week. "Have children report on days they take baths at home. The *type of home* will determine whether to expect more than two baths a week. Do not demand too much." They kept hair neat, brushed teeth twice a day ("Check this habit individually, in order not to cause embarrassment"); they wore clean socks and underwear at least after bathing. Acquiring these basic skills was the heart of primary teaching.[19]

By the end of sixth grade, ideal students shined their shoes, cared for their clothes, bathed themselves, kept school desk tidy, covered sneezes unconsciously, and refrained from contact with diseased others or their belongings. "Be careful, however, not to hurt the feelings of the child with the skin trouble." Though new skills were necessary for this age, the emphasis shifted to attitudinal factors and internal controls. "It is essential to make the children *want to do* the things they are taught. Intelligence determines what an individual *can do,* instincts and emotional equipment determine what he *will do.* . . . The self-activity of the children must be aroused. They must get the beliefs strongly tied up with the emotions. This will help them to establish more firmly the habits begun in earlier grades."[20]

By the end of the ninth grade, successful educators had indoctrinated their charges, not merely with wanting to be clean, but with a sense of distinct discomfort when habits were violated by themselves or their peers. The processes of socialization to soap-and-water attuned students to the larger meaning of looking one's best and paying proper attention to personal hygiene. Knowing chapter and verse of the cleanliness catechism—fearing unclean toilets, respecting the unseen bacterial enemies around them, meticulous about their appearance and environment—they also appreciated the part that habits played "in acquiring a satisfactory job after leaving school." By then, out on their own, alone and unaided, they would not think twice about consuming soap frequently for the rest of their days.[21]

The inculcation of cleanliness required both reward and punishment. First-grade teachers were advised to create a town with Sunshine Avenue, Fruit Street, Milk Street, and such; each child constructed a house of folded paper, put his or her name on it, and chose a boulevard on which to place it. If a child failed in any one habit, his house was "removed from Health Town until he had again proved himself worthy to have a residence there." But the efficacy of positive rather than negative reinforcement was continually reiterated. Morning inspections had to be "a period of rejoicing over cleanliness rather than searching for dirt." The teacher had to see that the children observed ascribed practices "as a matter of course, *never as punishment.*" Games and gentle encouragements were a part of the fun. By the time students reached junior high school, one might reward their initiative with lunch. In at least one case of effective conditioning reported to the institute, 475 pupils washed at four sinks in ten-to-twelve minutes before lunch. Student monitors dispensed colored "wash tickets" after children washed their hands. These tickets were collected at the cafeteria's entrance by two more student monitors, who barred the door to recalcitrants. The color of the tickets changed daily, and the order of using the colors altered each week. "The children are most interested in the system and would rather do anything than be deprived of the privelege [*sic*] of acting as monitor during the handwashing session." Armed with these aids and devices, educators could ensure that their wards would provide a ready market for soap makers as long as habits might last.[22]

But "all the church, community, and school influence in the world cannot make up for the start along the path of right habits that a good home training gives. That is largely up to the mothers." The crusade did not disregard them. The institute specifically warned teachers not to "create a dissatisfaction of the children with their parents"; instead, they had to advise a child "of the desirability and possibility of a clean, neat, sanitary, and attractive home no matter what the financial status," and help the child appreciate "that home conditions must necessarily change along with other conditions in the community, the school, and social customs." The institute conceded that "it would be futile to have the school advance beyond the understanding and interest of the home," if "permanent habits" were to be instilled. Teachers were instructed to "write letters home telling of the cleanliness habits the children are trying to establish. Write letters to mother asking her to help the children remember to practice the cleanliness habits at home." Assisting her offspring's memory, she might herself join the ranks.[23]

The institute did not only appeal to mothers' concern for their school children. She was the primary purchaser of soap, and as homemaker, its chief user. The institute realized that preaching wash! clean! scrub! was not the way to entice women to more soap consumption. Sophisticated solicitors of the purchaser's vote in the dollar democracy had come to appreciate that one did not scream orders and injunctions to increasingly oblivious consumers. Edward L. Bernays, the preeminent public relations counsel of the era, explained the difference between simple salesmanship and advertising psychology as fine art. The one promoter, pushing bacon, keeps exclaiming " 'Eat more bacon; eat *our* bacon.' " The wise persuader, on the other hand, "makes use of what the psychologist calls the conditioned reflex. He does not mention bacon at all. He does not mention anything, because he knows no one is interested in what he mentions." Instead, "he gets a number of physicians to say that people should eat heartier breakfasts. He manages a kind of vogue for heartier breakfasts, on the grounds of dietetic necessity. He knows that if people will eat heartier breakfasts they will think of bacon." The crusades of Cleanliness Institute were an uncanny mimicry of this hypothetical search for bacon sales. Weaving tales of woman's sphere and romance, the institute employed the conditioned reflex: extolling homemaker, it would sell soap by simple association. Making ample use of the press release and radio—this, after all, was public service—it broadcast a picture of American woman caring for her home, and loving every moment of the experience.[24]

"Surer than the appearance of the robin or the tender crocus leaves as the first sign of spring is woman's urge to clean house from attic to cellar." According to the institute's Department of Public Information, "With the first warm zephyr she throws open the windows, hums a glad little song, and reaches for the broom." The woman described in the institute's releases did not object to housework; she relished it. A "friend of mine" regarded "her gay-colored modern utensils as a rainbow spreading over her kitchen horizon. And when they need washing, she says the job is easier because they shine like the proverbial pot of gold when she takes them out of the soapy dishwater. You remember the old saying about the treasure at the end of the rainbow. Of course it is only a figure of speech which really means brighter days are ahead, but it can have a double meaning if pleasant thoughts make a rainbow over a lot of greasy pots." Using soap was more than good times and sunshine, though; the enterprise was downright healthy. "You 'just hate' the refrigerator job? Don't. It's marvelous exercise, for it brings nearly all your muscles into play. So down on your knees! Think of yourself as kneeling before the altar of beauty and health. Not for one single instant are you a slave to household drudgery. And when you know that the exercise is helping to give you a fine, shapely body, it will become good fun to reach and turn and twist and peer into the refrigerator."[25]

Cleanliness Institute did not mean to victimize women and children; it meant to sell soap. It was oddly quiescent when men were concerned. The association published some posters for the proletariat: "A Clean Machine Runs Better—Your Body is a Machine—KEEP IT CLEAN." But other than a speech here and there on industrial dermatitis, the institute made few pitches directly to men. Perhaps it worked behind the scenes, encouraging owners with the efficiency of a healthy work force, pushing facilities for soap consumption in factories more rigorously than the public pronouncements of the organization reveal. Only the soap industry knows. Otherwise, for males, the tale-of-soap-and-water must have come from the women, and men's previous experience at American education.[26]

Many no doubt saw the magazine ads. These were the most obvious pleadings of Cleanliness Institute. Inducements to frequent washing appeared regularly in periodicals and newspapers; paid-space ads were repeated over 250 million times in 1928 alone. *Cleanliness Journal* was also sent free to civic leaders, social workers, health officials, and such, throughout the late twenties and early thirties. As Bernays had discovered, "the most direct way to reach the mind of the herd is through its leaders—its group leaders." The Health Service of the institute lectured nursing and education associations, state medical societies, parent-teacher groups, women's clubs, industrial and civic organizations, state and local public health associations, summer institutes, YMCAs, industrial courses, and occasional high schools, colleges, and professional schools. "Field work is concerned chiefly with those persons who are in a position to influence the cleanliness habits of larger numbers."[27]

In addition to these campaigns, the organization underwrote a massive experiment in magazine advertising between July 1930 and November 1931. The results were well worth the investment. The venture sought to measure the effectiveness of advertising various messages, employing coupon returns as the index of reader responsiveness. Spending less than $500,000 to buy space for the investigation, the institute managed to elicit 685,154 individual requests for more than a million free booklets that acted as magnets. The average cost-per-response was a "surprisingly low" 72.9 cents; the ardor with which Americans reacted to the advertising was some 40 percent better than the typical rate-of-return calculated by Daniel Starch in his definitive *Analysis of 5,000,000 Inquiries.* Of course the coupon clippers — those who actually took the time to cut them out and mail them back to the institute — were but the tip of the iceberg of those moved by the material. "A coupon in all the advertisements not only did not weaken the sales message for those who did not clip coupons," advised the agency that evaluated the effort, "but actually strengthened the copy." The remarkable rate-of-return "supplied desirable proof that the very fundamental educational campaign being undertaken was indeed functioning, that it was of public interest, that it could be expected in time to have a very real influence on the average standard of cleanliness and the per capita consumption of soap."[28]

Three basic appeals were employed in the advertising experiment: loveliness, cleaning, and the bath. Using twenty-one different periodicals and as many different layouts to carry its messages, the institute discovered what soap makers suspected ever since they first associated beauty with bars of soap: when fishing for customers, the promise of "loveliness" was one of their most effective lures. The most popular single promotion was "how to" copy, entitled "For a more beautiful complexion." This cohort of ads offered respondents *The Thirty Day Loveliness Test,* a curious blend of Progressive concerns for efficiency and measurable results with the new cult of beauty. The second most popular group of appeals concerned bathing; *The Book About Baths* acted as enticement — a basic balneology on types of water, when to bathe, the marvels of brisk scrub-and-towelling. The least effective way to soft soap Americans, ironically, was the direct pitch to cleanliness. Perhaps the offer *A Cleaner House By 12 O'Clock* was too stark an expression of the institute's ideal housekeeper. Her home, as the title suggested, could never be clean, only "cleaner." Maybe if she did not quit at noon, her domain might approach the immaculate, but the booklet did not go so far. It concluded with a picture of Mrs. American Housewife washing the front door, bucket at her side. If the pamphlet strained the credulity of the consumer, however, the promotions still got results. The average inquiry-cost to the institute for all seven "cleaning" ads was only eight-four cents apiece, and they were the least successful group of solicitations.[29]

One cannot measure the influence of Cleanliness Institute on soap sales precisely. First of all, its records, aside from promotional literature, are sealed. That condition is no accident, as Flynn observed a half century ago. "There are fences built around the trade organizations. These organizations of merchants and manufacturers formed into trade groups are slowly developing into guilds. They attempt to fix prices, parcel out territory, curtail production, fix the terms of existence within the trade, and generally regulate competition. This is called 'self-government in industry.'" Flynn noted that "what is overlooked is that in fixing prices, production, and trade routes, a trade association is governing not merely itself but the public which does business with it. It is in reality assuming a function of the general government and this function it proposes to discharge in absolute secrecy." Soap makers would hardly risk an admission of doing something disreputable, let alone dirty.[30]

Individual producers, moreover, independent of this effort to provide "a basic and constant background for brand exploitation," advertised soap ardently in the 1920s. One must appreciate the impossibility of attempting to analyze the impact of cooperative campaigning discretely, and be advised against attributing overly much influence to associational activities while individual members were eagerly courting consumers. Cooperative campaigns aimed to register long-term gains, as much as to incite immediate advances. Borden did observe, however, that the primary object of most such ventures was not to raise prices. Most cooperatives, rather, had hopes "of increasing the amount of the product which may be sold at the current price. Usually by so doing they may use more completely their manufacturing and marketing facilities and thus increase profits." If this was the ultimate mark of success, soap makers met the measure with distinction. The price of soap held steady throughout the late twenties, while supply registered a marked advance. (Table 5.1.) Soap

TABLE 5.1   Characteristics of soap production, 1914–1929 (indexed to 1923)

Characteristic	1914	1919	1921	1923	1925	1927	1929
Physical volume of production	75.4	95.6	86.5	100.0	99.9	105.1	115.1
Volume of production/wage earner	90.8	79.9	88.9	100.0	110.3	133.0	139.9
Output/establishment	...	...	...	100.0	99.2	110.8	113.4
Wage earners/establishment	...	...	...	100.0	89.9	83.3	81.4
Selling price/unit	61.3	119.5	100.4	100.0	100.8	98.8	95.4
Cost of materials/unit	67.8	143.3	100.1	100.0	106.6	94.5	87.5
Fabrication costs and profit/unit	50.3	79.2	100.9	100.0	90.9	106.2	108.6
Labor costs/unit	51.4	106.4	104.9	100.0	89.2	90.3	77.9
Overhead and profits/unit	50.0	72.4	99.9	100.0	91.3	110.3	116.4

SOURCE: Frederick C. Mills, *Economic Tendencies in the United States* (New York: National Bureau of Economic Research, 1932), 194, 196, 224, 228, 229, 235, 237, 293, 296, 303, 306, 381, 388, 391, 406, 407, 599.
NOTE: 1923 = 100.

making remained a profitable enterprise despite earlier fears of a nation becoming too clean or cosmetic.[31]

In the 1880s, Henry Ward Beecher testified for Pear's. "If cleanliness is next to Godliness," he averred, "soap must be considered as a means of Grace." Some forty years later, in 1929, a critic could acclaim that in modern America, "cleanliness has become the substitute for godliness." In 1938, when the Scripps-Howard network canvassed the commodities in 53,000 homes in sixteen cities, soap ranked second only to bread-and-butter in the essentials of life. (Table 5.2.) The results of the survey may have been little more than pipe dreams; housewives inventoried their cupboards themselves after almost a decade of depression. But the virtually universal acknowledgment of soap on the homemakers' shelves evidenced, at the least, a recognition on their part that soap ought to be there. And "ought" enforces the mores.[32]

TABLE 5.2   A cupboard inventory of 53,000 homes in 16 cities, 1938

Item	Percent possessing	Intercity range
Toiletries		
toilet soap—cake	94.1	96.6–92.1
laundry chips, granules, flakes, or powders	91.4	93.2–86.2
toothpaste or tooth powder	89.4	95.3–81.4
face powder	82.0	88.0–72.0
laundry soap—bar	77.5	89.7–65.4
scouring powders	73.9	84.1–54.7
toothbrushes	69.0	84.9–55.3
toothpaste	64.6	87.4–57.5
cold cream	58.8	65.7–52.1
lipstick	58.0	71.0–47.6
safety-razor blades	55.7	67.0–44.9
dry rouge	54.7	68.5–44.0
liquid nail polish	51.4	62.4–42.3
shaving cream	48.0	56.0–41.3
cleansing cream	46.2	58.0–37.7
tooth powder	46.1	58.6–33.6
safety razors	39.8	51.3–28.8
body powder	38.3	50.9–30.7
vanishing cream	27.8	38.4–18.3
skin and tissue cream	22.7	36.5–16.3
paste rouge	15.5	18.8–10.0
electric razor	9.0	15.3– 3.7
Foodstuffs		
all-purpose flour	94.8	97.5–89.1
butter or oleo	94.5	97.1–89.5
baking powder	94.3	96.6–91.6
coffee	93.3	95.9–89.9
shortening or lard	91.6	97.1–80.5

TABLE 5.2 (*continued*)

Item	Percent possessing	Intercity range
hot or cold cereal	91.1	94.4–86.5
granulated sugar	90.9	95.5–85.9
butter	84.3	94.2–59.2
tea	77.5	88.0–51.8
gelatin desserts	64.2	73.8–53.3
salad dressing	59.8	75.9–29.0
canned milk	59.7	78.5–44.1
mustard	59.6	75.5–47.7
catsup	54.4	70.5–37.4
packed sliced bacon	51.3	66.7–34.4
packaged cheese	41.9	54.4–29.3
canned baked beans	40.3	60.6–26.7
tomato juice	39.8	58.0–22.8
canned tuna fish	27.2	60.2– 9.2
carbonated beverages	26.1	38.2–14.3
oleomargarine	25.1	65.6– 9.6
pineapple juice	22.9	37.6–10.1
canned dog food	19.2	30.9–14.0
Other		
refrigeration of some sort	91.4	97.2–60.4
home radio	91.4	95.9–86.1
automobiles	68.4	84.3–59.5
mechanical refrigeration	59.7	73.3–29.8
paper towels	18.7	32.9–10.1

SOURCE: Adapted from *Market Records: From a Home-Inventory Study of Buying Habits and Brand Preferences of Consumers in Sixteen Cities,* 2 vols. (New York: Scripps-Howard Newspapers), Vol. 1, 54–230.

NOTE: Sampled on the basis of census tract and rental value of home.

6

American Hygiene in an

Age of Advertisement

Advertising is a queer cross between a black art and a swindle.
—WALTER B. PITKIN, 1932

The advertiser system of doing business is economic progressivism.
Progress and progressiveness are of its essence. It breeds progress and it
thrives only under conditions which permit progress.
—*FIFTY YEARS 1888–1938*, 1938

dvertisers made the commercial a dynamic aspect of everyday life in twentieth century America, incessantly innovating in their search for sales. How any particular promotion worked, or why one ad sold where another did not, was indeed a murky science at best. "The data may be hard," Pope has determined, "but they float on quicksand."[1] One could study from now until forever and yet not know with certainty how best to move a line of merchandise. When someone hit upon a novel insight, a new approach, he could make millions, actually shaping wants and needs. On the other hand, and with the same technique, another seller could lose.

It was not entirely a gamble. Hunches were reinforced at the cash register or rejected. When Listerine's advertising interjected a new note in marketing, its success was sensational. A disinfectant that had been sold for decades to an indifferent market suddenly became something that millions of Americans simply had to have. A fearful, bashful preoccupation with their own natural odors, the need to remove or disguise them with chemical concoctions apparently more pleasing to society, began to pervade the common consciousness. As imitators clamored to cash in on the innovation, self-avoidance became a very big business. Deodorant sprays and soaps, antiperspirants, mouthwashes and breath fresheners, foot powders, scented shampoos, douches, clothes fresheners, deodorant cleansers, and air fresheners (from the spray-can variety to incense to automated spritzers), all of them came to have a prominent place in the everyday life of America. The degree of that desire to "deodorize" seemed so unsocial, or so minute, as to be almost indiscernible on an articulate level. People did not talk much about it. And yet, they washed, brushed, sprayed, gargled, splashed, douched, powdered, and gargled again with a day-by-day determination to avoid offending, to smell attractive, to win friends and influence people with olfactory innocuousness. By the 1980s, if one totaled consumer expenditures on products whose purpose was to alter one's smell, the aggregate was well in excess of $3.5 billion a year. By then, appealing to Americans' aversion to their natural odors was a fairly safe bet.[2]

Other promoters were more concerned with long-term prospects than with the immediate sales that the producers of Listerine intended to create. Other marketers viewed advertising as process, and thus elevated it into public relations. Thus the soap industry, in fashioning Cleanliness Institute, did not hope to achieve an overnight shift in the vagaries of soap consumption; it envisioned a day when the commodity would be so thoroughly integrated into everyday life that the habit of washing would take on the appearance of a biological function of the organism. The institute did not hope to foster conscious deliberation over a bar of soap, the way one might consume mouthwash in anticipation of the day's events. Nor did it care which brand Americans purchased, so long as they purchased it avidly. The trade association wanted Americans to wash quite unwittingly after toilet, to wash without thought before eating, to jump into the tub as automatically as one might awake each new day. This cultivation of the conditioned reflex required a far more elaborate scheme than running ads in the magazines, though the incessant drum beating of individual firms sustained the effort. In the end, the industry succeeded in making frequent soap consumption a normative accompaniment to daily reality. By the latter years of the twentieth century, for instance, nine-out-of-ten Americans claimed to take some sort of bath each and every day. Whether or not they actually did so, they implicitly acknowledged that such behavior was both appropriate and expected of them. In America, the Saturday night bath had evolved into a daily routine; what once might have seemed fetishistic had become overwhelmingly unexceptionable.[3]

Whatever the intended outcome, whether the advertiser sought to incite immediate sales or induce long-term change in patterns of consumption, there seemed to be a fundamental premise that governed the promoters of goods. The key was repetition. Its discovery pre-dated the age of distribution, and it eventually ensured that ads be everywhere. How one advertised seemed almost less significant than how often the message appeared. In 1891, Thomas Balmer undertook a pioneering investigation not of why ads succeeded, but of how ads failed. He uncovered three major causes. The first was insufficient space committed to the task, when an initial advertiser hoped to create an impression already extant. Secondly, the single insertion seemed doomed to fail. Balmer found the absurdity of running only one solitary ad so striking that he decided never to accept one-time insertions again, except as trial copy designed as a test in a series of ads. Lack of follow-up was the third factor he isolated. Bruce Barton unmasked "The Real Jesus" in the midtwenties and revealed that "He would be a national advertiser today, I am sure, as he was the greatest advertiser of his own day." Barton also revealed the striking similarity between the power of the parable and effective promotion. Each bore a brief message. The wording was simple: "All the greatest things in human life are one-syllable things — love, joy, hope, home, child, wife, trust, faith, God." The copy, moreover, was sincere. Finally, it repeated. And repeated. In a world awash in ads, the injunction carried even greater weight: repeat, reiterate, restate. As Barton put it, "Reputation is repetition."[4]

REPETITION AND REPUTATION, 1885

The first time a man looks at an advertisement, he does not see it.
The second time he does not notice it.
The third time he is conscious of its existence.
The fourth time he faintly remembers having seen it before.
The fifth time he reads it.
The sixth time he turns up his nose at it.
The seventh time he reads it through and says, "Oh brother!"
The eighth time he says, "Here's that confounded thing again!"
The ninth time he wonders if it amounts to anything.
The tenth time he thinks he will ask his neighbor if he has tried it.
The eleventh time he wonders how the advertiser makes it pay.
The twelfth time he thinks perhaps it may be worth something.
The thirteenth time he thinks it must be a good thing.
The fourteenth time he remembers that he has wanted such a thing for a long time.
The fifteenth time he is tantalized because he cannot afford to buy it.
The sixteenth time he thinks he will buy it some day.
The seventeenth time he makes a memorandum of it.
The eighteenth time he swears at his poverty.

The nineteenth time he counts his money carefully.
The twentieth time he sees it, he buys the article, or instructs his wife
    to do so.[5]

How copy was replicated altered with circumstance. Pavlov himself—his name rings a bell—appreciated that an identical stimulus
repeated too often bred contempt. An ad had to attract the attention
of its intended purchasers, and because people changed, advertising
copy did too, giving these pronouncements an undeniable historical
significance. Slosson thought them "witnesses to the tastes and standards of the times"; he argued that "because of this anxious study of
the whims and humors of the buying market, the advertisers are almost our best source as to the actual aspirations, standards and ideals
of the masses." He overstated his case; ads molded desires, fashioned
wants, and articulated ambitions just as they anticipated and
portrayed those elusive qualities of a people. More than mirror images, they were probably closer to being "a living force in the thought-
ways of our time." A survey of successful advertisers of toiletries in
the 1920s and 1930s, however, does reveal a few common themes,
some shared assumptions about Americans, their values, and what
would make them buy.[6]

   Most apparent is the appeal to women in general, and specifically
to mother and lover. By 1890, advertisers had come to appreciate that
"women bought at least four-fifths of all consumer merchandise."
Forty years later, women were still buying 85 percent of all the goods
sold at retail. It was no coincidence that women's magazines appeared
at the first glimmerings of a national marketplace, and that these were
the first genre to amass enormous circulations enumerated in millions
of readers. "Like all consumer magazines they were conceived and
founded for one purpose—to make money for their owners." Betty
Friedan, decoder of the Feminine Mystique, wondered why it was
never stated that what made women so central to the American
economy, that homemakers' central function, was "*to buy more
things for the house.*" She traced the mystique to the early 1950s,
pointing to a marked change in depictions of women and their sphere
in the articles appearing in women's magazines.[7]

   If Friedan looked at the ads that subsidized stories she analyzed,
she would have discovered that promotions articulated a rather un-
compromising view of woman many decades before the fifties.
Whether wife or mother, worker, friend, or lover, she was Consumer,
mediating between the world of goods and human desire. Whether
washing, wedding, cooking, caring, she was purchasing and employ-

ing commodities both for herself and on behalf of those dependent upon her vision. Marketers assiduously determined to focus her attention at the very dawn of the distribution age. In *Ladies' Home Journal* of the 1890s, Editor Bok took a frankly manipulative perspective. "At the same time that he was advising women about affairs of the heart, telling them how to dress, how to conduct themselves, how to feed their families, even how to bring up their children, he strove to effect changes in home architecture and home design," running photos of furniture, for instance, with captions like "This table is beautiful" or "This chair is ugly." Of the ads themselves in the 1890s, Pope has concluded that "with virtually no exceptions, advertising men depicted women as mindless, irrational, compulsive consumers, and recommended tailoring their advertisements accordingly." By 1912, another student of advertising insisted that illustrations were "particularly essential where goods are sold to women, who can reason as well as men, it is true, but whose judgements, nevertheless, are more likely to be based on emotions." Whatever the source of their decisions, their skill at consumption had to be highly refined. Only the suitable soap would make baby "coo with delight." (Fig. 6.1.) A seemingly minor omission in the employment of goods could have tragic consequences. Witness Edna, meticulous in almost every way, damned to a lifetime of loneliness for want of a simple act of consumption. (Fig. 6.2.) Compare her misfortunes to She who had mastered that single task. (Fig. 6.3.) Results of consumptive patterns were rarely only personal or self-contained; an offspring's adjustment might hang in the balance. (Fig. 6.4.) To entice and arrest them, pleadings to the consumers of consequence—appeals to immediate providers—were everywhere in evidence in the 1920s and 1930s.[8]

Another obvious appeal was the promise of upward mobility. The ideology was nothing new in America; it glued the country together before the existence of a national marketplace. By the teens and twenties, while discretionary income increased as never before for many Americans, the association of a product with prosperity was quite predictable. As defined by the ads, new hygienic practices offered a leg up the ladder of success. In the struggle to distance oneself from the crowd, to attain the pinnacle of fortune, washing would help. Just as bathing was a direct path to one's heart's desire, gargling could be the means to a material paradise. Throughout the years between the two world wars, the hook of more is not hard to find.[9] (Figs. 6.5 and 6.6.)

Yet, if a bottle of mouthwash could transform a dime-store clerk into a courtesan, reaching the top had become an ersatz accomplishment. As measured by the old standards of hard work, temperance,

Whenever soap comes in contact with the skin—use Ivory

Tнıɴк of all the little babies who coo with delight every morning in their bath because Ivory Soap feels so grateful to their delicate skins.

Think of all the people who owe their clear, fine-textured complexions and soft, lustrous hair to their habit of using Ivory Soap for toilet, daily bath and shampoo.

Think of all the housekeepers whose hands are white and comely because they use Ivory Soap for washing dishes and for cleaning.

Think how much of the clothing in almost every family is laundered safely and inexpensively with Ivory Soap.

Then you will realize how fortunate it is that there is at least one soap that has every one of the seven qualities necessary for complete efficiency, safety and satisfaction in any and all uses. Abundant lather, quick rinsing, purity, mildness, whiteness, fragrance and "it floats"— these seven essentials combine to make Ivory the ideal soap.

Ivory Soap comes in a convenient size and form for every purpose

Small Cake
For toilet, bath, nursery, shampoo, fine laundry. Can be divided in two for individual toilet use.

Large Cake
Especially for laundry use. Also preferred by many for the bath.

Ivory Soap Flakes
Especially for the washbowl washing of delicate garments. Sample package free on request to Division 7-E, Dept. of Home Economics, The Procter & Gamble Company, Cincinnati, Ohio.

IVORY SOAP .. 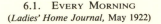 .. 99 $\frac{44}{100}$% PURE

6.1. Every Morning
(*Ladies' Home Journal*, May 1922)

6.2.   THE SECRET
(*Ladies' Home Journal,* May 1936)

Often a bridesmaid
but never a bride

EDNA'S case was really a pathetic one. Like every woman, her primary ambition was to marry. Most of the girls of her set were married—or about to be. Yet not one possessed more grace or charm or loveliness than she.

And as her birthdays crept gradually toward that tragic thirty-mark, marriage seemed farther from her life than ever.

She was often a bridesmaid but never a bride.

* * *

That's the insidious thing about halitosis (unpleasant breath). You, yourself, rarely know when you have it. And even your closest friends won't tell you.

Sometimes, of course, halitosis comes from some deep-seated organic disorder that requires professional advice. But usually—and fortunately—halitosis is only a local condition that yields to the regular use of Listerine as a mouth wash and gargle. It is an interesting thing that this well-known antiseptic that has been in use for years for surgical dressings, possesses these unusual properties as a breath deodorant.

It halts food fermentation in the mouth and leaves the breath sweet, fresh and clean. Not by substituting some other odor but by really removing the old one. The Listerine odor itself quickly disappears. So the systematic use of Listerine puts you on the safe and polite side.

Your druggist will supply you with Listerine. He sells lots of it. It has dozens of different uses as a safe antiseptic and has been trusted as such for half a century. Remember, Listerine is as safe as it is effective. Lambert Pharmacal Company, St. Louis, Mo.

This smart cosmetic bag
FREE →
with purchase of large size
LISTERINE
This offer good in U.S.A. only

Fits into purse, keeps powder, lipstick and other cosmetics in one place.

At your druggist's while they last

6.3. THAT TRAGIC THIRTY MARK
(*Ladies' Home Journal,* May 1936)

6.4. It's Nice to Be Liked
(*McCall's,* August 1940)

Within the illustration:

HEART'S DESIRE

A Kit for Climbers

Hard work, courage, common sense will prove stout aids on your way up in the world. But don't overlook another, one that is tied up with good manners—cleanliness.

Any way you look at it, clean habits, clean homes, clean linen have a value socially and commer-cially. How many successful men and women do you know who are not constantly careful of personal appearance and personal cleanliness?

In any path of life, that long way to the top is hard enough — so make the going easier with soap and water.

For Health and Wealth use SOAP & WATER

6.5. To THE TOP
(*Ladies' Home Journal,* August 1928)

Look at me now... Lily of the 5 & IO

IS IT really me?... here in a lovely house, with a car and servants... and the nicest man in the world for a husband? Sometimes I wonder...

It seems only yesterday that I was one of an army of clerks—and a very lonely one at that... only yesterday that Anna Johnson gave me the hint that changed my entire life. Maybe she told me because I was quitting and she wanted me to have a good time on my little trip to Bermuda that I'd skimped and saved for.

"Lil," she said, "in the three years we've been here, I've only seen you out with a man occasionally. I know it isn't because you don't like men..."

"They don't like *me*," I confessed.

"That's what *you* think... but you're wrong. You've got everything—and any man would like you if it weren't for..."

"If it weren't for what?"

"Gosh, Lil, I hate to say it... but I think I ought to..."

And then she told me... told me what I should have been told years before—what everyone should be told. It was a pretty humiliating hint to receive, but I took it. And how beautifully it worked!

On the boat on the way down to the Islands, I was really sought after for the first time in my life. And then, at a cocktail party in a cute little inn in Bermuda, I met HIM. The moon, the water, the scent of the hibiscus did the rest. Three months later we were married.

I realized that but for Anna's hint Romance might have passed me by.

For this is what Anna told me:

"Lil," she said, "there's nothing that kills a man's interest in a girl as fast as a case of halitosis (bad breath).* Everyone has it now and then. To say the least, you've

been, well... *careless*. You probably never realized your trouble. Halitosis victims seldom do.

"I'm passing you a little tip, honey—use Listerine Antiseptic before any date. It's a wonderful antiseptic and deodorant... makes your breath so much sweeter in no time, honest.

"I'd rather go to a date without my shoes than without Listerine Antiseptic. Nine times out of ten it spells the difference between being a washout or a winner."

And in view of what happened, I guess Anna was right.

Sometimes halitosis is due to systemic conditions, but usually and fortunately it is caused, say some authorities, by fermentation of tiny food particles in the mouth. Listerine quickly halts such food fermentation and then overcomes the odors it causes. Your breath becomes sweeter, purer, less likely to offend. Always use Listerine before business and social engagements. Lambert Pharmacal Co., St. Louis, Mo.

6.6.   IT SPELLS THE DIFFERENCE
(*McCall's*, November 1939)

and thrift, this rank revisionism in the formula for success bespoke an altered reading of the American dream. The nation's relationship with goods had altered in the aftermath of the industrial revolution. Once their producing lives were divorced from their consuming lives, Americans judged themselves primarily by their incomes and their expenditures. Veblen noted, before the twentieth century began, that individuals evaluated one another no longer by the work they performed so much as by what they owned. Perhaps people always looked to possessions as the measure of the person, but this took on a new twist after the machine age and assembly line restructured the nature of labor. Scientific management — assigning the worker a specified task with standard movement — exaggerated the effect. As Tugwell observed in 1927, "for the old morality of service, of workmanship, and of pride in skill, there is substituted the morality of display."[10]

The editors of *True Story,* whose very existence as a lower-class organ attested to the abundance of American society in the twenties, asserted that fairly clear class divisions dictated one's relationship to things. Although the middle class depended almost entirely on professional credentials for status, both the lower and upper strata derived esteem by what they had, not what they did. Either cohort could be deprived of employment or find new vocations, but so long as they retained their material belongings, their status remained essentially the same. Goods could be the route to more.[11]

These chroniclers of folk culture noted that the themes of manuscripts submitted to the periodical were far different by the late twenties than they had been a mere ten years before. Whereas previously their stories were "little more than a cry of common wants and pinching miseries," the New Era brought a novelty to the tales woven by the lowly. "Possessions, possessions, and more possessions run always between the lines. Love may be the theme, the trial or the triumph, but the outcome is possessions every time." Once one was measured by what one owned, while advertising strained to accommodate the glut of goods, promoters could use the promise of status to push their wares.[12]

Status strivings, however, are antithetical to mobility drives; the latter impulses hinge upon a willingness to shed and assume statuses as readily as one might change clothes. To the degree that a culture embraces individual movement up the scale of wealth, as Potter explained so carefully in *People of Plenty,* participants in the struggle must forego and indeed eschew the assurances of rank. The ascent to the summit is exclusive, not inclusive. Yet the ads teemed with appeals to prestige and common decency, to the certainties and satisfactions of circumstance.[13]

There may have been a new element at work in American culture in the 1920s, or really an old one made more pronounced. At least as measured in advertising copy, seeking the favorable evaluation of one's peers may have replaced upward mobility as the preeminent ambition in the American pantheon of values. Keeping up with the Joneses had become more important than beating them to the bank. David Riesman, Nathan Glazer, and Reuel Denny detected just such a fixation in many modern Americans, and labeled it "other direction."[14]

This was a preoccupation with capturing the good opinion of others and holding it hostage, particularly through careful, anxious, almost importunate manipulation of self. Rewards of the regimen were not measured internally, against some inner vision, but externally, in the approving gaze of those around one. The sudden enthusiastic embrace of toiletries itself may have testified to a shift in cultural priorities in the early twentieth century. These goods gratified a private need to placate one's public. Except when one looked in the mirror, hair care, white teeth, or colored cheeks were superfluous to self-perception. Intrinsic to the development of a deodorant market was an ability on the part of its votaries to project and to cater to aspects of themselves that were ascertainable mostly by others. In the case of mouthwash consumption, adherents had to be so attuned to appeasing others that they would routinely engage in a practice the results of which were, from the user's perspective, virtually imperceptible, because as the ads made clear, they could not sense their own breath. Benefits of the ritual were vicarious. But if one were other-directed, self-esteem came only by sufferance of one's associates. Courting their sensibilities rather than one's own was far from inconsequential; it was the hallmark of the type.

In their initial formulation, Riesman and his colleagues attributed the onset of other-direction in a society to "incipient population decline." If this were the proximate cause, it would not be too difficult to explain an outburst of other-directedness in the 1920s. But Riesman had to retract this line of analysis, and in a revision of *The Lonely Crowd,* acknowledged the shortcomings of "incipient population decline" as an explanatory device.[15]

Looking at the 1920s, one could suggest at least a slight alternative. A change in the structure of opportunity may have put a premium on winning the peer group's favor. Altered expectations of access to plenty may have redefined collective aspirations. The general prosperity of the country in the twenties may have made the prospects of individual mobility relatively more difficult to perceive. As Potter advised, "improvement in the standard of living of society at large should not be confused with the achievement of separate social advancement by individuals." To the degree that the good times were shared by the multitudes, a person's ability to rise even higher seemed correspondingly circumscribed. Just maintaining one's standing was an accomplishment. One might call it an apparent lapse in relative opportunity, or an assurance of social fixity, that triggered a move to strivings for status.[16]

Yesterday's indices of mobility had become common blessings; an automobile, a bank account, and a bathroom no longer verified much more than a widespread leap in the standard of living for the mass of Americans. The "white collar" was not a route to tomorrow, but a certitude of station today. It may be that this incidence of other-direction coincided with the adjustments made by a society heretofore geared to individual mobility, inviting a shared contentment with more of today. In any case, many advertisements appealed to yearnings for social place.

A reorientation of American character has been explicated quite eloquently by Christopher Lasch in his study of *The Culture of Narcissism*. He is quick to attribute his findings to the altered structure of opportunity that accompanied the shift from a producer to a consumer culture, as the subtitle of his work makes clear: *American Life in an Age of Diminishing Expectations*. In its essentials, the "new narcissus" he describes might be considered an elaboration and reformulation of Riesman's "other-directed" American.[17]

One must be careful not to confuse narcissism with mere selfishness, and even less with self-love. "The narcissist depends on others to validate his self-esteem. He cannot live without an admiring audience." In his desperate search for approval, he hones his manipulative skills, becoming "facile at managing the impressions he gives others." This personality type is, Lasch insists, a social phenomenon. Every society must prepare its members for the peculiar conditions in which they will have to cope, and every society will do so in an idiosyncratic manner. The net result is a characteristic personality structure. Although the predominant personality tendencies that Lasch explores did not appear full-blown until the latter half of the twentieth century, the shifting foundations of American culture that required a reorientation of self were well in place before their pathological manifestations became a clinical commonplace in those years since World War II.[18]

One witnesses the origins of the "culture of narcissism" in the personal grooming craze of the 1920s and 1930s. Advertising was both cause and effect. Just as it originated in the need to persuade more and more purchasers to acquire more and more things, it also provided a presentation of reality that suited the changing psychological constructs of those consumers. Psychiatrist Joel Kovel credits "the cultivation of infantile desire along with the usurpation of parental authority" by the media as a key to the development of the type. Stuart Ewen points directly to the advertising of the early twentieth century: "Ads of the 1920s were quite explicit about the narcissistic imperative." Nor was it entirely coincidental. Roland Marchand explained the strategy of merchandisers who deliberately relied on this sort of appeal. "People would certainly display more concern for the details of their appearance . . . if they could be induced to scrutinize themselves through the eyes of other people and to conceive of every aspect of external appearance as an index to their true character." For the advertisers themselves in the 1920s and 1930s, Marchand believes that this interpretation of social dynamics was already the simple truth of the world they knew. It was only a matter of time until it became "a common public perception of how society really worked." Lasch notes how this theme became increasingly strident; by the late twentieth century, advertising had defined "creation of the self as the highest form of creativity." By then, America's characteristic psychological type—the new narcissus—was in full flower.[19]

Of course a number of complementary explanations of changing cultural priorities have been adduced. T. J. Jackson Lears presents a fascinating analysis of the emergence of a therapeutic culture in the late nineteenth and early twentieth centuries, in some ways complementing Starr's work on the development of modern medicine. It was the articulation of this "therapeutic ideology," says Lears, that provided a philosophical rationale for the narcissistic preoccupations of modern Americans. Approaching the subject from another perspective, Horace Miner, in his ingenious account of "Body Ritual Among the Nacerima," noted the sado-masochistic urgings in American hygienic practices. Writing in the twenties, Philip Wagner insisted that "when future historians undertake to sum up the essential genius of the present decade, it is not at all unlikely that someone will suggest a preoccupation with oral matters as its most characteristic mood." Wagner did not pursue this highly suggestive assertion. If one were inclined to a Freudian bent, a fairly entertaining case could be made for a generalized occasion of oral fixation in America in the 1920s. Pointing not just to mouthwashes, toothbrushes, and lipsticks, this interpretation might account for the phenomenal rise in cigarette consumption as an index of oral gratification, as well as assessing the concurrent resurgence of kissing. Viewing these developments as evidence of oral character, the analysis might proceed to examine the consumptive patterns of eating and drinking and spending that offered immediate fulfillment of needs that had clearly ingestive components. Such an investigation would relate these practices to the narcissistic impulses in American society that Lasch describes so lucidly. The connections bear scrutiny; the "unsatisfied oral cravings" of the true narcissist are neurotic, and the personality type, in large part, consists in defenses "against feelings of oral deprivation." Such speculation, however, ranges beyond the scope of this inquiry.[20]

One of the first scholarly accounts of the decade, *The Great Crusade and After,* ended with a panegyric to material well-being. Preston William Slosson concluded his work by noting that, "Often in history the acid test of wealth has been applied to a favored class; alone in all nations and all ages the United States of the 1920s was beginning to apply that test to a whole people." The acid-test he mentioned was no metaphor. For years, Pebeco toothpaste included a packet of litmus papers with the purchase of a tube. Using the litmus, the consumer could test for "acid mouth," that deadly crippler of healthy teeth and gums. The acid test was but the most flagrant example of a trend interwoven in American toiletry advertising of the 1920s and 1930s. That theme, a lure of status yet distinct, was the pitch to the self-consciously civilized.[21]

This, after all, was the generation that believed it had discovered — with those new IQ tests — that even if a large number of them were moronic, Americans were the smartest people on earth. A simplistic, casual Darwinism, already a predominant means of ordering Americans' intellectual universe, was only exaggerated by the discovery. Off-hand references to an ostensible ethnic hierarchy, sloppy employment of Darwinian catch-phrases (race suicide, reversion to type, natural selection) crop up in seemingly incongruous places throughout the writings, minutes, and musings of the period. These were the people who barred admission into America to the alien characters who inhabited the rest of the planet, and enacted eugenics programs and marital restrictions at home to stem the threat of the feebleminded, the menace of inferiority, within.[22]

The technological advances that altered the most mundane aspects of life accentuated Americans' awareness of being different, better than their forebears, above the petty wants and mean concerns of the rest of the world. As the generation before it had seen fit to flatter itself as "Progressive," this generation went one step further, labeling not just themselves but their age. They proclaimed "the New Era."

Instead of burning a candle or stoking a kerosene lamp, these people flicked a switch to illuminate their world. They made toast. They changed the temperature of the very air by machine. Many housewives chased dirt no longer with brooms, but with vacuum wands plugged into an invisible network of electronic currents. For water, they merely turned on the tap. A trip to the toilet did not involve the out-of-doors, but crossing the hall to perhaps the most stunning architectural achievement of the twentieth century: the bathroom for everyone. Virtually free and widespread and intimate access to hot and cold running water was an epochal advance in the course of human history; it denoted a leap in the condition of man and woman across the millennia.[23]

Transportation and communication, too, had undergone a revolution. It was no longer an ordeal of horse-and-carriage for the average American; horsepower had first been harnessed in the automobile and then made accessible to consumers at a price the multitude could pay. For those without the ready cash, there was credit — on an unprecedented scale — extended to laborers who a decade before would have been lucky to get the time of day from a banker, let alone a loan. They went to movies, captured wave frequencies on their radio sets, and read of their heroes continent-hopping in airplanes through the magazines that inundated the nation with news of new and better merchandise awaiting a buyer.[24]

Although not impossible, it is hard to overestimate the transformations in everyday life of the early twentieth century. It was only natural for a people so blessed with material abundance and technological innovation to think themselves perhaps a cut above. Appealing to that quality became a common ingredient in toiletry ads, whether by instructing the unwashed how to whiten their teeth; or by revealing Cleopatra's beauty secret; disclosing day-to-day methods of tongue ablution; or by providing sundry other routes to refinement. (Figs. 6.7–6.10.)

Contributing to the cause of the self-consciously civilized, underwriting it, was the widespread — though at all times and strikingly unequal — distribution of discretionary income to purchase all the goods that industry could now deliver. The lower orders had the wherewithal to escape the oppression of base wants. They could now buy soaps and nail polish. Eye-to-eye, face-to-face with the well-to-do in the anonymous swarm of the cities, the crew had come "to eat at

All Races

are learning a new way to clean teeth

This new way to clean teeth is spreading all the world over. Leading dentists everywhere advise it. To millions of people it is daily bringing whiter, safer teeth.

Everyone should make this ten-day test. See and feel the benefits it brings. Compare the new way with the old.

To fight film

That viscous film you feel on teeth is their chief enemy. It clings to teeth, enters crevices and stays. It dims the luster, spoils the beauty and causes most tooth troubles.

Film is what discolors, not the teeth. Film is the basis of tartar. It holds food substance which ferments and forms acid. It holds the acid in contact with the teeth to cause decay.

Millions of germs breed in it. They, with tartar, are the chief cause of pyorrhea.

Much stays intact

The ordinary tooth paste does not effectively combat film. The tooth brush, therefore, leaves much of it intact. So teeth discolor and decay despite the daily brushing. Very few people escape.

Dental science has long sought ways to fight the film. Two ways have now been found. High authorities advise them. Many careful tests have proved them.

Both are embodied in a dentifrice called Pepsodent. And this modern tooth paste, nearly all the world over, is bringing a new dental era.

This pleasant ten-day test

We supply a pleasant ten-day test to everyone who asks. That test is most convincing. The results are a revelation.

Each use fights film in two effective ways. It also brings three other effects which authorities deem essential.

It multiplies the salivary flow. It multiplies the starch digestant in the saliva, to digest starch deposits that cling. It multiplies the alkalinity of the saliva, to neutralize the acids which cause tooth decay.

Thus every use immensely aids the natural forces designed to protect the teeth.

Send the coupon for a 10-Day Tube. Note how clean the teeth feel after using. Mark the absence of the viscous film. See how teeth whiten as the film-coats disappear.

Watch the five effects. Repeat them for ten days. Then let the clear results show you what this method means, both to you and yours. Cut out the coupon now.

Pepsodent
PAT. OFF.
REG. U.S.

The New-Day Dentifrice

A scientific film combatant, whose every application brings five desired effects. Approved by highest authorities, and now advised by leading dentists everywhere. All druggists supply the large tubes.

10-Day Tube Free 684

THE PEPSODENT COMPANY,
Dept. 121, 1104 S. Wabash Ave.,
Chicago, Ill.

Mail 10-Day Tube of Pepsodent to

....

Only one tube to a family

6.7. A NEW DENTAL ERA
(*Cosmopolitan,* November 1921)

Better than jewels
—that schoolgirl complexion

The girl with a clear, smooth skin, radiant with freshness and natural color, should leave jewels to those less fortunate. The charm of a perfect natural complexion attracts far more than elaborate dress and ornaments.

If your complexion lacks the beauty which women envy and men admire, don't depend on clothes and jewelry to draw attention from its defects.

Every woman can transform her bad complexion into a good one, for alluring freshness and clear color isn't a gift of Nature, but a matter of care.

How to have a perfect skin

No girl need be afflicted with a bad complexion, for improvement is simple and easy. Daily cleansing, gentle but thorough, is the secret.

You must use soap, for nothing else will remove the dirt, oil and perspiration which collect in the pores and cause most skin trouble.

Choose Palmolive, because its action is soothing. Harsh soap should never be used for washing the face.

Massage the smooth, creamy lather gently into the skin until it removes all clogging deposits. Don't forget your neck and throat. They are as conspicuous as the face for any lack in beauty.

Take a lesson from Cleopatra

With a world of ancient beauty arts at her command, she depended on cleansing with Palm and Olive oils to protect, improve and preserve the freshness and smoothness of her skin.

Careful rinsing leaves the skin stimulated, freshened and free from the accumulation which enlarges the pores, causes blackheads and carries infection.

Blended from the same oils

Palmolive Soap is blended from the same bland, soothing oils which adorned the sumptuous marble baths of Egyptians, Greeks and Romans.

But although very expensive, the gigantic volume in which Palmolive is produced keeps the price very low. Users profit by Palmolive popularity. The Palmolive factories, working day and night, and the importation of the rare oils in vast quantities, allow you to enjoy this finest facial soap for the modest price of 10 cents—no more than ordinary soap.

THE PALMOLIVE COMPANY, MILWAUKEE, U. S. A.
THE PALMOLIVE COMPANY OF CANADA, Limited, TORONTO, ONT.
Also makers of a complete line of toilet articles

Volume and efficiency produce
25-cent quality for only

10c

Copyright, 1922—The Palmolive Co.

6.8.   CLEOPATRA'S SECRET
(*Ladies' Home Journal*, 1922)

Simple new test
FOR BAD BREATH

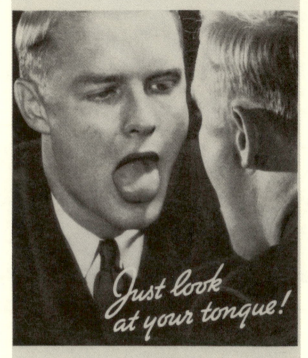

Just look at your tongue!

In 75% of cases of bad breath, science finds that the tongue is "coated." So make this test. Look in the mirror. If your tongue is "coated," you may be offending others unknowingly. Pepsodent Antiseptic offers you a pure, sweet breath at 1/3 the usual cost.

NOW you no longer need wonder if you have bad breath. Often your own mirror will tell you. If your mirror reveals a grey, "coated tongue," the chances are that your breath is impure. For recent investigations have shown that in 75% of cases of bad breath, a "coated tongue" condition was present.

The sensible way to guard against bad breath is to use Pepsodent Antiseptic . . . as thousands already do. Rinse out your mouth with Pepsodent. It acts to remove tiny food particles from between the teeth. It helps to cleanse the mucous membrane lining of the mouth . . . to sweep away dead cells and particles from the tongue. It kills the germs it reaches . . . the germs so often responsible for unpleasant breath odors. Your whole mouth feels more refreshed —you are confident that your breath cannot offend.

We do not claim that "coated tongue" always means bad breath. But take no chances. Use Pepsodent Antiseptic.

Goes 3 times as far . . . makes $1 *equal* $3

But in fighting "coated tongue" and halitosis, never forget the vital difference between mouth antiseptics. So many leading mouth antiseptics, you see, have to be used full strength to be effective. Pepsodent is safe when used full strength—yet it is powerful enough to be diluted with two parts of water and still *kill* germs in 10 seconds. Thus Pepsodent gives you 3 times as much for your money—offers added protection against unwholesome breath.

Look at your tongue TONIGHT. See what it tells about you. Then use Pepsodent Antiseptic to be sure your breath is above reproach. And always remember —a clean mouth and throat are among your best defenses against colds.

PEPSODENT ANTISEPTIC

6.9. TAKE NO CHANCES
(*Saturday Evening Post*, 3 November 1934)

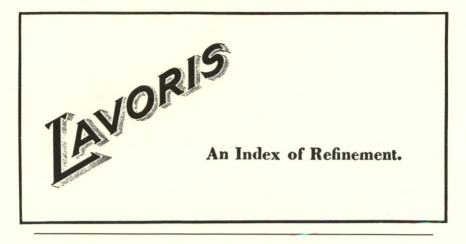

An Index of Refinement.

6.10. REFINEMENT
(*Saturday Evening Post*, 1 December 1934)

the Captain's table," or at least thought it had. Bewildered by how to act, what to do, what to wear, how to pose at the banquet so as not to expose their lowly roots, the wage earners in America were eager for an advertiser holding out the veneer of culture this vast population could now afford to purchase. With commodities provided by the toiletry industry, Americans could package the self, and by following the regimen espoused in the ads, they could learn how to promote themselves in the New Era.[25]

Something about the magazine itself may have encouraged visions of unparalleled prosperity and dreams of grandeur. The magazine was the harbinger of cosmopolitan culture, the vehicle of a nation whose material wealth was as undeniable as it was unprecedented, the carrier of wondrous invention and clever artifice even to people whose access to the marketplace was severely circumscribed. "Any issue of a national magazine is a world's fair, a bazaar filled with the products of the world's work: clothes and clocks and candle-sticks; soup and soap and cigarettes; lingerie and limousines — the best of all of them are there, proclaimed by their makers in persuasive tones." With a magazine, the most common consumers could bring the marketplace home, actually into their living rooms, to partake of the marvels of the American economy. "Modern machinery has made it not only possible but imperative that the masses should live lives of comfort and leisure, that the future of business lay in its ability to manufacture customers as well as products." By 1923, an economist could comment that, measured in dollars and cents, advertising was by far the most important form of education in the United States.[26]

The dollar democracy embraced everyone. As the champions of abundance, advertisers filled the magazines with fables that fashioned a new ethos of consumption. In his examination of its emergence in the ads of the New Era, Roland Marchand notes that among "the most pervasive of all advertising tableaux of the 1920s" was "the Parable of the Democracy of Goods." Each American was enjoined to share in the feast. The basic premise of this fiction was that "no discrepancies of wealth could prevent the humblest citizens . . . from retiring to a setting in which they could contemplate their essential equality, through possession of an identical product, with the nation's millionaires." The advertisers of toiletries, in particular, seized upon the counterpart to this doctrine — a negative corollary — which Marchand has labeled the "Democracy of Afflictions." The tyrannies of BO and bad breath and dirty hands observed no distinction of social class; every American was equally vulnerable to these debilities of everyday life. But the means of liberating oneself were also available universally. "The parable of the Democracy of Goods always remained implicit. . . . It assured readers that they could be as healthy, as charming, as free from social offense as the very 'nicest' (richest) people, simply by using a product that anyone could afford." Promoters reveled in the equity of the new order.[27]

One cannot confuse these egalitarian impulses with a glorification of the individual. Democracy was a tool of enforcement, not an exultation of freedom. Just as everyone could take part, one was also obliged to do so. Having been offered the opportunity to join in the banquet, all were expected to attend. The price of admittance was a rigorous adherence to a code of civility appropriate to an ever-increasing consumption of commodities; in its most elemental manifestation, this took the form of a style of grooming that meticulously suppressed any hint of nonconformity. Through the toiletry campaigns of the New Era, this commitment to a norm of innocuousness extended to include the most personal intimations of self. Individuality, heterogeneity, and eccentricity would continue to exist, to be sure, but only within the context of a consuming culture. One could choose to employ a particular brand of soap or an idiosyncratic scent of mouthwash to placate one's public, but that one would make such a choice was taken for granted. Apostasy from the discipline of consumption would not be tolerated. The ads were blunt about it. Your best friends would not tell you of your lapses. Instead they would leave you. Dissidents were outcast, ostracized, alone.[28]

Whether this outpouring of promotional literature was a cause for concern or a reason to celebrate resided with individual judgment. People have had serious reservations about advertising every since its beginnings. Edward L. Bernays tried to put those doubts into perspective. "You are full of terrors," he observed, "about the multitude of influences which propagandists shoot at the Mass Mind. I think you overlook the fact that if there were no such manipulators of public opinion the Mass Mind would still be at the mercy of quite as many influences; would be pulled about by quite as many forces—the fortuitous and whimsical forces of life and chance." Business could not run on chance or whimsy.[29]

NOTES

INTRODUCTION

1. One might consider television a form of liquid magazine. Both media serve the same function; both are structured to advertise goods. But one cannot push the comparison. In other respects, the magazine and the television are as different from one another as space is from time.

2. Daniel A. Pope, "The Development of National Advertising, 1865–1920" (unpublished Ph.D. diss., Columbia University, 1973), 1; of those 1500 exposures, the average American might recall 76.

3. Coolidge is quoted in *Congressional Record* (4 December 1928): 20; C. H. Sandage, "The Role of Advertising in Modern Society," *Journalism Quarterly* 28 (Winter 1951): 32.

4. George Soule observed that by 1929, American industry was simply unwilling to expand production further. "Nor was there any lack of funds for the purpose. As things stood at the end of the period, corporations had more money than they wished to use either for current production or for new investment. What was lacking was a sufficient market for the goods." *The Economic History of the United States* (New York: Holt, Rinehart, and Winston, 1947) Vol. 8: *Prosperity Decade: From War to Depression: 1917–1929,* by George Soule, 332; Ross M. Robertson, *History of the American Economy* 2d ed. (New York: Harcourt, Brace & World, 1964), 630; Wesley C. Mitchell, *Business Cycles: The Problem and Its Setting* (New York: National Bureau of Economic Research, 1927), 166. Also see Sidney Ratner, James H. Soltow, and Richard Sylla, *The Evolution of the American Economy: Growth, Welfare, and Decision Making* (New York: Basic Books, 1979), 383–84.

5. David M. Potter, *People of Plenty: Economic Abundance and the American Character* (Chicago: Univ. of Chicago Press, 1958), 166–68.

6. Daniel A. Pope, *The Making of Modern Advertising* (New York: Basic Books, 1983); also see "The Development of National Advertising 1865–1920," by Daniel A. Pope; Stephen Fox, *The Mirror Makers: A History of American Advertising and Its Creators* (New York: Vintage, 1985); Stuart Ewen, *Captains of Consciousness: Advertising and the Social Roots of the Consumer Culture* (New York: McGraw-Hill, 1976); T. J. Jackson Lears, "From Salvation to Self-Realization: Advertising and the Thera-

peutic Roots of the Consumer Culture, 1880–1930," in *The Culture of Consumption: Critical Essays in American History 1880–1980* (New York: Pantheon, 1983). Roland Marchand, *Advertising the American Dream: Making Way for Modernity, 1920–1940* (Berkeley: Univ. of California, 1985).

7. Fox, 64; Marchand, 16–17.

8. Potter, 193; Julian L. Simon offers a brief but suggestive economic analysis of the impact of advertising on the aggregate demand for goods in "The Effect of Advertising upon the Propensity to Consume," *Issues in the Economics of Advertising* (Urbana: Univ. of Illinois, 1970), 193–206.

9. Marchand, 18–20.

10. Stuart Ewen and Elizabeth Ewen, *Channels of Desire: Mass Images and the Shaping of American Consciousness* (New York: McGraw-Hill, 1982), 42.

11. Paul Starr, *The Social Transformation of American Medicine* (New York: Basic Books, 1982), especially 190 on handwashing and public health.

12. David Riesman, with Nathan Glazer and Reuel Denny, *The Lonely Crowd: A Study of the Changing American Character* (New Haven: Yale Univ. Press, 1961); John Higham and Paul K. Conkin, eds., *New Directions in American Intellectual History* (Baltimore: Johns Hopkins Univ. Press, 1979): " 'Personality' and the Making of Twentieth-Century Culture," by Warren I. Susman, 212, 221–22; Christopher Lasch, *The Culture of Narcissism: American Life in an Age of Diminishing Expectations* (New York: W. W. Norton, 1979).

CHAPTER 1

1. See Robert Wiebe, *The Search for Order, 1877 to 1920* (New York: Hill and Wang, 1967), particularly 2–4, 44.

2. For a succinct description of the revolution in communication, transportation, and the distribution of goods, see Samuel P. Hayes, *The Response to Industrialism 1885–1914* (Chicago: Univ. of Chicago Press, 1957). Also see Alfred D. Chandler, Jr., "The Beginnings of 'Big Business' in American Industry," *Business History Review* 33 (1959): 4; Stuart Bruchey, *Growth of the Modern American Economy* (New York: Dodd, Mead, 1975), 83, 85; Charles W. McCurdy, "American Law and the Marketing Structure of the Large Corporation, 1875–1890," *Journal of Economic History* 38 (1978): 632–33, 642. McCurdy has referred to this transformation of American law as "a doctrinal revolution."

3. Although Uneeda Biscuit met with success, a number of other optimistic producers did not—Uwanta Beer, *Ureada Magazine,* Itsagood Soap, Mustapha Biscuit. Chandler, "Beginnings," 12; *Fifty Years 1888–1938* (New York: *Printers' Ink,* 1938), 137.

4. Long before national advertising linked producers directly with consumers, jobbers acted as middlemen between local merchants and distant makers of goods. They handled commodities on consignment; being on the scene, these agents could know more about local demand than manufacturers. See Harold F. Williamson, ed., *The Growth of the American Economy* 2d ed. (New York: Prentice-Hall, 1951): "Domestic Trade and Marketing," by Theodore Marburg, 511–13; on risk, see William Trufant Foster and Waddill Catchings, *Profits* (Boston: Houghton Mifflin, 1925), 57–60.

5. *Fifty Years,* 67; Emerson P. Harris, "The Economics of Advertising," *Social Economist* 4 (March 1893): 173.

6. *Boston News-Letter,* 17 April 1704 to 24 April 1704, 2, quoted in Frank Presbrey, *The History and Development of Advertising* (New York: Doubleday, 1929), 126.

7. *Fifty Years,* 15; the first national ad, apparently, ran in *Atlantic Monthly* in 1860, see *Fifty Years,* 41. Theodore Peterson contends that the first ad in a periodical not a paper was run in 1741. See *Magazines in the Twentieth Century* 2d ed. (Urbana: Univ. of Illinois Press, 1964), 20. Many of the first magazines—*Harper's, Scribner's, Atlantic, Collier's*—were in a sense all advertisement for the publishing houses that produced them. Hugh E. Agnew and Warren B. Dygert, *Advertising Media* (New York: McGraw-Hill, 1938), 94. *Fifty Years,* 10–11, 22.

8 Chandler, "Beginnings," particularly 6–14; Bruchey, 102–3; also see Alfred D. Chandler, Jr., *The Visible Hand: The Managerial Revolution in American Business* (Cambridge: Belknap Press, 1977), 285–376, for a fuller discussion of "The Integration of Mass Production with Mass Distribution." Harris, 173; *Fifty Years,* 89.

9 James Playsted Wood, *Magazines in the United States* 3d ed. (New York: Ronald Press, 1971), 93; Algernon Tassin, *The Magazine in America* (New York: Dodd, Mead, 1916), 342; *Magazines in the Twentieth Century,* 3, 9; *Fifty Years,* 31.

10. *Fifty Years,* 31; *Magazines in the Twentieth Century,* 8–10; Tassin, 341; *Mc-Clure's* appeared for fifteen cents a copy with its issue of 28 May 1893; *Cosmopolitan* began charging twelve and one-half cents in July, and *Munsey's* cut-rate began in September-October of the same year; Howard W. Dickinson, *Crying Our Wares* (New York: John Day Co., 1929), 192.

11. Note that consolidation and national advertising were mutually reinforcing. As Marburg put it, 518–19, "concentration was a necessary condition to large scale advertising; but it is also true that the increase in advertising and the adaptation of the distributive organization to the handling of advertised products placed an even greater premium on large scale organization." Bruchey notes that the peak period of consolidation occurred in the years 1898 to 1902, p. 110. Also see *Magazines in the Twentieth Century,* 12, 22, 18; Tassin, 364, 340; Frank Luther Mott, *A History of American Magazines,* Vol. 4: *1885–1905* (Cambridge: Belknap Press, 1957), 15; Presbrey, 410; *Fifty Years,* 32, 40; Frederick Lewis Allen, "American Magazines, 1741–1941," *Bulletin of the New York Public Library* 45 (June 1941): 441.

12. Tassin, 340, 355; the most important difference between magazines and newspapers is that most periodical advertisers do national business, while most advertisers in newspapers (about 75 percent) are local stores. William H. Boyenton, *Audit Bureau of Circulations* (Chicago: Audit Bureau of Circulations, 1948), 105. Nonetheless, national advertisers came to spend millions of dollars on newspaper ads; for a brand breakdown of expenditures, with comparison figures for 1933, see "300 Largest Advertisers in Newspapers for 1934," *Printers' Ink* 170 (28 February, 7 March, 14 March 1935).

13. Boyenton, 4–6; *National Magazines as Advertising Media* (Philadelphia: Curtis Publishing Co., 1947), 8.

14. Charles O. Bennett, *Facts Without Opinion* (Chicago: Audit Bureau of Circulations, 1965), 3, 12–13; Daniel A. Pope, "The Development of National Advertising 1865–1920" (unpublished Ph.D. diss., Columbia Univ., 1973), 263. Mott, 16, argues that the first periodical to pass the million mark was *Comfort,* in 1895; *Fifty Years* asserts that *Ladies' Home Journal* was the first to amass a million circulation, 194; Peterson, 45, goes further than Mott to claim that *Comfort* was probably the only million seller in 1900; Wood, 96, states that the only million seller in 1900 was the *Ladies' Home Journal.*

15. Boyenton, 10–11, 22–23, 95; *A.B.C.: Self-Regulation in the Advertising & Publishing Industry* (Chicago: Audit Bureau of Circulations, 1947), 1, 11; Pope, 270.

16. Fulton Oursler, "American Magazines, 1741–1941," *Bulletin of the New York Public Library* 45 (June 1941): 450; *Scientific Space Selection* 2d ed. (Chicago: Audit Bureau of Circulations, 1937), 32. There were other forms of paid circulation, and the Bureau tried to classify them. Despite these efforts, the Bureau's standards admitted of deficiency. A magazine with only half its circulation paid for, and then at only half the price, could still have the same circulation as one whose entire issue was paid in full. The endless categorizations only underscored the fact that when one started talking about circulation, any statement required qualification. The A.B.C. could not remove all the confusion by tabulation. Nonetheless, the Bureau provided relatively hard data on the magazine and its reach in America. The degree to which one can imply readership from type of circulation is a question that cannot be answered satisfactorily. For purposes here, circulation, regardless of its possible origin, may be taken to mean readership. See Boyenton, particularly 50–66, for examples of publishers' statements and audit reports, and 113–18 for a glossary of the jargon. Also look through *What is Circulation* (Philadelphia: Curtis Publishing Co., 1923).

17. See Bennett, 39–70; *A.B.C.,* 1–3; *The Story of the Audit Bureau of Circulations* (Chicago: Audit Bureau of Circulations, on the occasion of the 40th anniversary [1954]), 24; *A.B.C. Auditing Practices* (Chicago: Audit Bureau of Circulations, [1942]), 2.

18. This is not meant to imply that every American read magazines. A study undertaken by the Association of National Advertisers and Curtis Publications determined that 25 percent of American homes did not read magazines with any regularity; see *A Study of Duplication of Magazine Circulations in Jefferson and Lewis Counties New York* (New York: Association of National Advertisers, 1928), 22; Agnew and Dygert, 108–13; population figures can be found in Richard B. Morris, *Encyclopedia of American History* (New York: Harper & Row, 1970), 468.

19. John Bakeless, "Economic Basis of the Magazine," *Magazine Making* (New York: Viking, 1931), 3–13. For a list of some of the more esoteric titles, along with figures concerning circulation and founding, see *A Rate and Circulation Study of 404 Class, Trade and Technical Publications* (New York: Association of National Advertisers, 1941). For publications with broader appeal, see *A Trend Study of 276 General Magazines* (New York: Association of National Advertisers, 1938).

20. "How Cities Differ in Their Magazine Reading Habits," *Sales Management* 38 (15 February 1936): 218–20.

21. Paul F. Lazarsfeld and Rowena Wyant, "Magazines in 90 Cities—Who Reads What?" *The Public Opinion Quarterly* 1 (October 1937): 33–34. The 90 cities included all cities with more than 100,000 population, excepting Boston (which could not be isolated from Greater Boston). A chief reason those in largest cities knew of the availability of goods apart from magazines was because the density of population facilitated other forms of advertisement such as the street-car and outdoor varieties. The larger the city, the larger the total advertising outlay per capita tended to be. Julian L. Simon, *Issues in the Economics of Advertising* (Urbana: Univ. of Illinois, 1970), 41–51; Pope, 26.

22. In any event, one realizes that correlation does not imply causation. See Lazarsfeld and Wyant, 29–41. Aggregate income was inferred from the number of tax returns filed. The numbers of married women, educational expenses, and of foreign-born did not correlate. Incidentally, the authors determined that Muncie, Indiana, "is, therefore, most typical in this group of cities in regard to its magazine circulation; it is really *Middletown.*"

23. Starch's method can be criticized on the basis of his calculation of income,

which was assigned on the basis of designated occupation. However, Starch's research design seems carefully controlled. Given the immaturity of the science of the mass survey in 1930, it may be the most considered evidence on this subject that one is likely to discover. For a discussion of method, see American Association of Advertising Agencies, *Magazine Circulations—Qualitative Analysis by Incomes of Readers* (New York: American Association of Advertising Agencies, 1930), 33–46. Note too that the data for *Gentlewoman* were for the last six months of 1929, rather than the first six months of 1930 (p. 6). On Starch's qualifications, see *The Cyclopaedia of American Biography,* Vol. F: *1939–1942* (New York: James T. White, 1942), 183–84. Also see Agnew and Dygert, 118.

24. Curtis is quoted in Agnew and Dygert, 31–32; on Bok's claim, see Edward Bok, *The Americanization of Edward Bok* (New York: Scribner's, 1920), 234; Mott, 32; on the *Journal*'s circulation, see above.

25. Robert S. Lynd, with the assistance of Alice C. Hanson (Jones), "The People as Consumers," in *Recent Social Trends in the United States: Report of the President's Research Committee on Social Trends* (New York: McGraw-Hill, 1933), 871–72. Peterson argues that the average advertising content of monthly magazines was 54 percent by 1908, and 65 percent by 1947, p. 23.

26. See Table 1.4, noting that 1931 was an unusually bad year. Agnew and Dygert, 94–95; there is some controversy regarding the *Harper's* rejection. Potter alludes to an offer by Howe Sewing Machines, rather than Singer, for back covers of the magazine, and dates it in the 1870s rather than 1869; see Potter, 169. Presbrey, 466, refers to a refusal from *Harper's,* also in the 1870s, but does not name the maker. Magazine circulation did fluctuate. After a setback in the early thirties, it climbed to surpass all previous levels by 1937. Advertising volume dropped sharply in the last quarter of 1929 through the first quarter of 1933. It was hit not only by the collapse of the marketplace, but by the concurrent growth of radio advertising, which climbed through 1931, dipped somewhat in 1932, then took off again. For changes in advertising volume from January 1921 through January 1935, see "Monthly Index of Magazine Advertising," *Printers' Ink* (14 March 1935): 79. Compare it with "Monthly Index of Radio Advertising," Ibid. (28 February 1935): 64.

27. See Table 1.5, noting that "automotive" includes passenger cars and tires; "toilet goods" does not include "soaps and cleansers." For earlier years and corresponding expenditures, see earlier (generally annual) editions. Cf. "1935 Magazine and Radio Expenditures Show Gains," *Sales Management* (15 January 1936): 112, for data based on a more inclusive survey of 123 publications, including 15 weeklies and semi-monthlies, and 108 monthlies. These calculations, provided by the Publishers' Information Bureau and a regular feature in *Sales Management,* were very close to Curtis's figures for 35 leading magazines, but the latter are more complete.

28. *Nationally Established Trade-Marks* (New York: Periodical Publishers Association, 1934), passim. *City Markets: A Study of Thirty-Five Cities* (Philadelphia: Curtis Publishing, 1932), 9. Details regarding their methodology are far from sufficient and their categorizations require some scrutiny, but the results seem suggestive. The consumer spending study, 1935–1950, included all principal advertising media, not just magazines, though periodicals were the most stable medium: "as consumer spending rose or fell, so did magazine income from advertising." See *Magazines in the Twentieth Century,* 46.

29. On the marvel of the American economy in the 1920s, one might begin with Thomas Nixon Carver, *The Present Economic Revolution in the United States* (Boston: Little, Brown & Co., 1925), and *Recent Economic Changes in the United States: Report*

of the Committee on Recent Economic Changes of the President's Conference on Unemployment 2 vols. (New York: McGraw-Hill, 1929). See also Arthur M. Schlesinger and Dixon Ryan Fox, eds., *A History of American Life* 13 vols. (New York: Macmillan, 1927–1948) Vol. 12: *The Great Crusade and After 1914–1928,* by Preston William Slosson, 363, 423.

30. See Wiebe, particularly "A New Middle Class," 111–32. Wiebe is the first to admit that, "in part, the new middle class was a class only by courtesy of the historian's afterthought." Professors of Marketing recommended trade publications as the best vehicles for "vanity ads," because "it is usually before one's competitors that one likes to appear important." Agnew and Dygert, 252; *Fifty Years,* 49.

31. See Figure 1.1. Note that this is a list of magazines most commonly subscribed to, as a function of income. The data do not mean that *Needlecraft,* for example, was a lower class organ, or that most of its circulation went to the lowest class. Both inferences would be inaccurate. The data do mean that of magazine subscriptions the poorest were able to come by, *Needlecraft* was one of their most popular. Frederick Dwight, "The Significance of Advertising," *Yale Review* 18 (August 1909): 199.

32. Slosson, 287; Karl W. Deutsch, *Nationalism and Social Communication: An Inquiry into the Foundations of Nationality* 2d ed. (Cambridge: M.I.T. Press, 1966), 97; Potter, 15–16; Daniel Boorstin, in his social portrait of modern America, discovered not one national community of consumers, but many. "These consumption communities were quick; they were nonideological; they were democratic; they were public, and vague, and rapidly shifting. Consumption communities produced more consumption communities. They were factitious, malleable, and as easily made as they were evanescent." Of course community is neither quick, nonideological, nor evanescent. But Boorstin's description of the pseudo-event in contemporary America is compelling. See *The Americans: The Democratic Experience* (New York: Random House, 1973), 89–90, and *The Image: or What Happened to the American Dream* (New York: Atheneum, 1962). Also see Otis Pease, *The Responsibilities of National Advertising: Private Control and Public Influence, 1920–1940* (New Haven: Yale Univ. Press, 1958), 198, 203.

33. Hornell Hart, "Changing Social Attitudes and Interests," *Recent Social Trends in the United States,* 383–442; William E. Leuchtenburg, *The Perils of Prosperity 1914–1932* (Chicago: Univ. of Chicago Press, 1958), 158, 290. Theodore P. Greene, *America's Heroes: The Changing Models of Success in American Magazines* (New York: Oxford Univ. Press, 1970), 61; Frederick Lewis Allen, "The American Magazine Grows Up," *Atlantic Monthly* 180 (November 1947): 81; Tassin, 355.

CHAPTER 2

1. The term "demand creation" refers here to the ability of an advertiser to effect demand for particular products. Advertising probably does not influence demand for all goods in general, that being a function of change in real net income.

2. Harold G. Vatter, investigating the ostensible revolution in consumers' durables that historians have associated with the decade, discovered that the "revolution" was qualitative rather than quantitative, more apparent than real: the substitution of vacuum for broom, or car for carriage. For structural change in this index, he feels that one must look to the middle of the nineteenth century. See "Has There Been a Twentieth-Century Consumer Durables Revolution?" *Journal of Economic History* 27 (March 1967): 1–16. Arthur M. Schlesinger and Dixon Ryan Fox, eds., *A History of*

American Life 13 vols. (New York: Macmillan, 1927–1948) Vol. 12: *The Great Crusade and After 1914–1928,* by Preston William Slosson, 162; *Recent Economic Changes in the United States: Report of the Committee on Recent Economic Changes of the President's Conference on Unemployment* 2 vols. (New York: McGraw-Hill, 1929), xv; Leo Wolman, "Consumption and the Standard of Living," *Recent Economic Changes,* 52; Wesley C. Mitchell, "A Review," *Recent Economic Changes,* 874; Paul M. Mazur, *American Prosperity: Its Causes and Consequences* (New York: Viking, 1928), 268; Percival White, "Figuring Us Out," *North American Review* 227 (1929): 68; Hugh E. Agnew and Warren B. Dygert, *Advertising Media* (New York: McGraw-Hill, 1938), 103.

3. The distribution of the prosperity of the twenties has been exaggerated. Suggesting that 40 percent of Americans still lived below minimum subsistence levels in 1929, Robert K. Murray attributed part of the hyperbole to a problem with the sources. The primary recipients of the economic advance, the middle and upper-middle classes, were also the most articulate and influential champions of the New Era. See his interview with John A. Garraty, ed., *Interpreting American History: Conversations with Historians* 2 vols. (New York: Macmillan, 1970) Vol. 2: "The Twenties," by Robert K. Murray, 158; U.S. Bureau of the Census, *Historical Statistics of the United States, Colonial Times to 1957* (Washington: GPO, 1960), 139, 152; Maurice Levin, Harold G. Moulton, and Clark Warburton, *America's Capacity to Consume* (Washington: The Brookings Institution, 1934), 18, 44. According to their estimations, per capita income corrected for changes in prices and population growth was up 38 percent, 1900–1929. The distribution of this income was concentrated in urban America. The 25 percent of the population that still lived on farms in 1929 had a per capita income of less than a third of the rest of the population. For primary popular accounts of the acceleration of American abundance, see Thomas Nixon Carver, *The Present Economic Revolution in the United States* (Boston: Little, Brown & Co., 1925) and *The American Economic Evolution* (New York: *True Story Magazine,* 1930). A respected secondary account appears as "The Second Industrial Revolution," in William E. Leuchtenburg, *The Perils of Prosperity 1914–1932* (Chicago: Univ. of Chicago Press, 1958), 178–203.

4. *Historical Statistics,* 510.

5. For a lucid discussion of standards of living, see Stanley Lebergott, *The American Economy: Income, Wealth, and Want* (Princeton: Princeton Univ. Press, 1976). He emphasizes the importance of relative rather than absolute change when considering these issues. In 1910, there was one automobile for every 265 Americans; by 1928, there was one for every six. By 1925, 68.3 percent of urban households had stationary bathtubs; American water consumption was two or three times greater than European levels. Frank Presbrey credits advertising as the chief cause of the widespread introduction of tubs in *The History and Development of Advertising* (New York: Doubleday, 1929), 425–27. Wolman, 59, 66, 69. "Changes in Minimum Standards of Living, 1869–1938," *Conference Board Studies in Enterprise and Social Progress: Selected Chapters in the Story of the American Enterprise System and Its Contribution to Prosperity and Public Welfare* (New York: National Industrial Conference Board, 1939), 142–53.

6. That average wage earners could not be reduced to the subsistence levels common to their counterparts of the 1870s, nor indeed to workers anywhere in the less developed world, caused consternation to an English observer of the Great Depression: "May it not be that countries that have not developed a very high standard of living are in point of real advantage in a better position than those who have? . . . What would it profit the country if our industries fell into decay to be able to boast that we continued

to maintain the highest standard of living of any country in the world up to the end?" *The Statist: An Independent Journal of Finance and Trade* 134 (26 August 1939): 256.

7. The 34 percent of their income which wage earners of the early thirties had to "dispose of" can be misleading. Along with average annual incomes, prices for items like housing and food plummeted. Costs of what had become essential over the years, however, did not decline at a similar rate. Although rents fell 39.2 percent between 1929 and 1935, for example, the costs of furnishing one's home declined only 8.9 percent. Although food consumed at home was down 15.9 percent in price, medical care costs declined a mere 2.1 percent. Gardiner C. Means went so far as to comment that "Indeed, the whole depression might be described as a general dropping of prices at the flexible end of the price scale and a dropping of production at the rigid end with intermediate effects between." See "Industrial Prices and Their Relative Inflexibility," *Senate Document* no. 13 (1935), 8. On Consumer Indexes, see *Historical Statistics,* 125–27; see also *Studies in Enterprise and Social Progress,* 147, 189. One must also recognize that expenses that were largely incidental to a wage-earning existence little more than a decade before—most notably the automobile and previous purchases on installment—were bills that had to be met by the 1930s. On retail credit, see note 31 below. The percentage of discretionary income in the 1930s, in other words, may have been larger than that of the 1920s, but smaller in terms of actual purchasing power. These computations, moreover, say nothing about the distribution of income in general. A gross rise in the percentage of discretionary income need not imply a net gain in the standard of living, and most certainly not for everyone. One must appreciate that the number of those stripped of income by unemployment, 1930–1935, ranged from 8.7 percent to 24.9 percent of the civilian labor force. New Deal innovations to stabilize the purchasing power of the unemployed had yet to take effect. These figures do not tell us that everyone was better off than ever, 1930–1935, so much as they reveal that the potential for an uneven distribution of income in America had never been so great.

8. For data on which Table 2.1 is based, see "Change in Minimum Standards of Living, 1869–1938," *Studies in Enterprise and Social Progress,* 150–51; see, for example, "Part 9: Comparative Economic Conditions in the United States and Other Countries" in the same volume, 257–323, for European comparisons; Wolman, 76; Morris A. Copeland, "The National Income and Its Distribution," *Recent Economic Changes,* 765. William Trufant Foster and Waddill Catchings, *Profits* (Boston: Houghton Mifflin, 1925), 224.

9. Robert S. Lynd, with the assistance of Alice C. Hanson (Jones), "The People as Consumers," in *Recent Social Trends in the United States: Report of the President's Research Committee on Social Trends* (New York: McGraw-Hill, 1933), 857. Emphasis theirs.

10. Lynd and Hanson, 857; Slosson, 167.

11. Rexford Guy Tugwell, *Industry's Coming of Age* (New York: Harcourt, Brace, 1927), 1–2, 26, 29–32, 35–41, 120–28; Stuart Chase, *The Tragedy of Waste* (New York: Macmillan, 1927), 165–67. On output of various industries, see Arthur F. Burns, *Production Trends in the United States Since 1870* (New York: National Bureau of Economic Research, 1934), particularly Table 44: "Continuous Production Series: 1870–1929," 284–304.

12. Edwin F. Gay, "Introduction," *Recent Economic Changes,* 1–6; see also *Recent Economic Changes,* xviii; Tugwell, 62–64, 92; Edward Marshall, "Machine-Made Freedom: An Authorized Interview with Thomas A. Edison," *Forum* 76 (October 1926): 482–97; Mazur, 82, 74, 79; Agnew and Dygert, 103–4.

13. Ralph M. Hower, *The History of an Advertising Agency: N. W. Ayer & Son at*

Work 1869–1949 2d ed. (Cambridge: Harvard Univ. Press, 1949), 126.

14. Hower, 301–2. Foster and Catchings, 224; George Gunton, "Demand and Supply," *Social Economist* 4 (May 1893): 290–91.

15. Mazur, 226; Roy Sheldon and Egmont Arens, *Consumer Engineering: A New Technique for Prosperity* (New York: Harper, 1932), 16, 17.

16. Daniel A. Pope's insightful account of "The Development of National Advertising 1865–1920" (unpublished Ph.D. diss., Columbia University, 1973) discusses the historical antecedents of many of the issues treated here. On Progressive developments and the "Creation of an Advertising Ideology," see particularly 68, 74–77, 78, 222, 313, 325, 413, 427. Also see Daniel A. Pope, *The Making of Modern Advertising* (New York: Basic Books, 1983). See also *Fifty Years 1888–1938* (New York: *Printers' Ink*, 1938), 136, 175, 182, which argues that the shift to salesmanship in ads occurred about 1902.

17. The government issued $21,478,356,250 in bonds to finance the war, and sold them all between May 1917 and April 1919. "The disposal of this vast amount of obligations was accompanied by direct sales to the people on an unprecedented scale." See James Truslow Adams and R. V. Coleman, eds., *Dictionary of American History* 6 vols. (New York: Charles Scribner's Sons, 1940) Vol. 3: "Liberty Loans," by Frederick A. Bradford, 271; for a primary account, see George Creel, *How We Advertised America* (New York: Harper and Brothers, 1920). Mazur, 57–58; Slosson, 61, 65; *Fifty Years,* 294; Pope, "Development," 330ff.

18. *A Table of Leading Advertisers* (Philadelphia: Curtis Publishing, 1926), 34; Mazur, 225.

19. Gerard B. Lambert, *All Out of Step: A Personal Chronicle* (New York: Doubleday, 1956), 22–24; "Magazine Advertising Develops New Use for Listerine," *Success Bulletin: Notes from the Book of Magazine Experience* (9 February 1925).

20. His autobiography is best read as an expression of the biases of class, sex, and race of an American elite. *All Out of Step,* particularly 47–48, 89–92.

21. *All Out of Step,* 97, 106; Gerard B. Lambert, "How I Sold Listerine," *The Amazing Advertising Business* (New York: Simon and Schuster, 1957), 49–51; also see Richard Wightman Fox and T. J. Jackson Lears, eds., *The Culture of Consumption: Critical Essays in American History, 1880–1980* (New York: Pantheon, 1983): "From Salvation to Self-Realization: Advertising and the Therapeutic Roots of the Consumer Culture," by T. J. Jackson Lears, 1–38.

22. John L. Scott, "The 'Wallflower School' of Advertising, or 'How to Become Popular in Ten Doses,' as Exposed and Expounded by Leading Copy Experts," *Sales Management* (13 November 1926): 867; Lambert, *All Out of Step,* 98, and "How I Sold Listerine," 49; "Magazine Advertising Develops New Use for Listerine," n.p.

23. Lambert, "How I Sold Listerine," 53, 55, and *All Out of Step,* 99. Emphasis his. Surveys indicate that Listerine did enjoy an unusually high distribution. Thus, in Appleton, Wisconsin, it was only one of forty drug products which had 100 percent distribution in that community's drug stores. In its survey of fourteen drug, department, and general stores in Findlay, Ohio, however, Dartnell discovered that only three of eighty-five nationally advertised drug products had universal distribution, one of them being Listerine. See "Dartnell Check-Up on Distribution of Advertised Products: Further Results of a Survey Covering the Distribution of Drugs, Clothing, Furniture, Dry Goods, Hardware, and Shoes in Appleton, Wisconsin," *Sales Management* (3 September 1927): 385–86; "Dartnell Check-Up on Distribution of Advertised Products: The Conclusion to the Survey of Findlay, Ohio, Covering the Drug, Furniture, Clothing, Shoe, and Dry Goods Lines," *Sales Management* (26 November 1927): 954.

24. *Cosmopolitan* (November 1921): 148; *Hearst-International Cosmopolitan* (September 1926): 145, 177; *Saturday Evening Post* (28 March 1928): 205; Ibid. (7 March 1925): 165; Ibid. (7 December 1929): 257; Ibid. (17 November 1934): 1; Ibid. (16 November 1929): 115; Ibid. (14 December 1929): 62; *Better Homes and Gardens* (April 1933): 5; Ibid. (May 1933): 3; Ibid. (September 1927): 25, emphasis theirs; Ibid. (December 1932): 37; *Ladies' Home Journal* (May 1936): 66. For an account of another firm that met with notable success by adopting an approach similar to Listerine's, see D. S. McNaughton and W. H. Herbert, "Astring-O-Sol Campaign Sells a Year's Quota in One Month," *Sales Management* (28 November 1929): 584–85, 595, 599; also see Philip Wagner, "Mouth Conscious America," *New Republic* (21 July 1926): 250–52.

25. *A Table of Leading Advertisers [1926]*, 30; *Leading Advertisers [1927]* (Philadelphia: Curtis Publishing, 1928), 32; *Leading Advertisers [1930]* (Philadelphia: Curtis Publishing, 1931), 24; *Leading Advertisers [1935]* (Philadelphia: Curtis Publishing, 1936), 8; *All Out of Step*, 116.

26. See Allan R. Barkley, "Halitosis Totters on Its Last Legs as Listerine Launches New Campaign," *Sales Management* (4 February 1928): 215–16, on the introduction of new appeals in Lambert Pharmacal's assault on halitosis; "How I Sold Listerine," 57; *All Out of Step*, 116; also see Otis Pease, *The Responsibilities of National Advertising: Private Control and Public Influence, 1920–1940* (New Haven: Yale, 1958), 134–37. In 1927, for example, monthly newspaper lineage underwritten by the firm went through three cycles: from 111,877 lines in January rising to 398,256 by May, dropping to 104,646 for June and building up to 435,101 lines in October, then nothing in November, followed by 584,190 in December; "Newspaper Lineage of Large National Advertisers," *Sales Management* (31 March 1928): 220.

27. Lambert, *All Out of Step*, 94–95, 98, 144, and "How I Sold Listerine," 56; "Magazine Advertising Develops New Use for Listerine," n.p.

28. "Magazine Advertising Develops New Use for Listerine," n.p.; Lambert, "How I Sold Listerine," 49, 58, 59.

29. Mazur, 69, 72; Tugwell, 104–5; *Fifty Years*, 89, 92–94, Chiclets, using ads, outsold the gum trust that thought it had gained mastery over its market; *Historical Statistics*, 526.

30. Mazur, 226; *Fifty Years*, 325.

31. Noting that "it is only within the last five years that instal[l]ment buying has become a respectable thing to do," Wilbur C. Plummer tracked the phenomenal growth of personal credit in "Social and Economic Consequences of Buying on the Instal[l]ment Plan," *Annals of the American Academy of Political and Social Science*, supplement to vol. 129 (January 1927). By then, 15 percent of all goods purchased at retail were bought on installment, and the trend was growing. See particularly 2–3, 10. Foster and Catchings, 62; Tugwell, 107; Mazur, 93–95, 98–99, felt that increases in retail sales were almost all attributable to installment purchasing. The authors of *Economic Evolution*, 68, 73, noted that 40 percent of this personal credit line was absorbed by labor. Also see Charles Merz, "Debts—Public and Private," *New York Times* (29 January 1933); Stanley Lebergott, *The Americans: An Economic Record* (New York: W. W. Norton, 1984), 436–38.

32. *Recent Economic Changes*, xviii, xix; Frederick C. Mills, *Economic Tendencies in the United States: Aspects of Pre-War and Post-War Changes* (New York: National Bureau of Economic Research, 1932), 245.

33. Levin et al., 126; Lynd and Hanson, 870, 877; Slosson, 369; *Fifty Years*, 397; also see Hower, 126.

34. Collis A. Stocking, "Modern Advertising and Economic Theory," *American*

Economic Review 21 (March 1931): 44–48, 50, 52, 54; Ralph Borsodi, *The Distribution Age: A Study of the Economy of Modern Distribution* (New York: D. Appleton, 1927), particularly 286.

35. Foster and Catchings, 7, 190–93; *Historical Statistics,* 526. Total volume of advertising would not exceed 1929 levels until 1947. For a seminal discussion of the nature of business cycles, see *Business Cycles and Unemployment: Report and Recommendations of a Committee of the President's Conference on Unemployment* (New York: McGraw-Hill, 1923): "Business Cycles," by Wesley C. Mitchell, 5–18.

36. To begin to understand the Great Depression, as Ross Robertson advises, one must "distinguish between the forces that brought a downturn in activity and those that turned a business recession into utter disaster." See his *History of the American Economy* 2d ed. (New York: Harcourt, Brace & World, 1964), 629–34. Fluctuations in the stock market are generally not considered to be causes of business fluctuations; the crash of 1929 was exceptional. The psychological impact need not be discounted, as Hubert Henderson explained in his classic introduction to *Supply and Demand* 2d ed. (Chicago: Univ. of Chicago Press, 1958), 28. Regardless of the collapse of confidence, the fiscal mismanagement of the Federal Reserve from 1929 to 1932 made recovery impossible. See W. Elliot Brownlee, *Dynamics of Ascent: A History of the American Economy* (New York: Alfred A. Knopf, 1974), particularly 286–93. In 1933, 24.9 percent of the civilian labor force was unemployed, *Historical Statistics,* 73; *Fifty Years,* 398; *Consumer Engineering,* 15–17; Foster and Catchings, 35. Lebergott, in *The Americans,* 436–38, argues convincingly that the overextension of credit must be viewed as a primary cause.

37. The firm was third in 1931–1932, fourth in 1933, and sixth in 1934–1935. *Leading Advertisers [1935],* 8. See for example *Ladies' Home Journal* (April 1915): 75, and *Saturday Evening Post* (29 January 1916): 1, compared to *Ladies' Home Journal* (May 1936): 66, and *McCall's* (November 1939): 3.

38. Wolman, 35, 37, 38, 41–42, 45, 47, 53. Based on receipts of four great urban markets (New York, Philadelphia, Chicago, Boston), consumption of poultry jumped from 214.1 million pounds in 1920 to 355.8 million pounds in 1926. For current opinion on the nature and causes of halitosis, see Julian W. Brandeis, "Unpleasant Breath," *Hygeia* (December 1933): 1072–73; Robert H. Brotman, "Halitosis," *Hygeia* (October 1932): 885–86; Don C. Lyons, "The Mouth: An Open Road to Health and to Disease," *Hygeia* (April 1931): 340–43.

39. Two-thirds of the population already lived in dry areas in 1920 and the remainder were accustomed to wartime restrictions. Slosson, 107, 119, 123; White, 67–68. For the impact of prohibition on other goods, see Herman Feldman, *Prohibition: Its Economic and Industrial Aspects* (New York: D. Appleton, 1927), passim.

40. Slosson, 156; Wolman, 53–55; *Leading Advertisers [1931],* 100; *Vanity Fair* (December 1931): 25; *Fifty Years,* 307, 395. For a history of cigarette advertising, see Pope, "Development," 173–220. Burns, 298–99.

41. Neil Borden, *The Economic Effects of Advertising* (Chicago: Richard D. Irwin, 1944), 294, 303; he notes that advertising did not stem declining sales in the worst years of the Great Depression (298).

42. Borden, 304–8; *Market Records: From a Home-Inventory Study of Buying Habits and Brand Preferences of Consumers in Sixteen Cities* Vol. 1 (New York: Scripps-Howard Newspapers, 1938), 1–24 on method; 206–13 on dental goods (pastes, brushes, and powders). On pastes, 64.6 percent reported possession; 69.0 percent of the homes reported at least one brush. Also see "Magazine Advertising Helps Teach Public to Use Toothbrush," *Success Bulletin* no. 70 (13 October 1924): n.p.; "Bristol-Myers

Company Successful in Entering a Crowded Field," *Success Bulletin* no. 90 (30 November 1925): n.p.; "Pepsodent Gains Leadership in Seven Years," *National Advertising: Notes from the Book of Experience* no. 33 (14 May 1923): n.p.

43. Slosson, 156; Lambert, *All Out of Step,* 89, 99; see for instance *Saturday Evening Post* (29 January 1916): 1. A columnist advised women to rinse their mouths regularly with "listerin" to avoid dentists' bills as early as 1897 in "Changes of Linen," *The New York Voice* (3 June 1897): 7.

44. Pope, "Development," 418, 420; *Fifty Years,* 362; D. B. Lucas and C. E. Benson, "The Historical Trend of Negative Appeals in Advertising," *Journal of Applied Psychology* 13 (August 1929): 347, 350, 355; D. B. Lucas and C. E. Benson, "The Relative Values of Positive and Negative Advertising Appeals as Measured by Coupons Returned," *Journal of Applied Psychology* 13 (June 1929): 296, 299; D. B. Lucas and C. E. Benson, "The Recall Values of Positive and Negative Advertising Appeals," *Journal of Applied Psychology* 14 (June 1930): 236. "Do not" was less effective than "Do," as in "don't forget to brush" versus "start brushing now."

45. See *Vanity Fair* (August 1931): 65, for a good example of this theme.

46. Tugwell, 109, suggested that the sudden switch from a rural to an urban economy made Americans particularly susceptible to ads; Leuchtenburg, 9; on conspicuous consumption, one might begin with Thorstein Veblen, *The Theory of the Leisure Class: An Economic Study of Institutions* (New York: Macmillan, 1899).

47. David Riesman, with Nathan Glazer and Reuel Denny, *The Lonely Crowd: A Study of Changing American Character* 3d ed. (New Haven: Yale Univ. Press); Christopher Lasch, *The Culture of Narcissism; American Life in an Age of Diminishing Expectations* (New York: W. W. Norton, 1979); John Higham and Paul K. Conkin, eds., *New Directions in American Intellectual History* (Baltimore: Johns Hopkins Univ. Press, 1979): " 'Personality' and the Making of Twentieth-Century Culture," by Warren L. Susman, 221.

48. Slosson, 134, 142, 144; Arthur M. Schlesinger, *Learning How to Behave: A Historical Study of Etiquette Books* (New York: Macmillan, 1946), 54–55; *Vanity Fair* (June 1931): 85; David M. Kennedy discusses romance in *Birth Control in America: The Career of Margaret Sanger* (New Haven: Yale Univ. Press, 1970), 128–30 and particularly 68–69 for a fascinating account of the impact of Freudian notions on the romantic impulses of the era. Impossible expectations may have had nothing to do with a rise in divorce; women's realistic aspirations had altered perceptibly. As Slosson observed, 134, "No longer was marriage the inevitable way of getting a living."

49. George B. Evans began taking out ads for Mum in 1902 and Odorono got its start around 1909. Both relied heavily on magazines for their success; indeed, Odorono "can be said to have been made by magazine advertising." See "Magazine Advertising Adds New Article to Woman's Toilet Case," *Success Bulletin* no. 61 (9 June 1924): n.p.; "School Girl Starting with $150 Adds New Item to Woman's Toilet Case," *National Advertising Bulletin* no. 41 (3 September 1923): n.p.; "Many Nationally Known Brands Have Won Their Markets by Advertising Without the Help of Salesmen," *Success Bulletin* no. 34 (28 May 1923): 1–4; *Fifty Years,* 392; *Ladies' Home Journal* (April 1915): 104; Ibid. (July 1915): 41, 46; Ibid. (July 1928): 148; Ibid. (September 1928): 162, 194; Ibid. (April 1936): 1; Ibid. (December 1936): 43; Ibid. (September 1936): 43; *Cosmopolitan* (July 1918): 157; Ibid. (August 1918): 126, 139; Ibid. (August 1920): 165; *Hearst-International Cosmopolitan* (July 1932): 141. As specialty brands appeared to satiate the increasing demand to deodorize, feminine deodorants began to advertise. For a Lysol ad discussing this need, see *Woman's World* (October 1929): 32, for one of

many examples of its approach. It warned women not to experiment with such a delicate matter but to rely on Lysol.

50. The word "perfume" derives from Latin *per* (through) and *fumare* (to smoke), although it seems to be traced to ancient methods of manufacture. Charles C. McGuirk, "A Subtle Something," *Saturday Evening Post* (4 December 1926): 72, 76; Slosson, 155; also see Chase, 90–91.

51. Franz Boas, *Anthropology and Modern Life* (New York: Norton, 1928), 154; Stocking, 49.

52. W. G. Sumner, "The Mores of the Present and the Future," *Yale Review* 18 (November 1909): 233–34, 238.

53. *Fifty Years,* paid space between 128–29: "To have great poets there must be great Audiences, too," by Crowell Publishing Company.

CHAPTER 3

1. For a sampling of contemporaneous opinion and scholarship concerning American women in the 1920s, see "The New Woman: A Symposium," *Current History* 27 (October 1927): 1–48; Viva B. Boothe, ed., "Women in the Modern World," *Annals of the American Academy of Political and Social Science* 143 (May 1929); V. F. Calverton and S. D. Schmalhausen, eds., *Sex in Civilization* (New York: Macaulay, 1930). During the 1920s, claims Sheila M. Rothman, conceptions of women's central role "moved from the nursery to the bedroom." *Woman's Proper Place: A History of Changing Ideals and Practices, 1870 to the Present* (New York: Basic Books, 1978), 177. A standard secondary survey of developments in the New Era is William H. Chafe, *The American Woman: Her Changing Social, Economic, and Political Roles, 1920–1970* (New York: Oxford, 1972). Instead of change, the picture he draws is one of continuity. Also see Estelle B. Freedman, "The New Woman: Changing Views of Women in the 1920's," *Journal of American History* 61 (September 1974): 372–93. For an analysis of changing ideals of beauty, see Lois W. Banner, *American Beauty* (New York: Alfred A. Knopf, 1983).

2. The suffrage campaigns were of course much more complex than this brief overview can convey. See Aileen Kraditor, *The Ideas of the Woman Suffrage Movement 1890–1920* (Garden City: Anchor, 1971), 217. Also see Eleanor Flexner, *Century of Struggle* (Cambridge: Belknap Press, 1959). Carl N. Degler, *At Odds: Women and the Family in America from the Revolution to the Present* (New York: Oxford, 1980). The Suffrage, says Degler, was "more radical than is generally supposed" (341–342, 349, 352).

3. Kraditor, 214; Arthur M. Schlesinger and Dixon Ryan Fox, eds., *A History of American Life* 13 vols. (New York: Macmillan, 1927–1948) Vol. 12: *The Great Crusade and After 1914–1928,* by Preston William Slosson, 135; also see J. Stanley Lemons, *The Woman Citizen: Social Feminism in the 1920's* (Urbana: Univ. of Illinois, 1973), 153–80, and Rothman, 136–52.

4. Lemons, 63; Hugh L. McMenamin, "Evils of Woman's Revolt Against the Old Standards," *Current History* 27 (October 1927): 31; one historian in particular who would take issue with McMenamin's indictment is James R. McGovern, "The American Woman's Pre-World War I Freedom in Manners and Morals," *Journal of American History* 55 (September 1968): 315–33. He asserts that especially for middle- and upper-class women, one must look to the Progressive Era—specifically between 1910 and

1920 — for the major shift in manners and morals. Others have insisted that something profound transpired in the attitudes of and about women after Suffrage. Banner has concluded that "by the mid-1920's it had become a matter of belief, proclaimed by press and radio, businessmen and politicians, that women had in fact achieved liberation." Going a step further, June Sochen asserts, "The flapper thought she was free." Lois W. Banner, *Women in Modern America: A Brief History* (New York: Harcourt Brace Jovanovich, 1974), 141–42; June Sochen, *The New Woman: Feminism in Greenwich Village, 1910–1920* (New York: Quadrangle, 1972), 148. Sochen argues that "the new woman was a sociological fact by 1910," pointing to the number of Ph.D.'s awarded women and confining her study to literary feminism in bohemian New York, ix, 126, 148. Joseph Collins, "Woman's Morality in Transition," *Current History* 27 (October 1927): 33–35, argued that although the "new ideal for women had its birth with the century," the change did "not come about gradually and insensibly, but overnight, as it were, in the span of one generation." Freedman, 387; although normative behavior changes relatively slowly, it seems clear that many observers were stunned by the transformations in the meaning of "womanhood" in the 1920s.

5. Charlotte Perkins Gilman, "The New Generation of Women," *Current History* 18 (August 1923): 736, 737; Mrs. Henry W. Peabody, "Woman's Morality a Light Through the Ages," *Current History* 29 (January 1924): 584, 589; Floyd Dell, "An Anti-Feminist Utopia," *Current History* 27 (November 1927): 10.

6. Stanley Lebergott, *The American Economy: Income, Wealth, and Want* (Princeton: Princeton Univ. Press, 1976), 16–18; Robert S. Lynd, with the assistance of Alice C. Hanson (Jones), "The People as Consumers," *Recent Social Trends in the United States: Report of the President's Research Committee on Social Trends* (New York: McGraw-Hill, 1933), 864; Gilman, 736; Beatrice Forbes-Robertson Hale, "Women in Transition," *Sex in Civilization,* 68–69; David M. Kennedy, *Birth Control in America: The Career of Margaret Sanger* (New Haven: Yale, 1970), 136; Collins, 37; Robert S. Lynd and Helen Merrell Lynd, *Middletown: A Study in Contemporary American Culture* (New York: Harcourt, Brace, 1929), 123–26; Robert S. Lynd and Helen Merrell Lynd, *Middletown in Transition: A Study in Culture Conflicts* (New York: Harcourt, Brace & World, 1937), 164–67. For the views of an educated reactionary, see David Snedden, "The Probable Social Consequences of the Out-Working of Well-Endowed Married Women," *Women in the Modern World,* 356–57, 358, 359; Beatrice Forbes-Robertson Hale, "The Women's Revolution," *Current History* 29 (October 1923): 21. "Feminism and Jane Smith," *Harper's Monthly* 155 (June 1927): 2, rejected feminism altogether because it denigrated mothers and neglected motherhood; when lists of "12 greatest women" appeared, only unmarried or childless women qualified. For the lists to which the author may have been referring, see "Twelve Greatest Women," *New York Times,* 25 June 1922. Look at Margaret Sanger, "The Civilizing Force of Birth Control," *Sex in Civilization* (New York: Macaulay, 1929), 525–37, for a brief expression of her views.

7. William F. Ogburn, with the assistance of Clark Tibbetts, "The Family and Its Functions," *Recent Social Trends in the United States: Report of the President's Research Committee on Social Trends* (New York: McGraw-Hill, 1933), 661; John Demos places the family in "Comparative Perspective" in *A Little Commonwealth: Family Life in Plymouth Colony* (New York: Oxford, 1970), 180–90, reaching much the same conclusion that as its social meaning waned, the family may have acquired psychological import. Charles Franklin Thwing, "The Family at the Parting of the Ways," *Current History* 19 (January 1924): 590–95; also see Christopher Lasch, *Haven*

in a Heartless World: The Family Besieged (New York: Basic Books, 1977). Viva B. Boothe, "Forward," *Women in the Modern World,* vii; Leta S. Hollingsworth, "The New Woman in the Making," *Current History* 27 (October 1927): 18. For a highly suggestive discussion, see Mary Hartman and Lois W. Banner, eds., *Clio's Consciousness Raised: New Perspectives on the History of Women* (New York: Harper & Row, 1974): "A Case Study of Technological and Social Change: The Washing Machine and the Working Wife," by Ruth Schwartz Cowan, 245–53; compare with Hildegarde Kneeland, "Is the Modern Housewife a Lady of Leisure?" *Survey Graphic* 62 (1 June 1929): 301–2, 331, 333, 336; also see W. Elliot Brownlee, "Household Values, Women's Work, and Economic Growth, 1800–1930," *Journal of Economic History* 39 (March 1979): 199–209. The Lynds noted that the introduction of new technologies did much to fragment the shared experiences of women in *Middletown,* 175; housework used to be "a craft passed down from mother to daughter"; the quality of performance consisted "in a narrower world of 'either-or'": the right way and the wrong way. Now there were a half dozen ways just to wash clothes. On home economics curricula, see Louise Stanley, "Home-Making Education in the College," *Women in the Modern World* (Philadelphia: American Academy of Political and Social Science, 1929), 361–67.

8. Collins, 39; Banner, *Women in Modern America,* 144; John B. Watson, with the assistance of Rosalie Rayner Watson, *Psychological Care of Infant and Child* (New York: W. W. Norton, 1928), especially 5, 7, 12–14, 37–39, 64, 76–82, 149–50, 166 on these issues. They seriously question "whether children should know their own parents." One must appreciate that behaviorism, like any psychological understanding that seeks a popular audience, is and was susceptible to rank reductionism, as this account intimates. Slosson, 147; also see Rothman, 209–18; she observes that "however strident the rhetoric or seemingly idiosyncratic the position, the Watson message, in fact, dominated the child-rearing literature of the 1920s" (211). Also see Barbara Ehrenreich and Deirdre English, *For Her Own Good: 150 Years of the Experts' Advice to Women* (Garden City: Anchor, 1978).

9. Hollingsworth, 19; Elsa Denison Voorhees, "Emotional Adjustment of Women in the Modern World and the Choice of Satisfactions," *Women in the Modern World,* 371; Carrie Chapman Catt, "Woman Suffrage Only an Episode in an Age-Old Movement," *Current History* 27 (October 1927): 4–5 notes that "the first and chief effect of the triumph of woman suffrage is one the general public has not noticed, or if so has not comprehended. A vast army has been demobilized. What became of the army?" Boothe, vi, reassures her readers that, "women are essentially the same today as they have always been," their problems different "only in the details of their manifestation." And yet she adds—parenthetically—that "with developments of modern psychological knowledge" women "may turn out to be much less different from men than was formerly supposed." Many people shared her ambivalence. B. June West, "The 'New Woman,'" *Twentieth Century Literature* 1 (July 1955): 67, observed that "The literature of the time pictures the 'new woman' insisting on her right to be a human being. . . . She emphasizes the identity of interests that all human beings have."

10. Martha Bensley Bruere, "The Highway to Woman's Happiness," *Current History* 27 (October 1927): 28; Joseph Jastrow, "The Implications of Sex," *Sex in Civilization* (New York: Macaulay, 1930), 128; Voorhees, 371.

11. Nancy F. Cott, *The Grounding of Modern Feminism* (New Haven: Yale University, 1987), particularly 6 for passages quoted.

12. Bok is quoted in James Playsted Wood, *Magazines in the United States* 3d ed. (New York: Ronald Press, 1971), 104. Although the theme may have been an old one,

by the late 1920s it was ubiquitous. See Ernest R. Groves, "The Personality Results of the Wage Employment of Women Outside the Home and Their Social Consequences," *Women in the Modern World,* 341–42; McGovern, 320, 322, 324, 333.

13. Anthony Ludovici, "Woman's Encroachment on Man's Domain," *Current History* 27 (October 1927): 23; Carroll Smith-Rosenberg, *Disorderly Conduct: Visions of Gender in Victorian America* (New York: Alfred A. Knopf, 1985), particularly 258, 272, 280–81.

14. Beatrice Forbes-Robertson Hale, "Women in Transition," 80–81; Dorothy Dunbar Bromley, "Feminist – New Style," *Harper's Monthly* 155 (October 1927): 554; Collins, 36, 40, notes that the change could not be permanent "and yet be so self-assured, self-satisfied and at the same time so conscious of itself." Magdaleine Marx, "Frenchwomen's Lack of Political Progress," *Current History* 27 (October 1927): 44–45, ascribed the lack to "timid bourgeois females haunted by the fear of losing their femininity or being otherwise compromised."

15. On the Ku Klux Klan, begin with Kenneth T. Jackson, *The Ku Klux Klan in the City, 1915–1930* (New York: Oxford, 1967), 4, 9, 14–15, 16, 18–19, 85; for an example of purity in ads, see *Ladies' Home Journal* (April 1922): 58–59; an ad for Fairy Soap extolling *"purity* whiteness" – "the choice of discerning people to whom *white cleanliness* is a natural habit" – faces an article on "College Women and Race Suicide." (Emphasis theirs.)

16. Frank Deford, *There She Is: The Life and Times of Miss America* (New York: Viking, 1971), 3, 5, 7, 8, 11, 41–42, 45, 59, 61, 65, 108, 113. "The formal pageant appears to be a modern creation with no obvious antecedents." It was initially part of a larger promotional scheme to retain Atlantic City's tourist trade beyond Labor Day and "began as a stated revue of bathing beauties on the beach." It made some attempt in 1923 to make the process scientific, introducing a rigorous 100-point system of judging: up to ten points each for eyes, facial expression, torso, legs, arms, hands, and "grace of bearing"; five points apiece for hair, nose, and mouth; and fifteen points for construction of head. The winner may have been more the eugenist's ideal than companionate dream; she was just turned sixteen, stood 5′1″ at 108 pounds, and measured 30-25-32.

17. Erving Goffman, *Gender Advertisements* (Cambridge: Harvard Univ. Press, 1979), 8; Louis Gottschalk, ed., *Generalization in the Writing of History: A Report of the Committee on Historical Analysis of the Social Science Research Council* (Chicago: Univ. of Chicago Press, 1963): "Generalizations about National Character: An Analytical Essay," by Walter P. Metzger, particularly 90–91 on "the dramaturgical model."

18. Lynd and Hanson, 898, 900; purses and pocketbooks were not only convenient containers; they too were gender-specific, providing a uniform for modern American women.

19. See *A Table of Leading Advertisers: Showing Advertising Investments of Advertisers Spending $20,000 and over in Thirty-two Leading National Publications* (Philadelphia: Curtis Publishing, 1927), 28–29. Data cover 1922–1926. "Toilet Goods" also includes goods like dentifrices whose consumption was not apparently gender-specific. Also see Lynd and Hanson, 874, for Crowell Publishing's computations although that classification, "Drugs and Toilet," is even more general. Also note Robert S. Lynd, "Family Members as Consumers," *Annals of the American Academy of Political and Social Science* 160 (March 1932): 91. Lynd's unattributed assertion that *Ladies' Home Journal* was running more ads for beauty than for food by 1931 will not stand scrutiny. See *Leading Advertisers [1931]* (Philadelphia: Curtis Publishing, 1932), 57, 115. According to these computations, the *Journal* carried $3,770,520 for "foods" in 1931 and $2,762,747 for "toilet goods."

20. Paula S. Fass, *The Damned and the Beautiful: American Youth in the 1920's* (New York: Oxford, 1977); passages quoted appear on 283, 284. On whiteness, see note 15 above.

21. Banner, 40, 133, 208; Karen Halttunen, *Confidence Men and Painted Women: A Study of Middle-Class Culture in America, 1830–1870* (New Haven: Yale University, 1982), 88–89, 160, 163.

22. Mary Douglas, *Purity and Danger: An Analysis of the Concept of Pollution and Taboo* (London: Routledge & Kegan Paul, 1966), 39, 67–68, 72, 94, 128, 140.

23. Ibid., 62–64; Ellen Ross and Rayna Rapp, "Sex and Society: A Research Note from Social History and Anthropology," *Powers of Desire: The Politics of Sexuality* (New York: Monthly Review, 1983), 51.

24. Charles J. McGuirk, "A Subtle Something," *Saturday Evening Post* 199 (4 December 1926): 73; figures are attributed to Ruth J. Maurer of the American Cosmeticians Society, although Slosson, 155, ascribes some identical calculations to the Foucaults, French perfumers.

25. Slosson, 155; Paul H. White, "Our Booming Beauty Business," *Outlook and Independent* 154 (22 January 1930): 133.

26. Middletown is Muncie, Indiana, subject of the sociological studies of Robert and Helen Lynd; see Lynd and Lynd, *Middletown,* 117; when speaking of beauty parlors in 1925, the Lynds enclosed the term in quotes; U.S. Bureau of the Census, *Census of Business: 1935, Service Estabishments* Vol. 2: *Statistics for States, Counties, and Cities* (Washington, D.C.: GPO, 1935), 143; Lynd and Hanson, 906; Lynd and Lynd, *Middletown in Transition,* 170–71; Banner, *Women in Modern America,* 143; Rothman, 180, 186.

CHAPTER 4

1. Dorothy Dunbar Bromley, "Feminist—New Style," *Harper's Monthly* 155 (October 1927): 552, 553, 557, 560.

2. *New York Times,* 11 May 1924; Paula S. Fass, *The Damned and the Beautiful: American Youth in the 1920's* (New York: Oxford, 1977), 280; also see James R. McGovern, "The American Woman's Pre-World War I Freedom in Manners and Morals," *Journal of American History* 55 (September 1968): 324–25 for developments in the teens.

3. St. Louis, National Hairdressers Association papers (hereafter N.H.A.), Second Session of the 4th Annual Convention, 9 September 1924, Minutes, 5, 6; Ethel Erickson, "Employment Conditions in Beauty Shops: A Study of Four Cities"; *Bulletin of the Women's Bureau* no. 133 (Washington, D.C.: GPO, 1935): "Letter of Transmittal," by Mary Anderson, v; Sophonisba P. Breckenridge, *Women in the Twentieth Century: A Study of Their Political, Social, and Economic Roles* (New York: McGraw-Hill, 1933), 134.

4. Carl N. Degler, *At Odds: Women and the Family in America from the Revolution to the Present* (New York: Oxford, 1980), 331, 349; N.H.A., Tuesday Morning Session, 3d Convention, 1923, Minutes, 15.

5. Lois W. Banner, *American Beauty* (New York: Alfred A. Knopf, 1983), 208–13; *American Hairdresser/Salon Owner: "A Century of Service"* (New York: Service Publications, 1978), 13. On hair fashion in the early nineteenth century, see Karen Halttunen, *Confidence Men and Painted Women: A Study of Middle-class Culture in America, 1830–1870* (New Haven: Yale, 1982), 84–86, 161, 163.

6. Banner, 210–11, 213; *"A Century of Service,"* 26.

7. N.H.A., 1st Convention, 1921, Minutes, 2; N.H.A., Tuesday Morning Session, 3d Convention, 1923, Minutes, 16.

8. N.H.A., Legislative Committee Meeting, 7 September 1924, Minutes, 33–34; on political corruption in the early 1920s, see Isabel Leighton, ed., *The Aspirin Age, 1919–1941* (New York: Simon and Schuster, 1949): "The Timely Death of President Harding," by Samuel Hopkins Adams, 81–104. The roll call of delegates at the first convention, per Minutes, 4, included representatives from local and regional associations in New York, St. Louis, New England, California, Chicago, Minnesota, Evansville, Colorado, Madison, Cleveland, Philadelphia, and Milwaukee.

9. John B. Watson, "Present Economic Conditions: Some Practical Lessons to be Drawn." An address given before the Associated Dress Industries of America, 22 November 1921. (New York: J. Walter Thompson, n.d.), 6–7.

10. N.H.A., 1st Convention, 1921, Minutes, 34; N.H.A., Executive Committee Meeting, 7 September 1924, Minutes, 73; N.H.A., 1st Convention, Minutes, 18, 20.

11. N.H.A., 2d Convention, 1922, Minutes, 150; Watson, 11.

12. N.H.A., 5th Convention, 1925, Minutes, 135–36, 139, 147.

13. N.H.A., 2d Open Session, 4th Convention, 1924, Minutes, 15; N.H.A., Wednesday Morning Session, 4th Convention, 1924, Minutes, 4–9; N.H.A., Executive Committee Meeting, 7 September 1924, Minutes, 67; the issue of fraudulent schools was a perennial in the early years. N.H.A., 6th Convention, 1926, Minutes, 258, 265; N.H.A., Tuesday Morning Session, 3d Convention, 1923, Minutes, 125; N.H.A., 6th Convention, 1926, Minutes, 71. On permanent waving, also see N.H.A., 1st Open Session, 4th Convention, 1924, Minutes, 35–36; although, as one delegate put it, permanent waving was "the worst abused thing I have ever heard of . . . the effect of incompetency, of untrained operators, and of unscrupulous individuals," it was also, as another added, "the most important remunerative department that we have in our business."

14. Lyon Gardiner Tyler, ed., *Narratives of Early Virginia, 1606–1625* (New York: C. Scribner's Sons 1907), 125–26. For a history of the Barbers' Union, see W. Scott Hall, "The Journeymen Barbers' International Union of America," *The Johns Hopkins University Studies in Historical and Political Science* Series 54 (Baltimore: Johns Hopkins Press, 1936), 299–407.

15. "This addition to your business will prove just as profitable as it is doing to the thousands of other barbers in the United States and Canada." "Big Opportunity for Barbers," *Barbers' Journal* 24 (March 1922): 14; "Helps Barbers Make Money," *Barbers' Journal* 24 (April 1922): 29; "Will Teach Barbers Beauty Culture," *Barbers' Journal* 24 (May 1922): 48; "With the Publisher," *Barbers' Journal* 24 (June 1922): 22.

16. N.H.A., 1st Convention, 1921, Minutes, 21; that hairdressers did not lead their own organization was one of the criticisms levelled at the N.H.A. from the beginning. *Beauty Culture* magazine, in a letter sent to all the delegates at the 2d Convention, argued that "ONLY AN ACTIVE HAIRDRESSER OF NATIONAL REPUTATION should be elected President, one without manufacturing, wholesale, or other personal interests; that all the offices should be filled only by responsible HAIRDRESSERS." These publishers were particularly annoyed that the national elected another printer and publisher as its president, named his publication the official organ, and took his lawyer—a "reputed" stockholder—as the association's counsel. That hairdressers—as distinguished from publisher or manufacturer or wholesaler—did not take a more active leadership could be attributed to a number of factors. Wholesalers' participation was essential, especially for financial support. Beyond their awareness of

the intricacies of the national market, the revenue received from them at conventions — at the trade exhibits — was essential to the solvency of the organization. Perhaps more important in accounting for the preponderance of people other than hairdressers at the top was that the hairdressers themselves — increasingly women — lacked the organizational expertise to run a national; they had difficulty creating the local units that the national was supposed to serve. Many women were new to business altogether, and had yet to master bookkeeping, let alone the complexities of national legislation. Perhaps the most compelling reason that hairdressers themselves were not better represented in the highest offices, though, was the time and money that those duties required. Snyder — who was indeed a hairdresser — declined renomination in 1924, unless he was paid; he made between $50 and $75 a day doing permanent waves before he became president, but the association demanded at least a third to a half of the president's time. The next president, C. W. Godefroy, was a manufacturer, and he retained the post for the next six years, then became chairman of the board for two more. Letter "To the Delegates" from Joseph Byrne, President, and Barbara Burke, Editor, Beauty Culture Publishing Company, N.Y., N.Y. (28 July 1922), 1; N.H.A., 2d Convention, 1922, Minutes, 80–81; N.H.A., Tuesday Morning Session, 3d Convention, 1923, Minutes, 54–55, 273–75; N.H.A., 1st Session, 3d Convention, 1923, Minutes, 53; N.H.A., 1st Session, 4th Convention, 1924, Minutes, 19–20; N.H.A., Friday Morning Session, 4th Convention, 1924, Minutes, 45–46; N.H.A., Friday Afternoon Session, 4th Convention, 1924, Minutes, 6.

17. N.H.A., 1st Convention, 1921, Minutes, 21; N.H.A., 2d Convention, 1922, Minutes, 78, 82, 86–87, 88, 90, 92; the remark on St. Louis's preeminence in the parlor goods trade was made by C. W. Godefroy, president of the St. Louis Association, then vice president of the national, and himself a producer of hair goods, 15.

18. N.H.A., 2d Convention, 1922, Minutes, 95, 97, 98–99, 207a (original pencil resolution appended to transcript); N.H.A., Tuesday Morning Session, 3d Convention, 1923, 3, 9; Kozlay reiterated the poolroom comparison, noting that the men customers themselves probably did not appreciate the women: "A barber shop has a free and easy atmosphere and the men don't like the ladies sitting around. They cannot do as they please — throw off their coats in the manner in which they do, and talk as they always talk in a barber shop."

19. N.H.A., 2d Convention, 1922, Minutes, 159; N.H.A., Elective Art Coiffure Departmental, 14 September 1926, Minutes, 6–7; N.H.A., Tuesday Morning Session, 3d Convention, 1923, Minutes, 10, 242; Fass notes that the new look "was indeed liberating, as it emphasized the woman's more informal existence and behavior. It allowed her to feel equal with men and unencumbered by a traditional symbol of her different role." Fass, 280.

20. "The Keith Decision," *The N.H.C.A. Bulletin* (August 1928): 4; *Reports of Cases Argued and Determined in the Supreme Court of the State of Kansas* (Topeka: Kansas State Printing Plant) Vol. 112: *Oct. 1, 1922–Feb. 28, 1923:* "Mary E. Keith, *Appellant,* The State Barber Board et al., *Appellees,*" 834–36; N.H.A., 7th Convention, 1927, Minutes, 70; "Keith Decision," 4, emphasis theirs; as President Snyder noted, 1st Open Session, 4th Convention, 1924, Minutes, 38, the decision "has been the means of the reversal of every case that has been found against a member of our association in a lower court."

21. St. Louis, National Hairdressers and Cosmetologists Association Papers (hereafter N.H.C.A.), 8th Convention, 1928, Minutes, 82–83; for the revised version of the Model Bill presented in 1924 and ratified in 1925 after consultations with the American Cosmeticians Society, see "Legislative Supplement to October, 1928, Issue,"

N.H.C.A. Bulletin 1 (October 1928): 22–27. The American Cosmeticians Society was an outgrowth of the Marinello, a beauty school; they also were especially concerned about schooling. N.H.A., Sub-Legislative Committee Meeting, 9 September 1924, Minutes, 14, 28–29; N.H.A., Legislative Committee Meeting, 7 September 1924, Minutes, 1–65; N.H.A., 5th Convention, 1925, Minutes, 74–75.

22. N.H.A., 5th Convention, 1925, Minutes, 215, 216, 219, 220, 222; N.H.C.A., 9th Convention, 1929, Minutes, 134; N.H.A., 5th Convention, 1925, Minutes, 134–36.

23. N.H.A., 5th Convention, 1925, Minutes, 68.

24. N.H.A., 7th Convention, 1927, Minutes, 63, 341; N.H.A., 6th Convention, 1926, Minutes, 83–84, 496; N.H.C.A., 9th Convention, 1929, Minutes, 143; N.H.A., 7th Convention, 1927, Minutes, 334, 339; N.H.A., 6th Convention, 1926, Minutes, 497; N.H.C.A., 9th Convention, 1929, Minutes, 137–38. Also see N.H.A., 5th Convention, 1925, Minutes, 63–64; the National also had to fight the interference of cities and local ordinances from time to time.

25. N.H.A., 7th Convention, 1927, Minutes, 326; N.H.A., 6th Convention, 1926, Minutes, 497; N.H.A., 5th Convention, 1925, Minutes, 82; N.H.A., 6th Convention, 1926, Minutes, 244–53, 255, 256. The distinction between doctor and "beauty culturist" was fuzzier in the beginning, when hairdressers only had a glimpse of the possibilities of their field. In 1922, a woman addressed the convention on "Featural Surgery," to alter noses, eyes, ears, and chins. She noted, when asked about her competence in surgery, that "I don't do the work, I just mark the skin and show the doctor how to do the work." She looked forward to regulations; "then we would not have any defective faces made." She observed that one really had to have a good surgeon; "I never touch the patient, I only help to tie the stitches." See N.H.A., 2d Convention, 1922, Minutes, 119–24. As time went by, the difference between cosmetic surgeon and cosmetologist may have become clearer, but not so between cosmetic and curative agents. See N.H.C.A., 9th Convention, 1929, Minutes, 131–34, for instance: In New Hampshire, for one case, the legislature attempted to place many substances "we" use under its Food and Drug Act, to be sold only by registered pharmacists. The result would have been turning a substantial volume of beauty sales over to drugstores. In the end, the bill was amended so as to be harmless to the hairdressers' and wholesalers' interests. In *NHCA's Golden Years* (Racine, Wisc.: Western Publishing, 1970), 20–21, a brief account of the association's encounter with the federal government over the Copeland Bill—amending the Food and Drug Act of 1906 to include cosmetics—credits the national with emasculating it. "That haircoloring was not banned from the American market must be credited by the industry of this committee. All of the amendments adopted in 1938 were substantially word for word the language offered in our presentation." Judging from the Association's achievements in the 1920s, one has little reason to doubt these conclusions.

26. N.H.A., Sub-Legislative Committee Meeting, 9 September 1924, Minutes, 28–29; N.H.A., 6th Convention, 1926, Minutes, 237, 238–40, 243.

27. See Table 4.1; *Golden Years,* 20; Hall notes, 367, that thirty states had license laws for beauty workers in 1936.

28. Other magazines in the trade included *Beauty Culture* and *Modern Beauty Shop; American Hairdresser* apparently retained a lead in circulation while it was the official organ but lost it thereafter to *Modern Beauty Shop.* See *A Rate and Circulation Study of 404 Class, Trade, and Technical Publications* (New York: Association of National Advertisers, 1941), 12; also see note 16 above; *Golden Years,* 11, 13, 19; also see *"A Century of Service",* passim; N.H.A., 7th Convention, 1927, Minutes, 351, 360; 5th Convention, 1925, Minutes, 155.

CHAPTER 5

1. New York, Soap and Detergent Association Archives (hereafter S.D.A.A.), Association of American Soap & Glycerine Producers, Inc., "Stabilizing Industry by Joining Product Appeal with Social Service. Brief and Supporting Data for American Trade Association Executives' Award 1931," 2–3. Statement quoted here appears in italics in original. This essay first appeared in slightly different form as "Lustrum of the Cleanliness Institute, 1927–1932," *Journal of Social History* 22 (Summer 1989): 613–30.

2. *Oxford English Dictionary* (Oxford: Claredon Press, 1933) Vol. 9: "Soap," 350–51; the first recorded English usage of the word soap was circa A.D. 1000; *Fifty Years 1888–1938* (New York: *Printers' Ink,* 1938), 23; "Local Candle Shop and Soap Factory Becomes Prominent National Advertiser: Each Procter & Gamble Advertised Product an Outstanding Success," *Success Bulletin: Notes from the Book of Magazine Experience* (New York: Periodical Publishers Association, 1 April 1928), n.p. On domestic soap making in the nineteenth century, see John Mack Faragher, *Women and Men on the Overland Trail* (New Haven: Yale, 1979), 56–57, 68, 221; also see R. Carlyle Buley, *The Old Northwest Pioneer Period 1815–1840* (Indianapolis: Indiana Historical Society, 1950), 223; Eugene D. Genovese, *Roll, Jordan, Roll: The World the Slaves Made* 3d ed. (New York: Vintage Books, 1976), 553. Alfred D. Chandler, Jr., *The Visible Hand: The Managerial Revolution in American Business* (Cambridge: Belknap Press, 1977), 296; also look at *Into a Second Century with Procter & Gamble* (Cincinnati: Procter & Gamble, 1944), an effort in public relations with a chronology of the firm on 44–50; and Alfred Lief, *"It Floats": The Story of Procter & Gamble* (New York: Rinehart, 1958), a popular history of the firm.

3. *Fifty Years,* 23; Frank Presbrey, *The History and Development of Advertising* (New York: Doubleday, 1929), 393.

4. Presbrey, 394; *Fifty Years,* 23, 24. For years common wisdom had it that Sapolio disappeared from the market because it failed to maintain its advertising. Donald S. Tull argues convincingly that the story is more complex. See "A Re-examination of the Causes of the Decline in Sales of Sapolio," *The Journal of Business* 28 (April 1955): 128–37.

5. *Fifty Years,* 23, 111; Presbrey, 395, 396; Frank Luther Mott, *A History of American Magazines,* Vol. 4: *1885–1905* (Cambridge: Belknap Press, 1957), 25–26.

6. Mott, 26, 30; *Fifty Years,* 122, 126, 129, 182, 205.

7. Walter B. Pitkin, *The Consumer: His Nature and His Changing Habits* (New York: McGraw-Hill, 1932), 45–47. In 1910, 1 percent of American families had automobiles; by 1930, 60 percent were so equipped. Stanley Lebergott, *The American Economy: Income, Wealth, and Want* (Princeton: Princeton Univ. Press, 1976), 290; on "Passenger car registration (per 1000 population)" and "Percentage of roads surfaced" in the early and mid-twenties, see *Recent Economic Changes in the United States; Report of the Committee on Recent Economic Changes, of the President's Conference on Unemployment* (New York: McGraw-Hill, 1929) Vol. 1: "Marketing," by Melvin T. Copeland, 339.

8. Pitkin, 45–48. On electrification, see *Historical Statistics of the United States, Colonial Times to 1957* (Washington: U.S. Bureau of the Census, 1960), 510, and "Socialization and Demand Creation."

9. Other factors also accelerated the slump. See Pitkin, 45–48.

10. On cosmetics, see "Cosmetics and the Crisis in Gender Identity"; as Ross M. Robertson notes, "Continual introduction of new goods and services means that the

demand for old ones must be restricted, and the faster the introduction of new commodities the greater the restrictive influence on old ones." In *History of the American Economy* 2d ed. (New York: Harcourt, Brace & World, 1964), 541.

11. "Stabilizing Industry," 2, 4. Cosmetics were a direct threat to washing. They concealed rather than cleaned. Removing them was easier with substances other than soap. St. Louis, National Hairdressers Association Papers, Wednesday Morning Session, 4th Annual Convention, Minutes, 33; N.H.A., 6th Annual Convention, 1926, Minutes, 243. The widespread acceptance of deodorants in the 1920s also threatened the demand for soap.

12. J. Donald Edwards, "The Position of the Soap Industry in World War I" (U.S. Bureau of Labor Statistics, September 1941), 1, 5, 10–13, 17, 21–22. On soap makers' earlier appreciation of a common interest in their market, see Victor S. Clark, *History of Manufactures in the United States,* Vol. 3: *1893–1928* (New York: McGraw-Hill, 1929), 265–66, and "A Soap Trust," *Printers' Ink* (31 October 1906): 28, which reported the rumor of a proposed combination to "include all the prominent advertised brands in the world," with J. Pierpont Morgan as the ostensible organizer.

13. *Fifty Years,* 283, 387; Mott, 33; Neil H. Borden, *Cases on Cooperative Advertising with Introduction and Commentaries,* Vol. 11 of *Harvard Business Reports* (New York: McGraw-Hill, 1932), 23–26. For an early explication of this approach to the marketplace, see Arthur Jerome Eddy, *The New Competition: An Examination of the Conditions Underlying the Radical Change that is taking Place in the Commercial and Industrial World—the Change From a Competitive to a Cooperative Basis* 5th ed. (Chicago: A. C. McClurge, 1916).

14. Paul M. Mazur, *American Prosperity: Its Causes and Consequences* (New York: Viking, 1928), 207, 221; Rexford Guy Tugwell, *Industry's Coming of Age* (New York: Harcourt, Brace, 1927), 110–14; Wesley C. Mitchell, "A Review," in *Recent Economic Changes in the United States: Report of the Committee on Recent Economic Changes of the President's Conference on Unemployment* (New York: McGraw-Hill, 1929), 865–66; Robert S. Lynd, with the assistance of Alice C. Hanson (Jones), "The People as Consumers," *Recent Social Trends in the United States: Report of the President's Research Committee on Social Trends* (New York: McGraw-Hill, 1933), 885, 887. For an analysis of the cotton industry's organization, see Louis Galambos, *Competition and Cooperation: The Emergence of a National Trade Association* (Baltimore: Johns Hopkins Univ. Press, 1966).

15. *New York Times,* 24 June 1927, 3; " 'Take-A-Bath' Week Starts," *New York Times,* 10 July 1927, 7; "Another Order of the Bath," *New York Times,* 17 August 1927, 23. The producers of 80 percent of the soap made in America were represented in the association that founded the institute; the president, Sidney M. Colgate, had been chairman of the Soap and Candle Industries War Service Committee; also on the board of directors were presidents, vice presidents, or spokesmen for Procter & Gamble, Fels, Lever Brothers, John T. Stanley, Palmolive-Peet, Armour, James S. Kirk & Co., Los Angeles Soap, and Swift & Co. S.D.A.A. "Association of American Soap and Glycerine Producers, Inc.," June 1928, n.p.

16. W. W. Peter, M.D., Dr. P. H., and Grace T. Hallock, *Hitchhikers: Patrolling the Traffic Routes to the Mouth and Nose* (New York: Cleanliness Institute, 1930), 47–50; the book was written for health officers, physicians, nurses, health workers, and teachers. S.D.A.A., Anne Raymond, "Reflections from the Mirror," 11, transcript of CBS radio broadcast delivered 25 June 1930 in thirty-six metropolitan areas.

17. "Association of American Soap", n.p.; S.D.A.A., "Suggestions from Teach-

ers (Kindergarten and Grades I and II) in the Use of the Animal Way" (New York: School Service, Cleanliness Institute, 1932), 5.

18. Roscoe C. Edlund, "Lave and Learn; Study Made by Cleanliness Institute Reveals that Hands of America's 25,000,000 School Children Are Not Washed as Often as Health and Decency Demand" (Albany: A.P.W. Paper Co., n.d.), 1–3; S.D.A.A., "Handwashing in Schools; Report of a Study Made by Cleanliness Institute" (New York: School Service, Cleanliness Institute, 1931), 1–6; S.D.A.A., "Clean Hands for Every School Child: Program Suggestions for Parent-Teacher Associations. To be read as a single address, or as three short addresses by three different persons. Questions for discussion have been added" (New York: School Service, Cleanliness Institute, n.d.), Part 2, 1.

19. "Association of American Soap," n.p.; Jean Broadhurst, *Pictures From the Animal Way,* with illustrations by Dorothy Double (New York: School Service, Cleanliness Institute, n.d.); according to an undated note attached to the cover in the archive copy, S.D.A.A., 264,868 copies were distributed on request for kindergarten, first, and second graders; "Suggestions from Teachers . . . ," 7; Margaret C. Munson, compiler, *Outline for Cleanliness Teaching, Based on an Analysis of 100 Courses of Study* 2d ed. (New York: School Service, Cleanliness Institute, 1932): "Section I–Kindergarten, Grades I, II, III," 4–17. Also see S.D.A.A., "Handwashing Methods from the School Service Correspondence of Cleanliness Institute" (mimeograph, n.d.), 1–6 on schools without running water, and 7–8 on schools with modern equipment. On aspects of best utilization of faucets and sinks, see "Handwashing in Schools," 12–15; at their experimental center in Newton, Massachusetts, the institute—along with twenty-one manufacturers and associations with interest in the issue—studied consumption per 100 handwashings as a function of type of soap, type and location of equipment, age and sex of students, type of water, and degree of supervision. The institute knew whereof it spoke.

20. Munson, "Section II—Grades IV, V, VI," 6–17; Grace T. Hallock, *After the Rain: Cleanliness Customs of Children in Many Lands* (New York: Cleanliness Institute, 1927), was written for 3rd, 4th, and 5th graders, introducing them to ethnic and racial variety as well as fairly severe sex roles; 300,000 copies were printed between November 1927 and September 1928, distributed at cost. Also see Mary Alice Kimball and Mary Hopkins Alden, *The Judd Family: A Story of Cleanliness in Three Centuries* (New York: Cleanliness Institute, 1932), for 6th and 7th graders, of which 200,000 copies were printed in 1932; S.D.A.A., Happy Goldsmith, "Learn the Art of Magic" (New York: Cleanliness Institute, 1928), is a fourteen-page pamphlet on hygiene made fun.

21. Munson, "Section III—Grades VII, VIII, & IX," 6–18; Grace T. Hallock, *A Tale of Soap and Water: The Historical Progress of Cleanliness* 2d ed. (New York: Cleanliness Institute, 1937), for the 7th, 8th, and 9th grades; also see "Word Book for a Tale of Soap and Water," (New York: Cleanliness Institute, 1932), a concordance to the text that shows that the word "civilization" appeared in the original on 3, 5, 10, 22, 28, 29, 30, 32, 34, 76, 93. Lillian B. Davis, "Prevention of Communicable Disease. A Junior High School Unit" (New York: School Service, Cleanliness Institute, 1932); Happy Goldsmith, "The Smart Thing to Do: An Engagement Book for Engaging Young Ladies" (New York: Cleanliness Institute, 1927), a fourteen-page pamphlet for young girls; Happy Goldsmith, "The Strange Case of Mr. Smith—An Amusing Story of a Cold Murder" (New York: Cleanliness Institute, n.d.); no one knows how much sickness soap and water could prevent, but 92 percent of communicable diseases, said

the brochure, "are passed on in the same way as your daughter's cold": unwashed hands were the carriers.

22. "Suggestions from Teachers," 12–13; Munson, "Section I," 6–7, emphasis hers; Mrs. Florence H. Hobson, "The Health and Cleanliness Chronicle of a Junior High Training School" (New York: Cleanliness Institute, 1929), 29; "Handwashing Methods," 8; "Cleanliness in Child Care and Training" (New York: Charles Francis Press for Cleanliness Institute, n.d.).

23. Mrs. A. E. P. Searing, "Cleanliness by Choice," in "Cleanliness in Child Care," 11; Munson, "Section I," 4, 10.

24. John T. Flynn, "Edward L. Bernays; The Science of Ballyhoo," *Atlantic Monthly* 149 (May 1932): 564. Also see John T. Flynn, "News by Courtesy," *Forum* 83 (March 1930): 139–43, for an elucidation of ways that publicity passes for news. According to one estimate, for instance, half the news in financial sections of New York newspapers originated as handouts of the banks, one-fourth from the tickers, one-fourth from reporters. Real estate sections were almost all publicity. The institute issued a steady stream of press releases, radio broadcasts, and filler for newspapers and radio.

25. S.D.A.A., "Helpful Hints on Household Cleanliness (second series), reprinted from Educational Material published by the Department of Public Information" (New York: Cleanliness Institute, n.d.), 9; "Picturesque Pots and Pans," *The Romance of Everyday Things* (second series); *6 Radio Talks Prepared by Cleanliness Institute* (New York: Cleanliness Institute, 1932), 1; "Kitchen Calesthenics," *Houseworking Your Way to Good Looks: 5 Radio Talks Prepared by Cleanliness Institute* (mimeograph: Cleanliness Institute, n.d.), 3–4. The distribution of this "educational material" is impossible to track, although the institute asserted that in 1928 alone, its news and feature stories were repeated fifty million times, see "Association of American Soap . . . ," 2; the literature surely would not lack for sponsors. The institute, furthermore, often did not demand attribution or acknowledgment of their "news stories" or broadcasts. As the message on the inside of the *Housekeeping Your Way to Good Looks* series advised, "The courtesy of credit to Cleanliness Institute as the source of this material will be appreciated but is not required." That series, incidentally, included lectures on "A Boat Ride in the Bedroom," "Beauty through Bathing the Bathroom," "Dance of the Mop and Duster," and "Good Form for Wash Day," in addition to "Kitchen Calesthenics." In *The Romance of Everyday Things* (first series): *7 Radio Talks prepared by Cleanliness Institute* (mimeograph: Cleanliness Institute, n.d.), listeners could learn of "Handkerchief Habits," "Tableware—Yesterday and To-day," "Old Time Table Linen," "About Beds," "Lingerie of Long Ago," "The Story of Soap," and "Tales of the Tub." The second series of scripts included, in addition to "Picturesque Pots and Pans," "The Glamour of Gloves," "Quaint Collars and Cuffs," "Magic Carpets," "Windows of the World," and "Changing Viewpoints on Keeping Clean." They were indeed entertaining, well-researched releases; their residual impact—to use soap lavishly—was quite real, if this reader's experience is representative. One can track two series of formal radio addresses the staff of the institute delivered in 1930. For Anne Raymond's presentation, see note 16. In addition to that monologue, the lectures and their air dates were: Adelbert A. Thomas, "The Search for Beauty," 4 June 1930; W. R. Redden, M.D., "Summer Camping and Cleanliness," 11 June 1930; Anne Raymond, "Your Child and You," 18 June 1930; Roscoe E. Edlund, "The Business of Cleanliness," 2 July 1930. All aired at 3:45 p.m., EDST, in thirty-six metropolitan areas. The second series aired at 3:30 p.m., EDST, in twenty-six metropolitan areas; speakers were Roscoe C. Edlund, "A Tale of Soap and Water," 2 April 1930; Anne Raymond, "A Trip Through the Looking Glass," 16 April 1930; W. W. Peter, M.D., Dr.

P.H., "A Doctor Looks at Cleanliness and Health," 30 April 1930; W. R. Redden, M.D., "The Proof of the Pudding," 7 May 1930; Sally Lucas Jean, "The Path of Happiness to Health," 14 May 1930; W. W. Peter, M.D., Dr. P.H., "Expanding Health Horizons," 28 May 1930. S.D.A.A. has copies of all transcripts. These various radio broadcasts might be considered as crude precursors to the soap operas of a later era.

26. S.D.A.A., for a collection of cleanliness posters; also see "Skin Troubles in Industry: What Personal Cleanliness Can Do for the Worker" (New York: Cleanliness Institute, n.d.); S.D.A.A., W. R. Redden, M.D., "Cleanliness in the Prevention of Industrial Dermatoses," Paper read at Newark Academy of Medicine, Newark, New Jersey (4 March 1931), 1, 9, 17, noted that skin troubles headed the list of industrial diseases; after American Cyanamid instituted new procedures—workers changing to work clothes at the outset, then bathing thoroughly before changing back into street clothes at the end of the shift—the incidence of dermatitis treated at the plant hospital dropped from 225 cases in 1929 to 29 cases in 1930.

27. "Association of American Soap . . . ," 1; *Cleanliness Journal* 6 vols. (1927–1932); Peter and Hallock, passim; W. W. Peter, M.D., Dr. P.H., *Policing the Mouth* (New York: Cleanliness Institute, 1930), 4; *Better Health through Cleanliness* 2d ed. (New York: Cleanliness Institute, 1931), 5; also published for presentation to group leaders was W. W. Peter, M.D., Dr. P.H., *Mastadons Microbes and Man* 2d ed. (New York: Cleanliness Institute, 1931). Flynn, "The Science of Ballyhoo," 566.

28. *Coupon Returns: One Advertiser's Experience* (New York: Newell-Emmett Co., 1932), 5–6, 60–61. Of course the 72.9-cent average disguised a wide spread among the various publications and advertisements. Indeed, the cost-per-return was as low as 14 cents in one instance, as high as $4.70 in another. "Surely here are differences worth the study of many advertisers."

29. *Coupon Returns,* 5, 7, 8, 56–60; *The Thirty Day Loveliness Test* (New York: Cleanliness Institute, 1930), went through six printings in 1930–1931. *The Book About Baths* (New York: Cleanliness Institute, 1930), also went through six printings. *A Cleaner House by 12 O'Clock* (New York: Cleanliness Institute, 1930), only went through five printings, 1930–1931; it depicted slovenly Mrs. Brown in contrast to fastidious Mrs. White. "When she leaves her house, she *has* just stepped out of her bath." (3, emphasis theirs.)

30. Flynn, "News by Courtesy," 142.

31. For annual advertising expenditures of individual firms, along with a breakdown by brand, see generally annual editions of *Leading Advertisers* (Philadelphia: Curtis Publishing), which analyzed outlays for space in about thirty of the largest circulation magazines. "Stabilizing Industry," 4; Borden, 7, 16, 21, 24; see Table 5.1.

32. See Table 5.2, bread being flour and baking powder, and butter including margarine too. Note that toilet soap had the least variation among cities of all goods listed. Beecher is quoted in Mott, 32; Percival White, "Figuring Us Out," *North American Review* 227 (1929): 69.

CHAPTER 6

1. Daniel A. Pope, "The Development of National Advertising, 1865–1920" (unpublished Ph.D. diss., Columbia University, 1973), 396. For the most thorough bibliography on advertising sources to appear to date, see Richard W. Pollay, ed. *Information Sources in Advertising History* (Westport, Conn.: Greenwood Press, 1979).

2. In 1981, expenditures on body deodorants, mouthwash, breath fresheners, deodorant soaps, feminine deodorants, and women's and men's fragrances totaled $3,681,134,000, per the "34th Annual Report on Consumer Spending," *Drug Topics* 126 (5 July 1982): 20, 56, 66, 71.

3. See data on personal grooming in Barry Tarshis, *The 'Average American' Book* (New York: Atheneum/SMI, 1979), 197–99. Also see Richard L. Bushman and Claudia L. Bushman, "The Early History of Cleanliness in America," *Journal of American History* 74 (March 1988): 1238.

4. Sidney Ratner, James H. Soltow, and Richard Sylla, *The Evolution of the American Economy: Growth, Welfare, and Decision Making* (New York: Basic Books, 1979), 382; James Playsted Wood, *Magazines in the United States* 3d ed. (New York: Ronald Press, 1971), 315; Pears soap advertised heavily for many years, but decided its brand was so well established that it stopped. Sales dropped $1,500,000 within a year. *Fifty Years 1888–1938* (New York: *Printers' Ink,* 1938), 119; Bruce Barton, *The Man Nobody Knows: A Discovery of the Real Jesus* (U.S.: Grosset & Dunlap, 1924/1925), 140, 146–54; Wood, 241; Pope, 320, found such a disproportionate number of ad men who were the sons of clergymen that he was forced to wonder, "Is advertising the secularized equivalent of preaching?"

5. Thomas Smith, *Hints to Intending Advertisers* (London, 1885).

6. Roy Sheldon and Egmont Arens, *Consumer Engineering: A New Technique for Prosperity* (New York: Harper, 1932), 104; Arthur M. Schlesinger and Dixon Ryan Fox, eds. *A History of American Life* (New York: Macmillan, 1927–1948) Vol. 12: *The Great Crusade and After 1914–1928,* by Preston William Slosson, 365; Fulton Oursler, "American Magazines, 1741–1941," *Bulletin of the New York Public Library* 45 (June 1941): 449.

7. *Fifty Years,* 38; Walter B. Pitkin, *The Consumer: His Nature and His Changing Habits* (New York: McGraw-Hill, 1932), 82; Pitkin's observations have a very uneven quality—at times very perceptive, other times incredibly foolish. On women, he seems downright misogynous. Wood, 117; Betty Friedan, *The Feminine Mystique* (New York: Dell, 1963), 197, emphasis hers.

8. Wood, 106, 108; Pope, 407, 415; also see Joseph E. Dispenza, *Advertising the American Woman* (Dayton: Pflaum, 1975); Robert Atwan, Donald McQuade, and John W. Wright, "Advertising and Social Roles," in *Edsels, Luckies, & Frigidaires: Advertising and the American Way* (New York: Dell, 1979), 2–43; For a sophisticated analysis, see Erving Goffman, *Gender Advertisements* (Cambridge: Harvard Univ. Press, 1979). Also see Janice Winship, "Handling Sex," *Media, Culture, and Society* 3 (January 1981): 25–41.

9. See Stephen Thernstrom, *Poverty and Progress: Social Mobility in a Nineteenth Century City* (New York: Atheneum, 1970).

10. Thorstein Veblen, *Theory of the Leisure Class* (1899); Rexford Guy Tugwell, *Industry's Coming of Age* (New York: Harcourt, Brace, 1927), 258–59.

11. *The American Economic Evolution* (New York: *True Story,* 1930), 9, 49–51, 52; *True Story* began in 1919, and in the twenties a number of other journals—like *True Confessions* and *Whiz Bang*—with a similar target market appeared; Frederick Lewis Allen, "The American Magazine Grows Up," *Atlantic Monthly* 180 (November 1947): 77–82; Oswald Garrison Villard, "Sex, Art, Truth, and Magazines," *Atlantic Monthly* 137 (1926): passim.

12. *Economic Evolution,* 9, 52.

13. David M. Potter, *People of Plenty: Economic Abundance and the American Character* (Chicago: Univ. of Chicago Press, 1954), 91–110.

14. David Riesman, with Nathan Glazer and Reuel Denny, *The Lonely Crowd: A Study of the Changing American Character* 3d ed. (New Haven: Yale Univ. Press, 1961), particularly 19–24 for "A definition of other-direction."

15. Riesman, particularly the preface, on the inadequacies of "incipient population decline."

16. Potter, 95.

17. Christopher Lasch, *The Culture of Narcissism: American Life in an Age of Diminishing Expectations* (New York: W. W. Norton, 1979), 88, 122, 123, 127.

18. Lasch, 7, 38, 82.

19. Joel Kovel, *A Complete Guide to Therapy* (New York: Pantheon, 1976), 252; Stuart Ewen, *Captains of Consciousness: Advertising and the Social Roots of the Consumer Culture* (New York: McGraw-Hill, 1976), 172, 179–80; Roland Marchand, *Advertising the American Dream: Making Way for Modernity, 1920–1940* (Berkeley: Univ. California Press, 1985), 210–16; Lasch, 90, 167–68.

20. Richard Wightman Fox and T. J. Jackson Lears, eds., *The Culture of Consumption: Critical Essays in American History, 1880–1980* (New York: Pantheon, 1983): "From Salvation to Self-Realization: Advertising and the Therapeutic Roots of the Consumer Culture, 1880–1930," by T. J. Jackson Lears, 1–38; Paul Starr, *The Social Transformation of American Medicine* (New York: Basic Books, 1982); Horace Miner, "Body Ritual Among the Nacerima," *American Anthropologist* 58 (1956): 503–7; Philip Wagner, "Mouth-Conscious America," *New Republic* 47 (21 July 1926): 250; Lasch, 74, 82, 98–99, 123.

21. Slosson, 438; for examples of Pebeco ads, see *Cosmopolitan* (September 1918): 136; ibid. (November 1920): 117; Arthur Kallet and F. J. Schlink, *100,000,000 Guinea Pigs* (New York: Vanguard, 1932), 4, 64–69, noted that although potassium chlorate had no more utility in the mouth than table salt, and though ingesting eight grams of it was fatal, a tube of Pebeco contained 30 grams of the poison. Ewen, particularly 41–48.

22. Begin with Richard Hofstadter, *Social Darwinism in American Thought* 2d ed. (Boston: Beacon Press, 1955); on immigration restriction, see John Higham, *Strangers in the Land: Patterns of American Nativism 1860–1925* 2d ed. (New York: Atheneum, 1963), and particularly 275 on IQ tests; also see Mark H. Haller, *Eugenics: Hereditarian Attitudes in American Thought* (New Brunswick: Rutgers Univ. Press, 1963).

23. The house that for decades remained unchanged "has been transformed in a generation by the introduction of a great variety of new functional fittings." In 1902, Standard Sanitary Manufacturing Company began a systematic campaign for "modern bathrooms"; by 1907, sales were up 400 percent. By 1929, 70 percent of urban homes had stationary bathtubs, and almost 25 percent of rural homes were so equipped. The kitchen, too, had been transformed. See Robert S. Lynd, with the assistance of Alice C. Hanson (Jones), "The People as Consumers," in *Recent Social Trends in the United States: Report of the President's Research Committee on Social Trends* (New York: McGraw-Hill, 1933), 857; Frank Presbrey, *The History and Development of Advertising* (New York: Doubleday, 1929), 425; *Fifty Years,* 154; Slosson, 138; Sheldon and Arens, 154–55, 156–57; the percentages of houses with indoor flush toilets registered a marked advance in the 1920s, from 20 percent in 1920 to 51 percent in 1930; by then, 85 percent of all urban homes were so equipped. By 1930, 30 percent of all homes had vacuum cleaners. See Stanley Lebergott, *The American Economy: Income, Wealth, and Want* (Princeton: Princeton Univ. Press, 1976), particularly 272, 287. On kitchens, also see Earnest Elmo Calkins, "The Truth About Advertising," *Atlantic Monthly* 137

(1926): 677, for a comparison of a kitchen of fifty years before with its contemporary counterpart; on the quality of meals prepared in those modern kitchens, see Leo Wolman, "Consumption and the Standard of Living," *Recent Economic Changes in the United States: Report of the Committee on Recent Economic Changes of the President's Conference on Unemployment* (New York: McGraw-Hill, 1929), 50.

24. On automobiles and credit, see discussion in Chapter 2, "Socialization and Demand Creation"; according to Theodore Peterson, *Magazines in the Twentieth Century* 2d ed. (Urbana: Univ. of Illinois Press, 1964), 50, roughly 60,000 homes had radio sets in 1922, and by 1932, 16,800,000 homes were so equipped; the number of stations, in the meantime, advanced from 30 to 608. *Fifty Years,* 372–77; "National Radio Market Grew in Four Years," *Success Bulletin: Notes from the Book of Magazine Experience* no. 83 (6 July 1925): n.p.; Hugh E. Agnew and Warren B. Dygert, *Advertising Media* (New York: McGraw-Hill, 1938), 105; the number of monthly journals available increased from some 3,415 titles in 1920 to 4,110 in 1930, per Peterson, 58.

25. For data on discretionary income, see discussion in Chapter 2, "Socialization and Demand Creation"; *Economic Evolution,* 22.

26. Barton, 139–40; *Fifty Years,* 397; Newel Howland Comish, *The Standard of Living: Elements of Consumption* (New York: Macmillan, 1923), 110.

27. Marchand, 217–22.

28. For a penetrating analysis of the coersive nature of democracy, see Michael Zuckerman, "The Social Context of Democracy in Massachusetts," *William and Mary Quarterly* 25 (1968): 523–44; on the tensions between individualism and individuality, refer to Richard Hofstadter, *The Progressive Historians: Turner, Beard, Parrington* (New York: Random House, 1968), 141–46.

29. Bernays is quoted in John T. Flynn, "Edward L. Bernays: The Science of Ballyhoo," *Atlantic Monthly* 149 (May 1932): 567–68.

A Selected Bibliography of Primary

and Secondary Sources

MANUSCRIPT AND ARCHIVAL SOURCES

New York. Soap and Detergent Association Archives. Public Papers and Publications
of Cleanliness Institute.
St. Louis. National Hairdressers and Cosmetologists Association Papers.

PERIODICALS AND ANNUALS

American Hairdresser. 1917–1930.
Barbers' Journal. Scattered issues.
Better Homes and Gardens. 1924–1940.
Cleanliness Journal. 1927–1932.
Cosmopolitan. 1915–1925.
Hearst—International Cosmopolitan. 1925–1940.
The Housewife (title varies). 1915–1923.
Ladies' Home Journal. 1915–1940.
Leading Advertisers (title varies). 1925–1936.
Literary Digest. 1915–1938.
McCall's. 1930–1940.
N.H.C.A. Bulletin. 1928–1929.
Printers' Ink. Scattered issues.
Sales Management. 1920–1930.
Saturday Evening Post. 1915–1940.
Soap Gazette and Perfumer. Scattered issues.
Success Bulletin: Notes from the Book of Magazine Experience (title varies). 1922–
    1928.
Vanity Fair. 1915–1936.
Woman's Home Companion. 1926–1940.
Woman's World. 1922–1940.

PRIMARY SOURCES

Agnew, Hugh E., and Dygert, Warren B. *Advertising Media.* New York: McGraw-Hill, 1938.

Allen, Devere. "Personal Decoration: Some Aspects of the Evolution of Adornment." *The World Tomorrow* 8(1925):76–79.

Allen, Frederick Lewis. "The American Magazine Grows Up." *Atlantic Monthly* 180(November 1947):77–82.

_____. "American Magazines, 1741–1941." *Bulletin of the New York Public Library* 45(June 1941):439–45.

American Association of Advertising Agencies. *Magazine Circulations—Qualitative Analysis by Incomes of Readers.* New York: American Association of Advertising Agencies, 1930.

The American Economic Evolution. New York: *True Story Magazine,* 1930.

"Andrew Jergens Company Increases Sales 3000% in Twelve Years." *Success Bulletin: Notes From the Book of Magazine Experience,* no. 1(28 August 1922).

"Another Order of the Bath." *New York Times* (17 August 1927):23.

Atkinson, Thomas G. *Psychological Laws Applied to Advertising: The Why and How of Advertising Methods. A Lecture.* Scranton: International Textbook Co., 1925.

"Attitude Test Shows Women and Old People Favor Advertising Most." *Sales Management* 38(1 January 1936):26.

Bakeless, John. *Magazine Making.* New York: Viking, 1931.

Barkley, Allan R. "Halitosis Totters on Its Last Legs as Listerine Launches New Cigaret [*sic*] Campaign." *Sales Management* 14 (4 February 1928):215–16.

Barnes, Harry Elmer. "Sex in Education." In *Sex in Civilization,* edited by V. F. Calverton and S. D. Schmalhausen, 285–348. New York: Macaulay, 1930.

Barton, Bruce. *The Man Nobody Knows: A Discovery of the Real Jesus.* New York: Grosset & Dunlap, 1924/1925.

Beard, Charles A., and Beard, Mary R. *The Rise of American Civilization.* Vol. 3: *America in Midpassage.* New York: Macmillan, 1939.

Boas, Franz. *Anthropology and Modern Life.* New York: Norton, 1928.

Bok, Edward. *The Americanization of Edward Bok.* New York: Scribner's, 1920.

Boothe, Viva B. "Forward." In *Women in the Modern World,* edited by Viva B. Boothe. Philadelphia: American Academy of Political and Social Science, 1929.

Brandeis, Julian W. "Unpleasant Breath." *Hygeia* 11(December 1933):1072–73.

Breckenridge, Sophonisba P. *Women in the Twentieth Century: A Study of Their Political, Social, and Economic Roles.* New York: McGraw-Hill, 1933.

"Bristol-Myers Company Successful in Entering a Crowded Field: Magazine Advertising Has Placed Ipana Toothpaste Among the Leading Dentifrices." *Success Bulletin: Notes from the Book of Magazine Experience,* no. 90(30 November 1925).

Bromley, Dorothy Dunbar. "Feminist–New Style." *Harper's Monthly* 155(October 1927):552–60.

Brotman, Robert H. "Halitosis." *Hygeia* 10(October 1932):885–86.

Bruere, Martha Bensley. "The Highway to Woman's Happiness." *Current History* 27 (October 1927):26–29.

Burns, Arthur F. *Production Trends in the United States Since 1870.* New York: National Bureau of Economic Research, 1934.

Calkins, Earnest Elmo. "The Truth About Advertising." *Atlantic Monthly* 137(1926):670–82.

Calverton, V. F. "Sex and Social Struggle." In *Sex in Civilization,* edited by V. F.

Calverton and S. D. Schmalhausen, 249–84. New York: Macaulay, 1930.

Carpenter, Charles E. *Dollars and Sense.* Garden City, N.Y.: Doubleday, Doran, and Co., 1928.

Carver, Thomas Nixon. *The Present Economic Revolution in the United States.* Boston: Little, Brown, & Co., 1925.

Catt, Carrie Chapman. "Woman Suffrage Only an Episode in an Age-Old Movement." *Current History* 27(October 1927):1–6.

Chamberlin, Edward Hastings. *The Theory of Monopolistic Competition.* 7th ed. Cambridge: Harvard University Press, 1956.

"Changes of Linen." *The New York Voice* (3 June 1897):7.

Chase, Stuart. *The Tragedy of Waste.* New York: Macmillan, 1927.

Chenery, William L. "American Magazines, 1741–1941." *Bulletin of the New York Public Library* 45(June 1941):445–48.

Cherington, Paul T. *The Consumer Looks at Advertising.* New York: Harper, 1928.

"Cigarette vs. Candy." *New Republic* 57(13 February 1929):343–45.

City Markets: A Study of Thirty-Five Cities. Philadelphia: Curtis Publishing, 1932.

Clark, Fred E. "An Appraisal of Certain Criticisms of Advertising." *American Economic Review* (Supplement) 15(March 1925):5–13.

Collins, Joseph. "Woman's Morality in Transition." *Current History* 27(October 1927):33–40.

Comish, Newel Howland. *The Standard of Living: Elements of Consumption.* New York: Macmillan, 1923.

Commons, John R. "Demand and Supply." *Social Economist* 4(May 1893):277–88.

The Complete Bachelor: Manners for Men. New York: D. Appleton, 1896.

Conference Board Studies in Enterprise and Social Progress: Selected Chapters in the Story of the American Enterprise System and Its Contribution to Prosperity and Public Welfare. New York: National Industrial Conference Board, 1939.

Cooley, Arnold James. *The Toilet and Cosmetic Arts.* London: Hardwicke, 1866.

Copeland, Melvin T. "Marketing." In *Recent Economic Changes in the United States: Report of the Committee on Recent Economic Changes of the President's Conference on Unemployment,* 321–424. New York: McGraw-Hill, 1929.

Copeland, Morris A. "The National Income and Its Distribution." In *Recent Economic Changes in the United States: Report of the Committee on Recent Economic Changes of the President's Conference on Unemployment,* 757–839. New York: McGraw-Hill, 1929.

"Coty, Inc. Accelerates Growth by Advertising." *Success Bulletin: Notes from the Book of Magazine Experience,* no. 110(24 January 1927).

Coupon Returns: One Advertiser's Experience. New York: Newell-Emmett Co., 1932.

Creel, George. *How We Advertised America.* New York: Harper and Brothers, 1920.

Cutler, J. H. "The Effectiveness of Page Size in Magazine Advertising." *Journal of Applied Psychology* 14(October 1930):465–69.

Decorum: A Practical Treatise on Etiquette and Dress of the Best American Society. New York: Union Publishing, 1880.

Dell, Floyd. "An Anti-Feminist Utopia." *Current History* 27(November 1927):10–14.

Dickinson, Howard W. *Crying Our Wares.* New York: John Day Co., 1929.

Dwight, Frederick. "The Significance of Advertising." *Yale Review* 18(August 1909):197–205.

An English Lady of Rank. *The Ladies' Science of Etiquette.* New York: Wilson and Co., 1844.

Erickson, Ethel. "Employment Conditions in Beauty Shops: A Study of Four Cities."

Bulletin of the Women's Bureau, no. 133. Washington, D.C.: GPO, 1935.

Fabricant, Solomon, with the assistance of Shiskin, Julius. *The Output of Manufacturing Industries, 1899–1937.* New York: National Bureau of Economic Research, 1940.

Feldman, Herman. *Prohibition: Its Economic and Industrial Aspects.* New York: D. Appleton, 1927.

"Feminism and Jane Smith." *Harper's Monthly* 155(June 1927):1–10.

Fifty Years 1888–1938. New York: *Printers' Ink,* 1938.

Fitzgerald, F. Scott. "Bernice Bobs Her Hair." In *The Bodley Head Scott Fitzgerald,* vol. 5, 84–112. London: The Bodley Head, 1963.

_____. "Echoes of the Jazz Age." *Scribner's* 90(November 1931):459–65.

Flynn, John T. "Edward L. Bernays: The Science of Ballyhoo." *Atlantic Monthly* 149 (May 1932):562–71.

_____. "News by Courtesy." *Forum* 83(March 1930):139–43.

Foster, William Trufant, and Catchings, Waddill. *Money.* Cambridge: Riverside Press, 1923.

_____. *Profits.* Boston: Houghton Mifflin, 1925.

Gay, Edwin F. "Introduction." In *Recent Economic Changes in the United States: Report of the Committee on Recent Economic Changes of the President's Conference on Unemployment,* 1–12. New York: McGraw-Hill, 1929.

The Gentleman's Pocket Companion, and Indispensable Friend. New York: Leavitt and Allen, [18 — —].

Gilman, Charlotte Perkins. "The New Generation of Women." *Current History* 18(August 1923):731–37.

_____. "Woman's Achievements Since the Franchise." *Current History* 27(October 1927):7–14.

Godfrey, Hollis. "The Function of Advertising in the Buyer's Market." *Advertising and Selling* 11(11 July 1928):26, 58–59.

Gompers, Samuel. "Self-Help is the Best Help." *American Federationist* 22(February 1915):113–15.

Gregory, Alyse. "The Changing Morality of Woman." *Current History* 29(November 1923):295–99.

Groves, Earnest R. "The Personality Results of the Wage Employment of Women Outside the Home and Their Social Consequences." In *Women in the Modern World,* edited by Viva B. Boothe, 339–48. Philadelphia: American Academy of Political and Social Science, 1929.

Gunton, George. "Demand and Supply." *Social Economist* 4(May 1893):288–96.

The Habits of Good Society: A Handbook for Ladies and Gentlemen. New York: Carleton, 1865.

Hale, Beatrice Forbes-Robertson. "Women in Transition." In *Sex in Civilization,* edited by V. F. Calverton and S. D. Schmalhausen, 67–81. New York: Macaulay, 1930.

_____. "The Women's Revolution." *Current History* 29(October 1923):16–22.

Harris, Emerson P. "The Economics of Advertising." *Social Economist* 4(March 1893):171–74.

Hart, Hornell. "Changing Social Attitudes and Interests." In *Recent Social Trends in the United States: Report of the President's Research Committee on Social Trends,* 382–443. New York: McGraw-Hill, 1933.

Henderson, Hubert. *Supply and Demand.* 2d ed. Chicago: University of Chicago Press, 1958.

Hollingsworth, Leta S. "The New Woman in the Making." *Current History* 27(October 1927):15–20.

"How Cities Differ in Their Magazine Reading Habits." *Sales Management* 38(15 February 1936):218–20.

"How Magazines Differ—As Shown by City Preferences." *Sales Management* 38(1 March 1936):296–97.

Hunter, Robert. *Poverty.* New York: Macmillan, 1904.

Into a Second Century with Procter & Gamble. Cincinnati: Procter & Gamble, 1944.

Jastrow, Joseph. "The Implications of Sex." In *Sex in Civilization,* edited by V. F. Calverton and S. D. Schmalhausen, 127–42. New York: Macaulay, 1930.

Kallet, Arthur, and Schlink, F. J. *100,000,000 Guinea Pigs.* New York: Vanguard Press, 1932.

———. "Poison for Profit." *The Nation* 135(21 December 1932):608–10.

———. "Quackery in the Ads." *Advertising and Selling* (1 September 1932):13–14, 25–26.

Keyserling, Count Hermann. "Caste in America." *Forum* 80(1928):103–6.

Kneeland, Hildegarde. "Is the Modern Housewife a Lady of Leisure?" *Survey Graphic,* no. 62(1 June 1929):301–2.

Lambert, Gerard B. *All Out of Step: A Personal Chronicle.* New York: Doubleday, 1956.

———. "How I Sold Listerine." In *The Amazing Advertising Business,* edited by the editors of *Fortune,* 47–59. New York: Simon and Schuster, 1957.

Lazarsfeld, Paul F., and Wyant, Rowena. "Magazines in 90 Cities—Who Reads What?" *The Public Opinion Quarterly* 1(October 1937):29–41.

"Lehn & Fink, Inc., Wholesale Druggists Becomes Lehn & Fink Products Company: Drugs Specialty Manufacturers." *Success Bulletin: Notes from the Book of Magazine Experience,* no. 98(17 May 1926).

Levin, Maurice; Moulton, Harold G.; and Warburton, Clark. *America's Capacity to Consume.* Washington, D.C.: The Brookings Institution, 1934.

Lloyd, J. William. "Sex Jealousy and Civilization." In *Sex in Civilization,* edited by V. F. Calverton and S. D. Schmalhausen, 233–46. New York: Macaulay, 1929.

"Local Candle Shop and Soap Factory Becomes Prominent National Advertiser: Each Procter & Gamble Advertised Product an Outstanding Success." *Success Bulletin: Notes from the Book of Magazine Experience* (1 April 1928).

Lucas, D. B., and Benson, C. E. "The Historical Trend of Negative Appeals in Advertising." *Journal of Applied Psychology* 13(August 1929):346–56.

———. "The Recall Values of Positive and Negative Advertising Appeals." *Journal of Applied Psychology* 14(June 1930):218–38.

———. "The Relative Values of Positive and Negative Advertising Appeals as Measured by Coupons Returned." *Journal of Applied Psychology* 14(June 1929):274–300.

Ludovici, Anthony. "Woman's Encroachment on Man's Domain." *Current History* 27(October 1927):21–25.

Lunettes, Henry. *The American Gentlemen's Guide to Politeness and Fashion.* New York: Derby & Jackson, 1857.

Lynd, Robert S. "Family Members as Consumers." *Annals of the American Academy of Political and Social Science* 160(March 1932):86–93.

Lynd, Robert S., and Lynd, Helen Merrell. *Middletown in Transition: A Study in Cultural Conflicts.* New York: Harcourt, Brace, and World, 1937.

Lynd, Robert S., with the assistance of Hanson (Jones), Alice C. "The People as Consumers." In *Recent Social Trends in the United States: Report of the President's Research Committee on Social Trends,* 857–911. New York: McGraw-Hill, 1933.

Lyons, Don C. "The Mouth: An Open Road to Health and to Disease." *Hygeia* 9(April 1931):340–43.

McAdoo, Fifi. "Dressing Down." *Vogue* 77(15 April 1931):89.

McDonough, Everett G. *Truth About Cosmetics.* New York: The Drug and Cosmetic Industry, 1937.

McGuirk, Charles J. "A Subtle Something." *Saturday Evening Post* 199(4 December 1926):31, 72–78.

McMenamin, Hugh L. "Evils of Woman's Revolt Against the Old Standards." *Current History* 27(October 1927):30–32.

McNaughton, D. S., and Herbert, W. H. "Astring-O-Sol Campaign Sells a Year's Quota in One Month." *Sales Management* 20(28 December 1929):584–85.

"Magazine Advertising Adds New Article to Woman's Toilet Case." *Success Bulletin: Notes from the Book of Magazine Experience,* no. 61(9 June 1924).

"Magazine Advertising Develops New Use for Listerine." *Success Bulletin: Notes from the Book of Magazine Experience* (9 February 1925).

"Magazine Advertising Helps Teach Public to Use Tooth Brush." *Success Bulletin: Notes from the Book of Magazine Experience,* no. 70(13 October 1924).

"Magazine Advertising Popularizes Novelty." *Success Bulletin: Notes from the Book of Magazine Experience,* no. 88(19 October 1925).

"Many Nationally Known Brands Have Won Their Markets by Advertising Without the Help of Salesmen." *Success Bulletin: Notes from the Book of Magazine Experience,* no. 34(28 May 1923):1–4.

Market Records: From a Home-Inventory Study of Buying Habits and Brand Preferences of Consumers in Sixteen Cities. 2 vols. New York: Scripps-Howard Newspapers, 1938.

Marshall, Edward. "Machine-Made Freedom: An Authorized Interview with Thomas A. Edison." *Forum* 76(October 1926):492–97.

Marx, Magdaline. "Frenchwomen's Lack of Political Progress." *Current History* 27(October 1927):41–48.

"Mary E. Keith, *Appellant,* The State Barber Board et al., *Appellees,*" In *Reports of Cases Argued and Determined in the Supreme Court of the State of Kansas.* Vol. 112: *Oct. 1, 1922–Feb. 28, 1923,* 834–36. Topeka: Kansas State Printing Plant.

"Mavis Appropriation Grows from $12,000 to $530,000 in Eight Years." *Success Bulletin: Notes from the Book of Magazine Experience,* no. 14(27 November 1922).

Mazur, Paul M. *American Prosperity: Its Causes and Consequences.* New York: Viking, 1928.

Means, Gardiner C. "Industrial Prices and Their Relative Inflexibility." *Senate Document,* no. 13. Washington: GPO, 1935.

Mills, Frederick C. *Economic Tendencies in the United States: Aspects of Pre-War and Post-War Changes.* New York: National Bureau of Economic Research, 1932.

Mitchell, Wesley C. "Business Cycles." In *Business Cycles and Unemployment: Report and Recommendations of a Committee of the President's Conference on Unemployment,* 5–18. New York: McGraw-Hill, 1923.

———. *Business Cycles: The Problem and Its Setting.* New York: National Bureau of Economic Research, 1927.

———. "A Review." In *Recent Economic Changes in the United States: Report of the*

Committee on Recent Economic Changes of the President's Conference on Unemployment, 841–910. New York: McGraw-Hill, 1929.

"Monthly Index of Magazine Advertising." *Printers' Ink* 170(14 March 1935):79.

"Monthly Index of Radio Advertising." *Printers' Ink* (28 February 1923):64.

Murray, John Allen, ed. *George Washington's Rules of Civility and Decent Behavior in Company and Conversation.* New York: G.P. Putnam's Sons, 1942.

Nationally Established Trade-Marks. New York: Periodical Publishers Association, 1934.

National Magazines as Advertising Media. Philadelphia: Curtis Publishing, 1947.

"National Radio Market Grew in Four Years." *Success Bulletin: Notes from the Book of Magazine Experience,* no. 83(6 July 1925).

"1935 Magazine and Radio Expenditures Show Gains." *Sales Management* 38(15 January 1936):12.

"99% Distribution Secured and Maintained for 30 Years on Packers Tar Soap." *Success Bulletin: Notes from the Book of Magazine Experience,* no. 28(5 March 1923).

Nourse, Edwin G.; Tryon, Frederick G.; Drury, Horace B.; Leven, Maurice; Moulton, Harold G.; and Lewis, Cleona. *America's Capacity to Produce.* Washington, D.C.: The Brookings Institution, 1934.

Ogburn, William F., with the assistance of Tibbetts, Clark. "The Family and Its Functions." In *Recent Social Trends in the United States: Report of the President's Research Committee on Social Trends,* 661–708. New York: McGraw-Hill, 1933.

Oursler, Fulton. "American Magazines, 1741–1941." *Bulletin of the New York Public Library* 45(June 1941):448–56.

Peabody, Mrs. Henry W. "Woman's Morality: A Light Through the Ages." *Current History* 29(January 1924):584–89.

"Pepsodent Gains Leadership in Seven Years: Breaks Into Field Already Crowded with Advertisers." *National Advertising: Notes from the Book of Experience,* no. 33(14 May 1923).

"Perspiration Deodorant." *Hygeia* 16(April 1938):368.

Phillips, M. C. *Skin Deep.* New York: Vanguard Press, 1934.

Pitkin, Walter B. *The Consumer: His Nature and His Changing Habits.* New York: McGraw-Hill, 1932.

Plummer, Wilbur C. "Social and Economic Consequences of Buying on the Instal[l]ment Plan." *Annals of the American Academy of Political and Social Science* (Supplement) 129(January 1927).

Popenoe, Paul. "Is There a Scarcity of Good Husbands?" *New York Times Magazine* (29 December 1935):6, 14.

A Rate and Circulation Study of 404 Class, Trade, and Technical Publications. New York: Association of National Advertisers, 1941.

Recent Economic Changes in the United States: Report of the Committee on Recent Economic Changes of the President's Conference on Unemployment. 2 vols. New York: McGraw-Hill, 1929.

Recent Social Trends in the United States: Report of the President's Research Committee on Social Trends. 2 vols. New York: McGraw-Hill, 1933.

Roosevelt, Theodore. "Rural Life." *The Outlook* (27 August 1910):919–22.

Sanger, Margaret. "The Civilizing Force of Birth Control." In *Sex in Civilization,* edited by V. F. Calverton and S. D. Schmalhausen, 525–37. New York: Macaulay, 1929.

"School Girl Starting with $150 Adds New Item to Woman's Toilet Case." *National Advertising Bulletin,* no. 41(3 September 1923).

Scientific Space Selection. 2d ed. Chicago: Audit Bureau of Circulations, 1937.

Scott, John L. "The 'Wallflower School' of Advertising, or 'How to Become Popular in Ten Doses,' as Exposed and Expounded by Leading Copy Experts." *Sales Management* 11(13 November 1926):867.

Sheldon, Roy, and Arens, Egmont. *Consumer Engineering: A New Technique for Prosperity.* New York: Harper, 1932.

Slichter, Sumner H. *Modern Economic Society.* New York: Henry Holt, 1928.

Snedden, David. "The Probable Social Consequences of the Out-Working of Well-Endowed Married Women." In *Women in the Modern World,* edited by Viva B. Boothe, 349–60. Philadelphia: American Academy of Political and Social Science, 1929.

"A Soap Trust." *Printers' Ink* 57(31 October 1906):28.

"Standards of Living." *The Statist: An Independent Journal of Finance and Trade* 134(26 August 1939):255–56.

Stanley, Louise. "Home-Making Education in the College." In *Women in the Modern World,* edited by Viva B. Boothe, 361–67. Philadelphia: American Academy of Political and Social Science, 1929.

Stevens, William Oliver. *The Correct Thing: A Guide Book of Etiquette for Young Men.* New York: Dodd, Mead, 1936.

Stocking, Collis A. "Modern Advertising and Economic Theory." *American Economic Review* 21(March 1931):43–55.

A Study of Duplication of Magazine Circulations in Jefferson and Lewis Counties New York. New York: Association of National Advertisers, 1928.

Sullivan, Mark. *Our Times 1900–1925.* Vol. 6: *The Twenties.* New York: Charles Scribner's Sons, 1932.

Sumner, William Graham. *Folkways: A Study of the Sociological Importance of Usages, Manners, Customs, Mores, and Morals.* 1906. Reprint. New York: Dover, 1959.

————. "The Mores of the Present and the Future." *Yale Review* 18(November 1909):233–45.

"'Take-a-Bath' Week Starts." *New York Times* (10 July 1927):7.

Tassin, Algernon. *The Magazine in America.* New York: Dodd, Mead, 1916.

"300 Largest Advertisers in Newspapers for 1934." *Printers' Ink* 170(28 February, 14 March 1935).

Thwing, Charles Franklin. "The Family at the Parting of the Ways." *Current History* 19(January 1924):590–95.

A Trend Study of 276 General Magazines. New York: Association of National Advertisers, 1938.

Tugwell, Rexford Guy. *Industry's Coming of Age.* New York: Harcourt, Brace, 1927.

"Twelve Greatest Women." *New York Times* (25 June 1922).

U. S. Bureau of the Census. *Census of Business: Service Establishments.* Vol. 2: *Statistics for States, Counties, and Cities.* Washington, D.C.: GPO, 1935.

U. S. Bureau of the Census. *Historical Statistics of the United States, Colonial Times to 1957.* Washington, D.C.: GPO, 1960.

Vaile, Roland S. "The Effects of Advertising During Depressions." *Printers' Ink* 154 (1 January 1931):41–44.

Vanderbilt, Amy. *Amy Vanderbilt's Complete Book of Etiquette: A Guide to Gracious Living.* Garden City, N. Y.: Country Life Press, 1952.

"Vanity, Modesty and Cancer." *Hygeia* 11(April 1933):300–302.

Veblen, Thorstein. *The Theory of the Leisure Class: An Economic Study of Institutions.* 2d ed. New York: Macmillan, 1912.

Verrill, A. Hyatt. *Perfumes and Spices.* Boston: L. C. Page and Co., 1940.

Villard, Oswald Garrison. "Sex, Art, Truth, and Magazines." *Atlantic Monthly* 137(1926):388–98.

Voorhees, Elsa Denison. "Emotional Adjustment of Women in the Modern World and the Choice of Satisfactions." In *Women in the Modern World,* edited by Viva B. Boothe, 368–73. Philadelphia: American Academy of Political and Social Sciences, 1929.

Wagner, Philip. "Mouth-Conscious America." *New Republic* 47(21 July 1926):250–52.

Watson, John B. "Present Economic Conditions: Some Practical Lessons to be Drawn." An address before the Associated Dress Industries of America, 22 November 1921. New York: J. Walter Thompson, n.d.

Weiss, E. B. "An Analysis of 300,000 Inquiries." *Printers' Ink* 155(21 May 1931):3–6.

What Is Circulation. Philadelphia: Curtis Publishing, 1923.

White, Paul H. "Our Booming Beauty Business." *Outlook and Independent* 154(22 January 1930):133–35.

White, Percival. "Figuring Us Out." *North American Review* 227(1929):65–71.

White House Conference on Child Health and Protection. *The Young Child in the Home: A Survey of Three Thousand American Families. Report of the Committee on the Infant and Preschool Child.* New York: D. Appleton-Century, 1936; New York: Arno Press, 1972.

Wolman, Leo. "Consumption and the Standard of Living." In *Recent Economic Changes in the United States: Report of the Committee on Recent Economic Changes of the President's Conference on Unemployment,* 13–78. New York: McGraw-Hill, 1929.

SECONDARY SOURCES

A.B.C. Auditing Practices. Chicago: Audit Bureau of Circulations, [1942].

A.B.C.: Self-Regulation in the Advertising & Publishing Industry. Chicago: Audit Bureau of Circulations, [1947].

Adams, James Truslow, and Coleman, R. V., eds. *Dictionary of American History.* 6 vols. New York: Charles Scribner's Sons, 1940.

American Hairdresser/Salon Owner: "A Century of Service." New York: Service Publications, 1978.

Atwan, Robert; McQuade, Donald; and Wright, John W. *Edsels, Luckies, and Frigidaires: Advertising the American Way.* New York: Dell, 1979.

Banner, Lois W. *American Beauty.* New York: Knopf, 1983.

———. *Women in Modern America: A Brief History.* New York: Harcourt Brace Jovanovich, 1974.

Barton, Michael. "The Study of American Everyday Life." *American Quarterly* 34(1982):218–21.

Bennett, Charles O. *Facts Without Opinion.* Chicago: Audit Bureau of Circulations, 1965.

Bernard, Jessie. *American Family Behavior.* New York: Harper, 1942.

Boorstin, Daniel J. *The Americans: The Democratic Experience.* New York: Random House, 1973.

_____. *The Image: or What Happened to the American Dream.* New York: Atheneum, 1962.

Borden Neil H. *The Economic Effects of Advertising.* Chicago: Richard D. Irwin, 1944.

_____. *Harvard Business Reports.* Vol. 11: *Cases on Cooperative Advertising.* New York: McGraw-Hill, 1932.

_____. *Problems in Advertising.* 3d ed. New York: McGraw-Hill, 1937.

Bossard, James H. S., and Boll, Eleanor S. *Ritual in Family Living: A Contemporary Study.* Philadelphia: University of Pennsylvania, 1950.

Boyenton, William H. *Audit Bureau of Circulations.* Chicago: Audit Bureau of Circulations, 1948.

Bradford, Frederick A. "Liberty Loans." In *Dictionary of American History,* Vol. 3, 271. New York: Charles Scribner's Sons, 1940.

Brownlee, W. Elliot. *Dynamics of Ascent: A History of the American Economy.* New York: Alfred A. Knopf, 1974.

_____. "Household Values, Women's Work, and Economic Growth, 1800–1930." *Journal of Economic History* 39(March 1979):199–209.

Bruchey, Stuart. *Growth of the Modern American Economy.* New York: Dodd, Mead, 1975.

Buitenhuis, Peter. "The Selling of the Great War." *The Canadian Review of American Studies* 7(Fall 1976):139–50.

Buley, R. Carlyle. *The Old Northwest Pioneer Period 1815–1849.* 2 vols. Indianapolis: Indiana Historical Society, 1950.

Bushman, Richard L., and Bushman, Claudia L. "The Early History of Cleanliness in America." *Journal of American History* 74(March 1988):1213–38.

Calhoun, Arthur W. *A Social History of the American Family from Colonial Times to the Present.* 1917. Reprint. New York: Barnes and Noble, 1945.

Chafe, William H. *The American Woman: Her Changing Social, Economic, and Political Roles, 1920–1970.* New York: Oxford, 1972.

Chandler, Alfred D., Jr. "The Beginnings of 'Big Business' in American Industry." *Business History Review* 33(1959):1–31.

_____. *The Visible Hand: The Managerial Revolution in American Business.* Cambridge, Mass.: Belknap Press, 1977.

Clark, Victor S. *History of Manufactures in the United States.* Vol. 3: *1892–1928.* New York: McGraw-Hill, 1929.

Cowan, Ruth Schwartz. "A Case Study of Technological and Social Change: The Washing Machine and the Working Wife." In *Clio's Consciousness Raised: New Perspectives on the History of Women,* edited by Mary Hartman and Lois W. Banner, 245–53. New York: Harper and Row, 1974.

The Cyclopaedia of American Biography. Vol. F: *1939–1942.* New York: James T. White, 1942.

Deford, Frank. *There She Is: The Life and Times of Miss America.* New York: Viking, 1971.

Degler, Carl N. *At Odds: Women and the Family in America from the Revolution to the Present.* New York: Oxford, 1980.

Demos, John. *A Little Commonwealth: Family Life in Plymouth Colony.* New York: Oxford, 1970.

Deutsch, Karl W. *Nationalism and Social Communication: An Inquiry into the Foundations of Nationality.* 2d ed. Cambridge: M.I.T. Press, 1966.

Dispenza, Joseph E. *Advertising the American Woman.* Dayton: Pflaum, 1975.

Douglas, Mary. *Purity and Danger: An Analysis of the Concept of Pollution and Taboo.* London: Routledge & Kegan Paul, 1966.

Durstine, Roy S. "Advertising." In *America Now: An Inquiry into Civilization in the United States,* edited by Harold E. Stearns, 164–81. New York: Charles Scribner's Sons, 1938.

Edwards, J. Donald. "The Position of the Soap Industry in World War I." U.S. Bureau of Labor Statistics, September 1941.

Ehrenreich, Barbara, and English, Deirdre. *For Her Own Good: 150 Years of the Experts' Advice to Women.* Garden City: Anchor, 1978.

Engel, James F.; Kollat, David T.; and Blackwell, Roger D. *Consumer Behavior.* New York: Holt, Rinehart, and Winston, 1968.

Ewen, Stuart. *Captains of Consciousness: Advertising and the Social Roots of the Consumer Culture.* New York: McGraw-Hill, 1976.

Ewen, Stuart, and Ewen, Elizabeth. *Channels of Desire: Mass Images and the Shaping of American Consciousness.* New York: McGraw-Hill, 1982.

Faragher, John Mack. *Women and Men on the Overland Trail.* New Haven: Yale University Press, 1979.

Fass, Paula S. *The Damned and the Beautiful: American Youth in the 1920's.* New York: Oxford, 1977.

Flexner, Eleanor. *Century of Struggle.* Cambridge, Mass.: Belknap Press, 1959.

Foner, Eric. *Free Soil, Free Labor, Free Men: The Ideology of the Republican Party Before the Civil War.* New York: Oxford, 1970.

Fox, Richard Wightman, and Lears, T. J. Jackson, eds. *The Culture of Consumption: Critical Essays in American History, 1880–1980.* New York: Pantheon, 1983.

Fox, Stephen. *The Mirror Makers: A History of American Advertising and Its Creators.* New York: Vintage, 1985.

Freedman, Estelle B. "The New Woman: Changing Views of Women in the 1920's." *Journal of American History* 61(September 1974):372–93.

Friedan, Betty. *The Feminine Mystique.* New York: Dell, 1963.

Friedl, Ernestine. *Women and Men: An Anthropologist's View.* New York: Holt, Rinehart, and Winston, 1975.

Galambos, Louis. *Competition and Cooperation: The Emergence of a National Trade Association.* Baltimore: Johns Hopkins University Press, 1966.

Galbraith, John Kenneth. *The New Industrial State.* New York: Houghton Mifflin, 1967.

Garraty, John A., ed. *Interpreting American History: Conversations with Historians.* 2 vols. New York: Macmillan, 1970.

Genovese, Eugene D. *Roll, Jordan, Roll: The World the Slaves Made.* 3d ed. New York: Vintage Books, 1976.

Goffman, Erving. *Gender Advertisements.* Cambridge: Harvard University Press, 1979.

Goldmark, Josephine. *Impatient Crusader: Florence Kelley's Life Story.* Urbana: University of Illinois Press, 1953.

Gottschalk, Louis, ed. *Generalization in the Writing of History: A Report of the Committee on Historical Analysis of the Social Science Research Council.* Chicago: University of Chicago Press, 1963.

Greene, Theodore P. *America's Heroes: The Changing Models of Success in American Magazines.* New York: Oxford, 1970.

Hall, W. Scott. "The Journeymen Barber's International Union of America." In *The Johns Hopkins University Studies in Historical and Political Science,* series 54, 299–407. Baltimore: John Hopkins University Press, 1936.

Haller, Mark H. *Eugenics: Hereditarian Attitudes in American Thought.* New Brunswick: Rutgers University Press, 1963.

Halttunen, Karen. *Confidence Men and Painted Women: A Study of Middle-Class Culture in America, 1830–1870.* New Haven: Yale University Press, 1982.

Hartman, Mary, and Banner, Lois W., eds. *Clio's Consciousness Raised: New Perspectives on the History of Women.* New York: Harper & Row, 1974.

Hayes, Samuel P. *The Response to Industrialism 1885–1914.* Chicago: University of Chicago Press, 1957.

Higham, John. *Strangers in the Land: Patterns of American Nativism 1860–1925.* New York: Atheneum, 1974.

Hofstadter, Richard. *The Progressive Historians: Turner, Beard, Parrington.* New York: Random House, 1968.

––––––. *Social Darwinism in American Thought.* 2d ed. Boston: Beacon Press, 1955.

Hollander, Anne. "A Pretty Girl . . . " *Commentary* 53(February 1972):94–96.

Howe, Louise Kapp. *Pink Collar Workers: Inside the World of Women's Work.* New York: Putnam, 1977.

Hower, Ralph M. *The History of an Advertising Agency: N. W. Ayer & Son at Work 1869–1949.* 2d ed. Cambridge: Harvard University Press, 1949.

Huff, Darrell. *How to Lie with Statistics.* New York: W. W. Norton, 1954.

Jackson, Kenneth T. *The Ku Klux Klan in the City, 1915–1930.* New York: Oxford, 1967.

Kennedy, David M. *Birth Control in America: The Career of Margaret Sanger.* New Haven: Yale University Press, 1970.

Kolko, Gabriel. *The Triumph of Conservatism.* New York: Macmillan, 1963.

Komisar, Lucy. "The Image of Woman in Advertising." In *Woman in Sexist Society,* edited by Vivian Gornick and Barbara K. Moran, 207–17. New York: New American Library, 1972.

Kovel, Joel. *A Complete Guide to Therapy.* New York: Pantheon, 1976.

Kraditor, Aileen. *The Ideas of the Woman Suffrage Movement, 1890–1920.* Garden City, N.Y.: Anchor, 1971.

Lasch, Christopher. *The Culture of Narcissism: American Life in an Age of Diminishing Expectations.* New York: W. W. Norton, 1979.

––––––. *Haven in a Heartless World: The Family Besieged.* New York: Basic Books, 1977.

Lebergott, Stanley. *The American Economy: Income, Wealth, and Want.* Princeton: Princeton University Press, 1976.

Leighton, Isabel, ed. *The Aspirin Age, 1919–1941.* New York: Simon and Schuster, 1949.

Lemons, J. Stanley. *The Woman Citizen: Social Feminism in the 1920's.* Urbana: University of Illinois Press, 1973.

Lerner, Gerda. *The Majority Finds Its Past: Placing Women in History.* New York: Oxford, 1979.

Leuchtenburg, William E. *The Perils of Prosperity, 1914–1932.* Chicago: University of Chicago Press, 1958.

Lief, Alfred. *"It Floats": The Story of Procter & Gamble.* New York: Rinehart, 1958.

McCurdy, Charles W. "American Law and the Marketing Structure of the Large Corporation, 1875–1890." *Journal of Economic History* 38(1978):631–49.

McGovern, James R. "The American Woman's Pre-World War I Freedom in Manners and Morals." *Journal of American History* 55(September 1968):315–33.

McLaughlin, Terence. *Dirt.* New York: Stein and Day, 1971.

McLuhan, Marshall. *Culture Is Our Business.* New York: McGraw-Hill, 1970.

_____. *Understanding Media: The Extensions of Man.* New York: Chelsea House, 1969.

McLuhan, Marshall, and Fiore, Quentin. *The Medium is the Massage: An Inventory of Effects.* New York: Bantam, 1967.

Marburg, Theodore. "Domestic Trade and Marketing." In *The Growth of the American Economy,* edited by Harold F. Williamson, 511–33. New York: Prentice-Hall, 1951.

Marchand, Roland. *Advertising the American Dream: Making Way for Modernity, 1920–1940.* Berkeley: University California Press, 1985.

Metzger, Walter P. "Generalizations about National Character: An Analytical Essay." In *Generalization in the Writing of History: A Report of the Committee on Historical Analysis of the Social Science Research Council,* edited by Louis Gottschalk, 77–102. Chicago: University of Chicago Press, 1963.

Mills, Frederick C. *Economic Tendencies in the United States.* New York: National Bureau of Economic Research, 1932.

Miner, Horace. "Body Ritual Among the Nacerima." *American Anthropologist* 58(1956):503–7.

Morgan, Winona L., and Leahy, Alice M. "The Cultural Content of General Interest Magazines." *Journal of Educational Psychology* 25(October 1934):530–36.

Morris, Richard B. *Encyclopedia of American History.* New York: Harper & Row, 1970.

Mott, Frank Luther. *American Journalism: A History of Newspapers in the United States Through 250 Years, 1690–1940.* New York: Macmillan, 1941.

_____. *A History of American Magazines.* Vol. 4: *1885–1905.* Cambridge, Mass.: Belknap Press, 1957.

NHCA's Golden Years. Racine, Wisc.: Western Publishing, 1970.

Oxford English Dictionary. Oxford: Clarendon Press, 1933.

Pease, Otis. *The Responsibilities of American Advertising: Private Control and Public Influence, 1920–1940.* New Haven: Yale University Press, 1958.

Peterson, Theodore. *Magazines in the Twentieth Century.* 2d ed. Urbana: University of Illinois Press, 1964.

Pollay, Richard W., ed. *Information Sources in Advertising History.* Westport, Conn.: Greenwood Press, 1979.

Pope, Daniel A. "The Development of National Advertising, 1865–1920." Ph.D. diss., Columbia University, 1973.

_____. *The Making of Modern Advertising.* New York: Basic Books, 1983.

Potter, David M. *People of Plenty: Economic Abundance and the American Character.* Chicago: University of Chicago Press, 1958.

Presbrey, Frank. *The History and Development of Advertising.* New York: Doubleday, 1929.

Project Associates, Inc. *The Cosmetic Benefit Study.* Washington, D.C.: The Cosmetic, Toiletry, and Fragrance Association, [1978/1979].

Ratner, Sidney; Soltow, James H.; and Sylla, Richard. *The Evolution of the American Economy: Growth, Welfare, and Decision Making.* New York: Basic Books, 1979.

Riesman, David, with Glazer, Nathan, and Denny, Reuel. *The Lonely Crowd: A Study of Changing American Character.* 3d ed. New Haven: Yale University Press, 1961.

Robertson, Ross M. *History of the American Economy.* 2d ed. New York: Harcourt, Brace and World, 1964.

Ross, Ellen, and Rapp, Rayna. "Sex and Society: A Research Note from Social History and Anthropology." In *Powers of Desire: The Politics of Sexuality,* edited by Ann Anitow, Christine Stansell, and Sharon Thompson, 51–73. New York: Monthly Review Press, 1983.

Rothman, Sheila M. *Woman's Proper Place: A History of Changing Ideals and Practices, 1870 to the Present.* New York: Basic Books, 1978.

Sandage, C. H. "The Role of Advertising in Modern Society." *Journalism Quarterly* 28(Winter 1951):31–38.

Schlesinger, Arthur M. *Learning How to Behave: A Historical Study of Etiquette Books.* New York: Macmillan, 1946.

Schlesinger, Arthur M., and Fox, Dixon Ryan, eds. *A History of American Life.* 13 vols. New York: Macmillan, 1927–1948.

Schudson, Michael. "Criticizing the Critics of Advertising: Towards a Sociological View of Marketing." *Media, Culture, and Society* 3(January 1981):3–12.

Shapiro, Stephen Richard. "The Big-Sell—Attitudes of Advertising Writers about Their Craft in the 1920's and 1930's." Ph.D. diss., University of Wisconsin, 1969.

Simon, Julian L. *Issues in the Economics of Advertising.* Urbana: University of Illinois Press, 1970.

Sinclair, Andrew. *The Emancipation of the American Woman.* New York: Harper and Row, 1965.

Slosson, Preston William. *The Great Crusade and After 1914–1928.* Vol. 12 of *A History of American Life.* New York: Macmillan, 1930.

Smith, Helen Evertson. *Colonial Days and Ways, as gathered from family papers.* New York: The Century Press, 1900.

Smith-Rosenberg, Carroll. *Disorderly Conduct: Visions of Gender in Victorian America.* New York: Knopf, 1985.

Snitow, Ann; Stansell, Christine; and Thompson, Sharon, eds. *Powers of Desire: The Politics of Sexuality.* New York: Monthly Review Press, 1983.

Sochen, June. *The New Woman: Feminism in Greenwich Village, 1910–1920.* New York: Quadrangle, 1972.

Soule, George. *Prosperity Decade: From War to Depression, 1917–1929.* New York: Holt, Rinehart and Winston, 1947.

Stabile, Toni. *Cosmetics: The Great American Skin Game.* New York: Ballantine, 1973.

Starr, Paul. *The Social Transformation of American Medicine.* New York: Basic Books, 1982.

Stearns, Harold E., ed. *America Now: An Inquiry into Civilization in the United States.* New York: Charles Scribner's Sons, 1938.

The Story of the Audit Bureau of Circulations. Chicago: Audit Bureau of Circulations, on the occasion of the 40th Anniversary, [1954].

Susman, Warren I. " 'Personality' and the Making of Twentieth-Century Culture." In *New Directions in American Intellectual History,* edited by John Higham and Paul K. Conkin, 212–34. Baltimore: Johns Hopkins University Press, 1979.

Tarshis, Barry. *The 'Average American' Book.* New York: Atheneum/SMI, 1979.

Thernstrom, Stephen. *Poverty and Progress: Social Mobility in a Nineteenth Century City.* New York: Atheneum, 1970.

"34th Annual Report on Consumer Spending." *Drug Topics* 126(5 July 1982).

Thure, Karen. "Martha Harper Pioneered in the Hair Business." *Smithsonian* 7(September 1976):94–100.

Vatter, Harold G. "Has There Been a Twentieth Century Consumer Durables Revolution?" *Journal of Economic History* 27(March 1967):1–16.

Walsh, Margaret. "The Democratization of Fashion: The Emergence of the Women's Dress Pattern Industry." *Journal of American History* 66(September 1979):299–313.

Walton, Clarence, and Eells, Richard, eds. *The Business System: Readings in Ideals and Concepts.* 3 vols. New York: Macmillan, 1967.

West, B. June. "The 'New Woman.'" *Twentieth Century Literature* 1(July 1955):55–68.

Wiebe, Robert H. *The Search for Order, 1877–1920.* New York: Hill and Wang, 1967.

Williamson, Harold F., ed. *The Growth of the American Economy.* 2d ed. New York: Prentice-Hall, 1951.

Winship, Janice. "Handling Sex." *Media, Culture, and Society* 3(January 1981):25–41.

Wood, James Playsted. *Magazines in the United States.* 3d ed. New York: Ronald Press, 1971.

———. *The Story of Advertising.* New York: Ronald Press, 1958.

INDEX

Acid test, 110

Advertising
  as agency of socialization, vii, x–ix,
    xi–xiv, 21–22, 26, 34–37, 43–44,
    45–46
  and brand recognition, 16–17, 28,
    39–40
  cooperative, 80, 85, 92
  and industrial consolidation, 121n.11
  national, origins of, 6–7, 26–27
  negativity in, 40–42
  in periodicals, volume of, 14–16, 28,
    123nn.26–28, 129n.35
  and promise of upward mobility, 99
  psychology, 17, 27, 40–42, 89, 90,
    96–98
  radio, 128n.26
  of toiletries
    appeals to status, 106–7
    common themes, 98–108
    volume of, 55
  traditional, 5–6, 21, 26
  women as depicted in, 98–106

Alcohol consumption, 33, 39, 49

American Association of Advertising
  Agencies, 12

American character, xix, 42, 106–15

American Cosmeticians Society, 138n.21

American Hairdresser, xvii, 61, 62, 64,
  75, 136n.16, 138n.28

American Magazine, 18

American Medical Association, 74

Association of American Soap and
  Glycerine Producers, 79, 83, 85
  founding of, 79
  member firms, 140n.15

Audit Bureau of Circulations, 8–9,
  122n.16

Automobiles, 82, 111, 125n.5, 139n.7

Babbitt's Best Soap, 81

Balmer, Thomas, 97

Banner, Lois, 51, 55–57, 64, 132n.4

Barbers and barbershops, xvi–xvii, 62,
  68–73, 75, 77, 137n.18
  female invasion of, 62–63, 66, 68–72,
    137n.18
  "immorality" of female invasion of,
    69–70

Barbers' Journal, 68, 69

Barton, Bruce, 97

Bath, ix, 87, 91

Bathing, frequency of, 87, 96

Bathrooms, ix, 125n.5, 145n.23

Beauty Culture, 136–7n.16

Beauty schools, 68

Beauty shops, xvi–xvii, 59, 61–77,
  135n.26
  and acceptance of cosmetics, 74–75
  competition with barbers, 68–72
  itinerant and bedroom beauticians, 67
  number of, 75, 76
  popular knowledge of, 59, 63